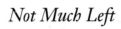

Not Much Left

Not Much Left

The Fate of Liberalism in America

Tom Waldman

UNIVERSITY OF CALIFORNIA PRESS

Berkeley   Los Angeles   London

University of California Press, one of the most distinguished
university presses in the United States, enriches lives around
the world by advancing scholarship in the humanities, social
sciences, and natural sciences. Its activities are supported by
the UC Press Foundation and by philanthropic contributions
from individuals and institutions. For more information, visit
www.ucpress.edu.

University of California Press
Berkeley and Los Angeles, California

University of California Press, Ltd.
London, England

Library of Congress Cataloging-in-Publication Data

Waldman, Tom, 1956–
    Not much left : the fate of liberalism in America / Tom
Waldman.
        p.   cm.
    Includes bibliographical references and index.
    ISBN: 978-0-520-24770-3 (cloth : alk. paper)
    1. United States—Politics and government—1945–1989.
    2. United States—Politics and government—1989–
    3. Liberalism—United States—History—20th century.
    4. Liberalism—United States—History—21st century.
    5. Presidents—United States—Election—History—20th
century.   6. Presidents—United States—Election—
History—21st century.   7. Political campaigns—United
States—History—20th century.   8. Political campaigns—
United States—History—21st century.   9. Popular
culture—Political aspects—United States—History—20th
century.   10. Popular culture—Political aspects—United
States—History—21st century.   I. Title.
    E839.5.W33   2008
    320.510973—dc22   2007037348

Manufactured in the United States of America

17   16   15   14   13   12   11   10   09   08
10   9   8   7   6   5   4   3   2   1

This book is printed on Natures Book which contains 50%
post-consumer waste and meets the minimum requirements
of ANSI/NISO Z39.48–1992 (R 1997) (*Permanence of Paper*).

To Theodore Waldman (1925–2005)

CONTENTS

ACKNOWLEDGMENTS

Different people dream different things. It has long been a dream of mine to write a book about contemporary politics. I am one of those people who relish political discussions, and have been lucky for most of my life to have been surrounded by others who feel the same way. I can't remember a time when I was not fascinated by politics and history. My parents knew what they were doing when for my eighth birthday they gave me Winston Churchill's *Illustrated History of the Second World War*—the first book that I could not put down.

It is only appropriate that I begin by thanking my parents, Ted and Nancy Waldman, who without pressing the point made it clear in our house that politics mattered. Though I was a kid through much of the 1960s, I was made very aware of what was happening in American society thanks to countless family discussions over breakfast, lunch, and dinner. A considerable portion of this book grew out of my vivid and firsthand memories of that era, despite the fact that I was too young to be drafted and too young to smoke pot.

I want to also acknowledge the people who willingly and enthusiastically shared their experiences of being politically active during the late 1960s and 1970s. It is not in my nature to romanticize the 1960s, but it is true that things were different then. I can't imagine sitting down twenty-five years from now with people who were politically active during the George W. Bush administration—liberal or conservative—and finding their stories to be as compelling as the ones told to me by those who marched for civil rights and against the war, who joined the McGovern campaign, or who instead embraced the conservative reaction to the rise of the New Left. I am grateful to Bill Rosendahl, Zev Yaroslavsky, Linda Griego, William Voegeli, Marc Haefele, Rick Tuttle, Lillian T., Michael Dukakis, Scott Schmidt, Stephen Vittoria, Richard Katz, Donzaleigh Abernathy, Derek Shearer, U.S. senator Sherrod Brown, and Morley Winograd for taking the time to sit with me and share their political biographies. This book would simply not exist without their participation.

I would like to single out Santa Monica Superior Court Judge Terry Friedman, who not only graciously sat for an interview in his chambers, but at the end of our time together gave me a box crammed with incredible memorabilia from the McGovern campaign. The original documents, press clippings, and newsmagazines contained in his personal collection were a tremendous help to me in recreating the political environment of 1972 and conveying the hope and promise of McGovern's candidacy. I am profoundly grateful to Judge Friedman for his generosity.

It was my great fortune to have close friends involved or interested in politics who were more than willing to read the manuscript. Ira Levine was one such volunteer, always available to read chapters and offer suggestions. Heather Rothman transcribed numerous interviews and contributed her own trenchant observations about the past, present, and future of liberalism. Then there was Tom Link, who selflessly and frequently took time from his own busy schedule to read drafts of the manuscript and provide detailed comments. Tom's emotional and intellectual support meant so much to me as I struggled to bring this project to completion.

I would like to also thank Joe Domanick, who steered me toward the University of California Press and provided excellent suggestions regarding the structure and content of the text; Jim Parish, who has been so kind over the years to offer his sage advice about both staying focused and navigating the tricky world of publishing and publishers; and my former journalism professor, Jack Langguth, a dear friend—and mentor—for more than twenty-five years.

As a journalist, magazine writer, and author, I have worked with some very good editors. But with all due respect to the others, Naomi Schneider is special. Even in an age of instant communication, I was continually astonished at her habit of reading and responding to fifty, a hundred pages or more within forty-eight hours. In relatively few words Naomi could tell me precisely what was needed to make the book better. It seems almost superfluous to say that her instincts were invariably correct.

Finally, thanks to my wife and two sons for their unflagging support and encouragement throughout this entire process. I could not have crossed the finish line without them.

Introduction

Quiet Americans

April 26, 2007, should have been a great day for liberals in the United States. By a margin of 51 to 46, the U.S. Senate voted to provide about one hundred billion dollars to fund the wars in Afghanistan and Iraq, while also establishing a timetable for withdrawing troops from Iraq by March of the following year. A day earlier, the House of Representatives had approved a similar measure. Neither the certainty of a presidential veto nor the inevitable accusations of "surrender" or "defeat" on talk radio, Fox News, and in the halls of Congress deterred the Democrats from near-unanimous support of the legislation. Of the forty-nine Democrats in the Senate in 2007, forty-eight supported the bill, and the remaining one abstained. The approval of two Republicans and one independent guaranteed its passage.

For the first time in thirty-four years, or since the beginning of Richard Nixon's second term as president, a majority of the United States Congress had recorded its opposition to an ongoing war. The situation in Iraq had deteriorated to the point that Democrats, in 2007, seemingly embraced comparisons with the peace movement of the 1960s and early 1970s. As the reporter Noam Levey commented, "By explicitly setting the terms for an end to U.S. involvement in a war, this Congress has gone further than any since the Vietnam era."[1]

Since the ignominious fall of Saigon in 1975, mainstream Democrats had grown increasingly reluctant to trumpet their party's role in bringing to an end U.S. involvement in the war in Vietnam. They were particularly wary of recalling the efforts of George McGovern, who in 1972 ran on a platform that called for all U.S. troops to come home from Vietnam within three months of his inauguration as president. If not for the memoirs of unrepentant liberals, aging radicals, and ex-hippies, one could almost conclude that mainstream Democrats were embarrassed by or ashamed of their party's antiwar stance during the period 1968–73.

On the evening of April 26, after the Senate had cast its vote, the eight Democratic candidates for president convened at South Carolina State University for the first debate of the campaign. Four of them—Hillary Clinton, Barack Obama, Joe Biden, and Christopher Dodd—had voted a few hours earlier for the legislation. But if they expected to be greeted with expressions of gratitude from the other candidates, they were mistaken. Two other contenders, the former Alaska senator Mike Gravel and the Ohio congressman Dennis Kucinich, criticized the quartet for voting to continue to provide funds for the war under any circumstances.

In 2003–04, Kucinich had run for president as an antiwar candidate. At that time Republicans constituted the majority in the House and the Senate, and most Americans still believed that victory was achievable in Iraq. Yet Kucinich was not going to soften his message just because the political environment had shifted in his favor four years later. His 2008 campaign was not about saying "I told you so," but, once again, extricating U.S. forces from Iraq as quickly as possible. Kucinich was no longer being unfairly perceived—even in Democratic circles—as simply the "left-wing nut" whose defeatist foreign policy would be a disaster for U.S. interests around the world. And, frankly, because the congressman could not win, he had nothing to lose. As long as he remained in the 2008 race, Clinton, Obama, Dodd, Biden, New Mexico governor Bill Richardson, and former North Carolina senator John Edwards could expect a spirited attack from the left for their views on the war over the previous five years. None of them could ever be as antiwar as Dennis Kucinich.

Other issues were discussed at the debate. In most cases, the "liberal" position was expressed without qualification by at least one of the major candidates. Edwards, who in the spring of 2007 was considered, along with Clinton and Obama, one of the leading Democratic presidential contenders, pushed his proposal for universal health care. He would pay for the plan by ending President Bush's tax breaks for all Americans making in excess of two hundred thousand dollars per year. The former senator went ahead with the idea despite knowing full well that (*a*) he would be attacked by conservatives for endorsing another form of "socialized medicine," and (*b*) in 1993–94, Hillary Clinton had attempted a major reform of the health care system in the United States, with famously disastrous results. Nearly fifteen years later, Clinton was still enduring the negative political consequences of that searing experience.

Yet Edwards assumed the risks, which on the surface seemed to contradict the advice of the smooth handlers who, in this era, frame political campaigns at all levels of government. He clearly sensed, however, that after six years of the George W. Bush administration, even moderate voters would be amenable to an idea that had been identified with American liberalism since Harry Truman was president. By comparison, the other major candidates proceeded cautiously on health care; they acknowledged the system had to be fixed but were unwilling to match what some commentators called Edwards's "radical" proposal. (One can better understand Senator Clinton's caution in view of what happened at the beginning of her husband's administration.)

The occupant of the White House in 2007, whom George McGovern, among others, called the worst president in U.S. history, had spawned the most liberal-sounding field of Democratic presidential candidates of any since 1972. Given the record of the Bush-Cheney regime, the candidates apparently concluded that the careful and uninspiring rhetoric of recent Democratic campaigns no longer matched the mood of the party. An extended era of well-meaning moderation and apologetic liberalism might well be coming to a close.

The day after the South Carolina debate, major newspapers around the country published the obligatory photo of the candidates standing together on stage; six white males, one Latino, one woman, and one African American. Women had run for president in the recent past (Shirley Chisholm in 1972, Elizabeth Dole in 2000), as had African Americans (Shirley Chisholm in 1972, Jesse Jackson in 1984 and 1988, and Al Sharpton in 2004). Bill Richardson, however, was the first Latino presidential candidate of note. As more Latinos are elected to powerful posts, one could safely predict others would soon follow Richardson's example.

Most important, however, was the very real possibility that the United States would elect an African American or a woman as president in 2008. In the race for the Democratic nomination, Clinton and Obama had been consistently ranked 1–2 in most polls, and they were well ahead of the competition—except Edwards—in the category of money raised. Though historically significant, the candidacies of Chisholm, Jackson, and Sharpton were viewed as symbols of progress on issues of race and gender rather than as viable challenges to the nomination. But for Clinton and Obama, anything short of victory in the primary and general elections would be considered a failure and would be hugely disappointing to their millions of supporters. Some fifty years after the beginning of the modern civil rights movement, and forty years after the advent of women's liberation, the country had cleared another hurdle in the ongoing quest for full equality between white heterosexual males and everyone else. Senator Obama had not been born when Rosa Parks refused to surrender her seat on that bus; nevertheless, his rapid rise and potent candidacy represented a continuation of her legacy. Not coincidentally, Obama was the preferred candidate of older white male liberals such as McGovern and Bill Moyers, whose political views were formed during the heyday of post–World War II liberalism, including during the civil rights movement.

. . .

These were the main reasons why 4/26/2007 should have been a glorious day for liberals across the United States. There was just one problem: where were the liberals? Let's start with the aforementioned 2008 presidential candidates, none of whom through, April 2007, had used "liberal" to describe his or her political views. In their reluctance to utter that word, they were merely following a pattern that first became apparent some twenty-five to thirty years earlier. The "disappearing liberal" has been a phenomenon of U.S. political life since the late 1970s, roughly coinciding with the emergence of the proud conservative in the Barry Goldwater–Ronald Reagan mold. Ever since George McGovern was crushed by President Nixon in the 1972 race, liberals have been the rootless drifters of American politics. The Democratic Party shunned them, and so did the far left—such as it existed during the 1980s, 1990s, and 2000s. As gays rushed out of the closet, liberals rushed in, making sure to lock the door behind them. The "L-word" has over time become just about the worst thing you could call your opponent—even in a Democratic primary.

Of course, conservatives since the 1980s have done their part to humiliate, disgrace, and destroy liberals and liberalism. Sean Hannity, the popular right-wing host of a talk radio program and the Fox News show *Hannity and Colmes*, wrote a book a year after 9/11 that implied that liberalism was hardly better than terrorism, because there is not much difference between killers and those who would appease them. Other conservative writers and commentators picked up on this theme. Karl Rove made a speech in which he declared that "therapy" is how liberals would prefer to deal with terrorists. He offered no evidence for this theory, but antiliberal bigotry is so prevalent in modern America that many people believed it nevertheless. In truth, 9/11 simply provided one more opportunity for conservatives to advance their standard view that liberals will ruin this country, if not by offering an olive branch to terrorists, than through their support for abortion, gay rights, civil liberties, and the welfare state.

. . .

Not Much Left: The Fate of Liberalism in America examines liberalism's decline in the United States during the final third of the twentieth century and the first several years of the twenty-first, concluding with its potential for revival. The story begins in the pivotal year of 1968, when the antiwar presidential candidacies of Eugene McCarthy and Robert Kennedy galvanized college-age supporters who wanted to see an immediate end to U.S. involvement in the war in Vietnam. Senator Kennedy's assassination in June of that year, and McCarthy's seeming indifference to actually winning the nomination, helped clear the path for Vice President Hubert Humphrey to become the Democratic nominee. The antiwar left, bitterly disappointed that the establishment's choice had prevailed and furious at the vice president's refusal to renounce the Johnson administration's Vietnam policy, either harassed Humphrey at campaign appearances or opted to sit out the election until the very end. By the time these "kids" awoke to the reality that their action and inaction was helping the campaign of Richard Nixon, it was too late to save the Democrat.

The indifference, or in some cases disloyalty, displayed by antiwar liberals toward the Humphrey candidacy outraged Cold War liberals and organized labor, both of whom regarded the vice president as one of the greatest Democrats and greatest Americans of the twentieth century. President Nixon was such a despised figure to Democrats of all kinds that he was unable to exploit this growing schism as successfully as did the far more likeable Ronald Reagan a decade later. But in the period from 1968 to 1972, as the war in Vietnam continued and women, gays, African Americans, and Latinos sought greater representation in the Democratic Party, the divide between Us and Them, or Them and Us as the case may be, became ever more pronounced. Then the Democrats nominated George McGovern for president.

Not Much Left examines at length the 1972 McGovern campaign, which was a watershed in the history of liberalism after the 1960s. The campaign put an official stamp on the changes and movements that had been bubbling to the surface of American culture and society over the previous seven years. This was the new incarnation of liberalism. For several months in 1972, the Democratic Party was under the leadership of a generation dismissive of bellicose anti-communism; skeptical of the idea that the United States was always in the right; contemptuous of the perceived sexual mores and social habits of their elders; and convinced that the idea "All men are created equal" included females, homosexuals, and people of color.

The book offers profiles of men and women who worked on the McGovern campaign, and believed in the candidate's cause, but from the perspective of thirty years later questioned whether the tactics and platform were in the best interests of the party and the country. McGovern has argued as recently as 2007 that his landslide defeat in 1972—Nixon won every state but Massachusetts—was due mainly to the Eagleton affair, which I will cover in chapter 6. But many Democrats, including those who backed McGovern, interpreted the vote as a wholesale repudiation of the candidate and his (liberal) politics. After all, this was an impatient generation, accustomed to getting its way. McGovern's huge loss did not conform to the blueprint for revolutionary change. By contrast, Goldwater Republicans, who experienced a defeat of similar proportions in 1964, stuck with their cause and were rewarded with the election of Ronald Reagan as president sixteen years later.

Following the collapse of McGovern and McGovernism, the Democratic Party, beginning with Jimmy Carter in 1976, embarked on a thirty-year project to distance itself from the legacy of Great Society liberalism and the New Left. Some of those who led the effort had been antiwar activists and were veterans of the civil rights movement. But as these men and women sought lifelong careers in politics, they grew increasingly worried that they would become victims of their political and cultural histories. It was not difficult for the opposition to willfully misinterpret and misrepresent the legacy of 1960s liberalism. The attacks had begun during the McGovern campaign, when centrist Democrats and Republicans succeeded in linking antiwar liberalism with anti-Americanism and, what might be termed, sexual liberalism with decadence and perversion.

In fact, McGovern has become so identified with his views against the war that it is easy to forget that the 1972 Democratic platform was also the first to formally endorse reproductive rights and equality for sexual minorities. And though there was no empirical evidence that liberals had more sex or better sex than conservatives, liberals did consider sexual freedom and sexual satisfaction as quintessential ingredients of the Good Life.

Beginning in the late 1970s, liberals—feminists in particular—began to openly express discomfort with the sexualizing of American society. In its early stages, feminism promoted the idea of good sex as liberating for women, as opposed to the old brand that was seemingly indifferent or hostile to a woman's special needs in the bedroom. Having tried to enlighten the masses—male and female—about these issues, some feminists subsequently adopted a harshly critical view of (hetero) sexual relations, especially between college students. According to this new way of thinking, men were not just animals, but criminally inclined beasts. In some cases, feminists agitated for laws and regulations that would stop men before they went too far—the definition of *too far* sometimes including a lingering look. Along with political correctness, this attitude was indicative of a disturbing trend within post-1960s liberalism to restrict rather than safeguard personal freedom.

Though minorities and women gradually improved their position in society beginning in the 1970s, political correctness and similar protective measures implied that their situation remained precarious. "Outsiders" were being sent mixed messages by women, minorities, and gays: namely, We are gaining strength but we still need to be handled with care. Many older liberals balked at the notion that they had to constantly watch what they said in the presence of members of these groups.

Not Much Left also takes note of the rise—largely unforeseen by liberals and conservatives—of the religious right in U.S. politics, which was a response to the social liberalism of the early 1970s. I have spoken with shrewd, politically astute Democrats who are completely flummoxed by the power and size of this voting bloc. They knew very well that the standard liberal views on abortion and gay rights were controversial, but they never anticipated that as a consequence millions of evangelicals would consistently vote Republican, or vote at all. And unlike reforming the welfare system or supporting the death penalty, there was little, if anything, liberals and other Democrats could offer these voters to get them to reconsider. Even the brain trust behind the Democratic Leadership Council—formed in the mid-1980s as a means of repositioning the Democrats closer to the ideological center on the economy and foreign policy—did not develop a viable "Third Way" alternative on social issues. Bill Clinton, who was the first president of the DLC, argued in the 1992 campaign that abortion should be "safe, legal, and rare," but this was little more than a crafty politician trying to have it both ways.

The team that ran Clinton's race in 1992 was obsessed with the idea that he should avoid making the mistakes of the 1988 nominee, Michael Dukakis. One of the worst of these involved allowing his opponent, Vice President George H. W. Bush, to define Dukakis as an l-i-b-e-r-a-l. *Not Much Left* will argue that the 1988 campaign represented the modern-day low point in the public's perception of liberals and liberalism. The contempt and disrespect shown toward Dukakis ushered in a new era of liberal-bashing, where you could say almost anything about liberals and get away with it. Today there are no speech codes or pressure groups to protect liberalism from being thoroughly trashed on radio and television, and even liberals do not insist on political correctness for liberals. No shock jock will lose his job because he demeans liberals. The nonresponse to the "L word" starting in the late 1980s created the perception that liberals were weak, lazy, or indifferent. And if liberals would not even come to the defense of liberalism, how could we trust them to stand up to the Soviet Union, international terrorists, street hoodlums, or man-hating feminists?

The two phrases I remember best from the 1992 Clinton campaign are, "It's the economy, stupid" and "The forgotten middle class." Neither can stand up to "Ask not what your country can do for you . . ." but this was a different candidate and a different Democratic Party. Although as a teenager Clinton admired President Kennedy, and although he worked in the McGovern campaign while attending law school, he deliberately steered the party away from some of the core principles developed during the 1960s and 1970s. This was especially true in the case of the U.S. economy, where on trade and other issues Clinton espoused views that were anathema to labor. For union members, this was no longer the Democratic Party of Roosevelt, Truman, and Humphrey. Still, the Clinton campaign gambled correctly that after twelve years of Ronald Reagan and George Bush, labor had nowhere else to go.

In charting the rightward shift of Democratic economic policies from the early 1970s to the mid-1990s, *Not Much Left* profiles a man named Morley Winograd, who supported the presidential bids of all three Kennedy brothers and became a high official in the DLC. Winograd's political odyssey began in his home state of Michigan in the 1960s, when he was part of the antiwar contingent within the Democratic Party. But by the early 1970s Winograd had become appalled at the arrogance of the young activists who sought to wrest control of the Michigan Democratic Party from the old guard, labor in particular. Winograd sided with the unions in this battle, and he did not support McGovern in the 1972 primary.

Two decades later Winograd advocated free trade and other economic principles that he felt were best suited to the burgeoning Information Age. A century earlier, liberals were proponents of free trade. But ever since the New Deal, liberals had been inclined to support public sector intervention in the economy, including protectionism, while conservatives championed the cause of economic freedom (i.e., keeping the government out of the marketplace). Winograd's evolution symbolized the movement within the Democratic Party away from the economic orthodoxy that had prevailed since the 1930s. Clinton's memorable phrase from his 1996 inauguration speech, "The era of Big Government is over," encapsulated the economic views of Winograd and the New Democrats.

The book will examine the status and stature of liberalism during the Clinton years. Though liberals may have gone into hiding, liberalism did not disappear. As noted, on the social issues, liberals and the Democrats in general stood firm. In addition, the effort by Hillary Clinton to reform the health care system was in the spirit of FDR-Truman liberalism, as was her husband's support for family leave protections and raising the minimum wage. Both Clintons also had a tendency to speak in the language of the New Left, and they possessed the proper pop culture credentials. There were enough vestiges of liberalism and the counterculture within the Clinton White House that in 1994 an emergent group of Republicans, who adored Ronald Reagan and Jesus Christ in equal measure, were able to gain control of the House of Representatives by targeting the "immorality" of the 1960s.

. . .

When I began work on this book in the late spring of 2005, liberalism looked to have no future. George W. Bush was a mere six months out of winning his second term, the Republicans were still the majority in the House and Senate, and Karl Rove was talking seriously about establishing a Republican majority that would last throughout the century. The Democratic Party appeared to be bereft of ideas, candidates, and compelling causes. If they couldn't succeed in 2004, what hope was there that things would improve in the next two, four, or eight years? Democrats had so despised and feared Bush that the 2004 campaign brought back into politics many who had drifted away over the previous decades. These reemergent Democrats contributed money, walked precincts, made phone calls, and sent out blast e-mails. In the end, John Kerry came very close to beating an incumbent president during wartime. Still, the slim margin of defeat made it only more difficult for Democrats to get out of bed on that Wednesday morning.

What I did not anticipate, nor did many of the experts looking ahead to 2006 and 2008, is the extent to which the rapidly deteriorating situation in Iraq would turn the electorate against Bush and the Republicans. In the first few years after 9/11, the United States seemed to be a country made up almost entirely of diehard patriots. They believed Bush and the administration's claim that the 9/11 terrorists were linked to Saddam Hussein; that Al Qaeda was close to acquiring nuclear weapons; and that Saddam possessed weapons of mass destruction. And they also believed Bush, Cheney, and Paul Wolfowitz's assertion that the United States could occupy Iraq without significant resistance ("We will be greeted as liberators," said the vice president) and transform that country and the entire Middle East into a haven for Western-style democracy.

Even when the occupation of Iraq proved to be more difficult than advertised, it did not appear that Bush or the GOP would suffer serious political consequences. After all, conservatives had about them an aura of invincibility that did not show up in the standard political analysis. They threw the Democrats out of the House in 1994; defeated Al Gore in a disputed election in 2000; won a U.S. Senate seat in Georgia two years later by claiming that the Democratic incumbent, a paralyzed Vietnam veteran, was coddling terrorists; and reelected what many liberals called "the worst president in American history" in 2004. Over the next eighteen months, conservatives secured their long-sought majority in the U.S. Supreme Court. What would they conquer next? Despite some predictions to the contrary, in the weeks leading up to the 2006 midterm elections it did not seem possible that the Democrats could take back control of the House of Representatives. Surely, on the day of the vote, the GOP would pull off another miracle, probably due to its having mobilized millions of evangelicals in the last minute to both campaign and go to the polls. One reason offered by the experts for a possible Democratic triumph was the many Democratic candidates to run in districts in the south and the west who did not agree with the liberal position on abortion, gay rights, or gun control. They correctly noted that many within the party hierarchy would rather topple the right-wing leadership in the House than fret over running candidates who swore by the party platform. I was with Democrats on election night 2006, and they all praised the brilliance of this strategy. It will be interesting to see if they feel the same way in November 2008.

Not Much Left concludes with a discussion of the condition of liberalism in the aftermath of the 2006 elections. While it is too early to say whether liberalism has come full circle since 1968, the existence of a potent antiwar movement and the enthusiasm of at one least one major presidential candidate to provide universal health care and end poverty suggest that a resurgence is possible. But no one was willing to acknowledge it publicly on April 26, 2007.

. . .

From 1932 to 1972, U.S. history is in many respects the history of liberalism: the New Deal, the Fair Deal, the New Frontier, the Great Society, the civil rights movement, the antiwar movement, women's liberation, gay liberation, and environmentalism. As the pundit and scholar Max Lerner wrote in 1957, *prior* to the liberal triumphs of the 1960s, "liberalism has furnished the dominant political and intellectual climate of America."[2] If the right-wing conservative reaction that began with the election of Ronald Reagan as president in 1980 had continued unabated to 2020 it would not have come close to matching the accomplishments of liberals during the earlier forty-year cycle.

But no political movement can triumph strictly by invoking its glorious past. A December 2004 Pew study surveying two thousand people revealed that on the basis of six questions covering economic and social issues, 18 percent could be categorized as liberal, 15 percent conservative, 16 percent populist, 9 percent libertarian, and 42 percent ambivalent. Despite this breakdown, the report also noted that when asked to describe their ideology, the conservatives outnumbered the liberals by a margin of

2 to 1. Even many of the people who held liberal views did not consider themselves liberal.

In his 2004 book *The Essential America*, George McGovern wrote: "The negative associations of the word [liberalism] are now so pronounced that some political campaigners assert that the opponent has been practicing 'liberalism'—as though that were sufficient to consign the guilty 'liberal' to ridicule and defeat."[3] Since McGovern's landslide defeat in 1972 many liberals have retreated, floundered, gone into hiding, reinvented themselves, or switched sides. Yet the idea and legacy of liberalism are so ingrained in the American experience that nothing can take their place. Progressivism, the Left, or New Democrats are weak substitutes; how many know what these terms actually stand for? In a culture largely bereft of serious political debate, liberalism is the all-purpose definition for everything to the left of the center.

. . .

In looking at liberalism over the past thirty-five years, I offer some reasons for its prolonged downturn in electoral politics:

(1) By the early 1970s, liberalism had exhausted its supply of Big Ideas. This was not unexpected given that the period 1955–70 had produced social and political change on a scale rarely equaled in the first two centuries of the United States. These fifteen years of activity in retrospect seem like fifty or one hundred, especially given the stagnation on the left since the middle of the 1970s. In the United States, politics is run like a business: you must continuously offer the people something new and exciting since even dedicated voters boycott boring elections. By the middle of the 1970s, after a decade of movements and causes that actually did lead to the remaking of American society, liberals faced this disconcerting question: How do we follow *that?* A good answer was not forthcoming.

(2) In November 1972, George McGovern lost to President Nixon by a final score of forty-nine states to one. Liberals had never before

suffered such a shattering defeat. Given the size of the loss and the personality and political history of the man at the top of the opposing ticket, November 7, 1972, has since been regarded as one of the bleakest days in the modern history of the Democratic Party. Why did Nixon win by such a huge margin? After all, here was a candidate who only a decade ago suffered his own humiliating defeat in the California governor's race, vowing at that time never to return to politics. He escaped with a narrow victory in the presidential election of 1968, only to annihilate McGovern four years later. One explanation is that the voters overwhelmingly rejected the new edition of American liberalism: pro-affirmative action, pro-choice, pro-gay rights, pro-peace in foreign affairs, enamored of social engineering, and anti-death penalty.

(3) Support for abortion and to a lesser extent gay rights—both of which were included for the first time in the 1972 Democratic Party Platform—would, within a few years, motivate millions of evangelical Christians to get actively involved in politics on the Republican side. This unexpected gift to the GOP altered the balance of power between the two parties, and, when combined with the Democrats' strong support for civil rights since the early 1960s, made it virtually impossible that a majority of the South would back the Democratic ticket in national elections. Whether from a personal indifference toward religion or a fear of upsetting both God and the electorate, liberals have failed miserably to counter the power of the religious right. In many campaigns, they simply capitulate, mixing joyous testimonials to the power of prayer and the necessity of faith with a quiet and hedged endorsement of legal abortion and, less often, gay marriage.

(4) The size of the defeat in 1972 persuaded many Democrats that McGovern-style liberalism—especially in the area of foreign affairs—must end if the party genuinely desired a return to power. According to this reasoning, Nixon did not so much win the 1972 election as McGovern lost it. In the view of many Democrats, the only way to prevent a recurrence was to change both the message and the messenger.

. . .

In contrast to popular perception, conservatives do not despise all liberals. For example, they admire and more importantly support—with rhetoric, money, and, on occasion, arms—liberals in Iran, Iraq, North Korea, and other countries run by oppressive regimes hostile to the United States. Leaders such as George W. Bush who promote the spread of democracy around the world are in fact counting on local liberals to do the difficult and dangerous work of advocating for and instituting free elections, freedom of the press, freedom of religion, and other freedoms that are the backbone of political culture in the United States and Western Europe. And because they believe in preserving the status quo, conservatives in these countries, whether self-proclaimed or defined that way by outsiders, are anathema to American conservatives.

Not Much Left defines liberalism as the ideology that during the whole of American history has been committed more than any other to the ideas of freedom and progress. As noted, one of the themes developed in this book is that many liberals since the mid-1970s forgot about this longstanding dedication to freedom and instead embraced political correctness, intrusive regulations against sexual harassment, and other practices that ran counter to the proud history of their movement. This new version exposed liberalism to widespread ridicule and contempt—even from other liberals.

There is a corollary definition of liberalism that will be explored throughout the text: the idea of liberalism as not just representing change, but change of a particular kind. After all, seemingly every politician in the United States today describes him or herself as "an agent of change." But change means something different for liberals than it does for conservatives. When Ronald Reagan talked about change in 1980, he meant taking a giant step backward, particularly in the areas of economic and foreign policy. His overriding goal was not to make America great, but to make America great *again*, by curbing or eliminating liberal domestic programs and, five years after the Communist victory in

Vietnam, reviving the myth of U.S. military might. In the end, Reagan won because a majority of the voters were tired of "progress."

On the other hand, when liberals advocate for change, they define it in terms of new ideas, and implementing untested or retooled policies. Liberals are by nature both optimistic and impatient; they believe in a better world, but they are also incapable of remaining silent and standing still. *Not Much Left* endorses the notion of liberalism as the ideology that is most committed to the idea of change as *forward* motion. In the liberal universe, tomorrow will not look like today, and it will certainly not look like yesterday.

· · ·

Finally, *Not Much Left* treats the fate of liberalism as a historic event. I use anecdotes, analysis, and first-person interviews to construct a narrative of why and how liberalism suffered a steady decline in strength and influence from the early 1970s to the middle of the second term of George W. Bush. To an extent, liberalism's downslide mirrors that of the Democratic Party, which also experienced a difficult couple of decades following the McGovern-Nixon race. But at the same time, the only two Democrats elected president since 1972, Jimmy Carter and Bill Clinton, were both southerners who consciously separated their own politics from various aspects of modern liberalism. This act of distancing was not the only reason they won, but it helped.

The book is not, in the strict sense, a prescriptive. It does not tell liberals—wherever they may be—what policies to pursue or positions to adopt in order to acquire political power. There are plenty of other books on the market with that purpose. Instead, *Not Much Left* seeks to explain why an ideology associated with some of the most significant legislation and social, political, and cultural movements of twentieth-century America, and espoused by FDR, Truman, and LBJ, should have become irrelevant, ineffective, and despised during the past thirty-five years. As we shall see, it is liberalism and liberals that are in large part to blame.

CHAPTER ONE

In Locke's Step

Disheartened liberals and disgruntled ex-liberals in the early twenty-first century should take some comfort in the fact that liberalism in America has a longer and more glorious history than the competition. It is older than socialism and conservatism—the beginnings of which are often traced to the Anglo-Irish statesman Edmund Burke's classic work *Reflections on the Revolution in France* (1790)—and has outlasted fascism and communism. One could argue that liberalism's protean qualities as much as its inherent appeal account for its longevity and significance and explain the constant fear of conservatives that at any moment liberalism will reemerge as a powerful force in American politics. After all, the ability of liberalism (and leading liberals in the United States) to respond effectively and forcefully to changing times and national crises, especially during the 1930s and the early 1960s, is among its most notable characteristics.

Many historians and political scientists trace the origins of liberalism or liberal thought to the English physician and philosopher John Locke (1632–1704). Locke's ideas on liberty, tolerance, and the rights of the individual exerted a profound influence on, among others, Thomas Jefferson and James Madison. Madison read Locke and various Enlightenment thinkers while a student at Princeton University in the early

1770s. In the words of the scholar Charles Murray, "We in the United States think of Locke as an intellectual inspiration of the American Founders, which he was."[1] The historian Peter Gay, editor of *The Enlightenment: A Comprehensive Anthology*, notes that Locke's correspondence in his *Letters Concerning Toleration* (1689) grew out of his "liberal political thought and Latitudinarian Protestantism." He adds, "Locke's plea is distinctly modern"; it holds that "it is not dissenters who threaten society, but society which by suppressing dissenters produces threats for itself."[2]

Reading Locke's original words, the contemporary reader can discern clear views on issues of critical importance to U.S. society, which in our time often divide the left and right, liberals and conservatives. As a prime example, Locke's thoughts on what we would today call the separation of church and state: "I esteem it above all things necessary to distinguish exactly the business of civil government from that of religion, and to settle the just bounds that lie between the one and the other. If this not be done, there can be no end put to the controversies that will be always arising between those that have, or at least pretend to have, on the one side, a concernment for the interest of men's souls, and, on the other side, a care of the commonwealth."[3] This passage could be on the wall at the national headquarters of People for the American Way.

Nearly ninety years after Locke wrote the *Letters*, as well as two other works that profoundly influenced eighteenth-century American political thought (*Essay Concerning Human Understanding* and *Two Treatises of Government*), the Declaration of Independence incorporated his ideas on the rights of man and provided the most famous phrase in U.S. history: "life, liberty, and the pursuit of happiness" (the last of which Locke called property)—the "unalienable rights." It would be presumptuous to call the Declaration of Independence a *liberal* document as the word is understood today. In the ongoing political tug-of-war between liberals and conservatives over possession of the Founding Fathers, both sides introduce impressive evidence to support their claims.

Yet the concept of "equality for all," a cornerstone of liberalism since the early 1960s, can be found within the Declaration of Independence. At the height of President Lyndon Johnson's Great Society, the historians Allan Nevins and Henry Steele Commager wrote: "There is the truth that all men are created equal—that all men are equal in the sight of God and equal before the law. There were, to be sure, even as Jefferson wrote, many inequalities in America: the inequality of rich and poor, of men and women, of black and white. But the failure of a society to live up to an ideal does not invalidate the ideal, and the doctrine of equality, once announced, worked as a leaven in American thought."[4]

Still, if one wishes to provide solid evidence of Jefferson's sympathetic disposition toward liberalism—as the term is understood today—there is perhaps no better example than a brief excerpt from a letter he wrote in 1816 to Samuel Kercheval: "But I know also, that laws and institutions must go hand in hand with the progress of the human mind. As that becomes more developed, more enlightened, as new discoveries are made, new truths disclosed, and manners and opinions change with the change of circumstances, institutions must advance also, and keep pace with the times."[5] Jefferson establishes a pattern of cause and effect in accordance with the view of liberals—people change, institutions follow—and includes the idea of progress, which is regarded as synonymous with liberalism.

. . .

Given that the Republican Party in the early twenty-first century stands for the Patriot Act, unlimited detention of suspected terrorists, and the use of torture under certain circumstances, it is ironic that Abraham Lincoln, the president most associated with the concept of freedom, was the first Republican ever elected president. The irony is not acknowledged by most Republicans today. The annual Lincoln Day Dinner remains a popular event in GOP circles, and even Republicans from below the Mason-Dixon Line pay homage to their leader, although usually not with the dedication and enthusiasm of their colleagues from the north.

Still, Lincoln was a Republican; whether he was also a liberal is not as apparent. Though the question is not without merit, one has to be careful to declare unequivocally that Abraham Lincoln fits the classic definition. Among other things, there is the risk of applying contemporary standards of liberalism, civil rights, and black-white relations to a political figure from the mid-nineteenth century. I can recall a radicalized black student from UC Berkeley condemning Lincoln as a racist and mocking Lincoln's role in ending slavery during an invited presentation to my seventh-grade history class in 1969. That guy would not have considered Lincoln a liberal, except perhaps in the pejorative sense.

It is natural to consider Lincoln's presidency as embodying the spirit of liberalism, if not its intent. Assessing the substance and tone of Lincoln's famous "house divided" speech, delivered in Springfield, Illinois, in 1858, the political scientists Morton Frisch and Richard Stevens offer this view: "His theme in that speech was that political events had been building up in such a way as to destroy the cause of human freedom forever, unless they were reversed."[6] Whether Lincoln's hatred of slavery stemmed from his love of black people—most historians think not—is beside the point when considering Lincoln's place within the history of American liberalism. Along with the mounting casualties, the prolongation of the Civil War saw a hardening of Lincoln's commitment to destroying the institution of slavery, and to extending an ever increasing number of freedoms to African Americans. The historian James McPherson observed, "In the last year of the war, the President [also] endorsed giving the right to vote to two overlapping groups: literate African-Americans and all black veterans of the Union army. . . . When Lincoln came under enormous pressure in the summer of 1864 to waive his insistence on Southern acceptance of the abolition of slavery as a precondition for peace negotiations, he eloquently refused to do so."[7]

In the decades after the Civil War, freed slaves living in the South experienced violence, racism, and both subtle and overt discrimination as politicians and once-fiery abolitionists in the North moved on to other issues. Adding to the injustice, the U.S. Supreme Court decision in *Plessy v. Ferguson* (1896) introduced the idea of "separate but equal" accommodations, which had a devastating impact on black communities across the South. As Hugh Brogan notes in his history of the United States, the Court "was entering into a conspiracy to deny adequate education to the blacks, because the Southern states had no intention of giving blacks equal facilities, even of they were separate, and the Court had no intention of inquiring whether they had done so or not."[8] Nearly a hundred years after the South surrendered to the North at Appomattox in April 1865, President Lyndon Johnson signed into law the Voting Rights Act, which represented the final historic achievement of the civil rights movement and a triumph for liberalism. Abraham Lincoln would probably have been surprised that it took an entire century for the South—and the rest of the country—to come around.

. . .

In his seminal work *Anti-Intellectualism in American Life,* Richard Hofstadter wrote about Woodrow Wilson, "He believed in small business, competitive economics, colonialism, Anglo-Saxon and white supremacy, and a suffrage restricted to men, long after such beliefs had become objects of mordant critical analysis."[9] Nearly a hundred years after Wilson was first elected president of the United States, the last four items on that list would make liberals cringe. Yet there has always been a degree of ambiguity about liberal presidents in the twentieth century. Not everything they believe in or support adheres to the post-1960s party line. Presidents Kennedy and Johnson expanded American involvement in Vietnam; President Carter boycotted the 1980 Moscow Olympics; and President Clinton successfully lobbied for passage of a welfare reform bill in 1996 that many liberals felt was cruel and punitive toward single mothers.

In many ways, however, Wilson fits the profile of a modern liberal. For one thing, he was a Democrat. We take it for granted today that the vast majority of liberals reside within the Democratic Party, but in the fifty years between the Civil War and Wilson's being elected president, two Republican presidents above all embodied the ideas of progress and freedom: Abraham Lincoln and Theodore Roosevelt. Wilson's ambitious agenda was dubbed the "New Freedom" program, thereby combining two words that have been closely associated with liberalism ever since. Twenty years later, President Franklin Roosevelt put forth the New Deal, and a quarter of a century after that momentous series of reforms, John F. Kennedy offered Americans a New Frontier.

Wilson's notable accomplishments included creation of the Federal Reserve System, the strengthening of antitrust legislation, and passage of the country's first federal law covering child labor, as well as a law establishing an eight-hour workday for railroad employees. In April 1917, a few months after being elected to a second term, Wilson engineered the entry of the United States into World War I. And notwithstanding the 1976 Republican vice presidential candidate Bob Dole's caustic remark that the twentieth century had been an era of "Democrat wars," Wilson's decision to align the United States with Britain, France, and Russia and against Germany and Austria was a monumental event in the history of European and American liberalism. As the classicist Victor Davis Hanson observed, World War I was "a war that was not so much a misunderstanding of like-minded aristocratically governed European constitutional states as a struggle for the liberal future of Europe itself."[10] Wilson's famous declaration that the "world must be made safe for democracy" was not just rhetoric.

The United States may have entered the war to "save democracy" abroad, but on the home front patriotic fervor and wartime hysteria led to some profoundly undemocratic and illiberal acts. The socialist presidential candidate Eugene V. Debs was put in prison for delivering a speech denouncing the war, and the Wilson administration signed into law both an Espionage Act and a Sedition Act. In the words of Brogan, "No one who weakened support for 'the boys' in uniform deserved any mercy."[11]

Casual students of American history know Wilson primarily for his

Fourteen Points, the ambitious plan to create a just and lasting peace for the peoples of Europe and, by extension, the United States. It is the last of the fourteen points that best reflects the thinking of modern liberalism: establishment of an association of nations "for the purpose of affording mutual guarantees of political independence and territorial integrity to great and small states alike." Wilson's concept, subsequently known as the League of Nations, would have effectively placed the United States at the head of a "world family" created to solve potential conflicts through peaceful negotiation instead of violence. This utopian ideal has been promoted by liberals and assailed by conservatives ever since it was propounded. In 1920 isolationist Republicans in the Senate were primarily responsible for the vote opposing U.S. participation in the League of Nations.

Some twenty-five years later, another liberal, Franklin Roosevelt, was the prime mover behind the United Nations. By the 1960s, the John Birch Society and other far-right conservatives were urging the United States to get out of the U.N. on the grounds that it was a nest of communist spies and routinely favored the Reds. Communism's collapse did nothing to modify the hostility of conservatives toward the U.N. The administration of George W. Bush, particularly such figures as Vice President Dick Cheney, Defense Secretary Donald Rumsfeld, and Ambassador John Bolton, held contempt for the organization and arrogantly challenged its authority. In their opposition to the Iraq war, liberals argued that the United States should have worked more closely with the U.N. on a strategy to contain if not counter the regime of Saddam Hussein.

. . .

Progressive was not always a euphemism for liberal in American history. In the period from 1895 to 1915, the term was a bona fide political movement. In national politics, progressives are identified primarily with Teddy Roosevelt (president from 1901 through 1908) and Wilson. Much of the progressive agenda was based on curbing the power of Big

Business—railroad companies in particular—"humanizing" the workplace, and protecting consumers.

Among Roosevelt's singular achievements was passage of the Hepburn Act of 1906, which bestowed upon the Interstate Commerce Commission the power to establish minimum and maximum railroad rates. Appalled—and goaded into action—by the publication of Upton Sinclair's novel *The Jungle*, an exposé of horribly unsanitary conditions in Chicago's stockyards, Roosevelt lobbied Congress to approve the Meat Inspection Act and the Pure Food and Drug Act. The latter prohibited the sale of adulterated products in interstate commerce. An ardent environmentalist, Roosevelt added nearly 150 million acres of open space to the government reserves of 45 million acres. Roosevelt's activism contrasts with the majority of Republican presidents who came after him throughout the twentieth century and into the twenty-first. Nonetheless, Republican senator John McCain (Arizona) considers Roosevelt one of the greatest Republican presidents of all time, right up there with Ronald Reagan.

The policies and programs of Roosevelt and Wilson helped to fundamentally change the definition of liberalism. During the nineteenth century, classic liberalism advocated free trade and unregulated markets. Subsequently, however, liberals have tended to support the rights of working people and unions when these rights are in conflict with big business. "When I was a young man in college, this nation was engaged in a great liberal crusade," said Wendell Willkie, the 1940 Republican nominee for president, during a speech that year in Toledo, Ohio. "Its leaders were three great Americans—all three very different in personality and background—Theodore Roosevelt, [Wisconsin governor] Robert La Follette, and Woodrow Wilson. Its objective was to free the American people from the excessive power of Big Business."[12] Willkie did not think so highly of his opponent in the 1940 election, Franklin Delano Roosevelt. A Republican criticizes a Democrat for destroying the true spirit of liberalism? To people whose experience with American politics begins with the Reagan presidency that would seem unlikely, if not impossible. Despite Willkie's objections, FDR thought of himself as liberal, and he regarded the New Deal as a great triumph for liberalism.

. . .

On August 24, 1935, nearing the end of his first term in office, fifty-three-year-old Franklin Delano Roosevelt gave an address to the Young Democratic Clubs of America. As often happens when an elected official speaks to young men and women who are preparing to embark on a life in public service and have shown an aptitude for politics, the president spoke from his heart about the evolution of his views. In a tone more regretful than apologetic, he confessed to an early ignorance of the connection between "lack of opportunity, lack of education" and both rural and urban poverty. But, in a rebuke to social Darwinist thinking, FDR told his audience that he came to understand that the poor were not born to be poor. It was government that in many cases had failed them, and it was government that could improve their desperate circumstances.

Later in the speech, FDR built upon this idea to offer a definition of New Deal liberalism that is no less relevant today: "The cruel suffering of the recent depression has taught us unforgettable lessons. We have been compelled by stark necessity to unlearn the too comfortable superstition that the American soil was mystically blessed with every kind of immunity to grave economic maladjustments, and that the American spirit of individualism—all alone and unhelped by the cooperative efforts of government—could withstand and repel every form of economic disarrangement or crisis."[13]

Throughout his administration, FDR reminded the American people that his policies and political philosophy were unquestionably liberal. His frequent and proud use of the words *liberal* and *liberalism* was as calculated as the efforts of post-McGovern Democrats to remove those words from their political vocabularies. Roosevelt also recognized that some would interpret government intervention in the economy as contradicting the classic notion that authentic liberalism demands a free-market economy. As a consequence, he emphasized the idea suggested in

Jefferson's letter near the start of the chapter: the equating of liberalism with progress. "In the coming primaries in all parties," said FDR in a June 24, 1938, Fireside Chat, "there will be many clashes between two schools of thought, generally classified as liberal and conservative. Roughly speaking, the liberal school of thought recognizes that the new conditions throughout the world call for new remedies."[14]

Another important reason that Roosevelt emphasized the quintessentially liberal character of the New Deal was to distinguish the program from communism and socialism, both of which were increasingly popular with American leftists in the 1930s. He wanted the public to be able to locate precisely the New Deal on the ideological spectrum, and not to be confused by propaganda and misinformation from the opposition. After all, in the 1930s conservative Republicans had already initiated the "red-baiting" of liberals and Democrats that would increase exponentially in the years immediately after World War II. Historian John White describes their tactics thus: "In a desperate attempt to regain the White House in 1936, the GOP drew a straight line between the New Deal and communism."[15] It was to counteract these claims that during that same 1938 Fireside Chat, FDR called communism "as dangerous as Fascism," which, with Hitler threatening Europe, was a damning indictment. How could any pro–New Deal leftists support communism after hearing that?

When Roosevelt took office in 1933, the unemployment rate was 25 percent, or some thirteen million workers. Hundreds of banks were failing every year. The Great Depression did not discriminate, affecting Americans of all races, ethnicities, religions, and regions. Over the next five years FDR and a Democratic-led Congress—under the banner of liberalism—approved a series of bills that transformed the relationship between the federal government and the national economy. As an example of liberalism in action, only the Great Society compares to the New Deal in terms of accomplishments. These include the Civilian Conservation Corps (1933); the Glass-Steagall Banking Act (1933), which separated investment from commercial banks and created the

Federal Deposit Insurance Corporation; the Securities and Exchange Commission (1934); the Federal Housing Administration (1934); the Social Security Act (1935); the Farm Security Administration (1937), which maintained migrant labor camps; and the Fair Labor Standards Act (1938), which established a bottom line for wages. By repeatedly linking the New Deal to liberalism, Roosevelt hammered home the idea that only liberalism was capable of both comprehending and aggressively responding to national economic crises. His programs also offered a powerful argument that liberalism represented the future, which was not immediately apparent during the Depression—even to true believing liberals. As Isaiah Berlin notes, "The most insistent propaganda in those days declared that humanism and liberalism were played out, and that the choice now lay between two bleak extremes—Communism and Fascism—the red and the black. To those where not carried away by the patter the only light that was left in the darkness was the administration of [Franklin] Roosevelt and the New Deal in the United States."[16]

The president implied that Americans were very fortunate that liberals held power in the 1930s. The mainstream alternative, pro–Big Business Republicanism, would in his view have condemned the country to an eternity of economic misery and hardship.

. . .

Freedom and progress—the dominant ideas behind liberalism—can coexist, but not always easily. Political correctness and hate speech codes are two modern-day examples: introduced presumably to end discrimination and bigotry, they also limit freedom of expression, which is unacceptable to many liberals. Regarding the economy, there are those who still argue that the New Deal was anathema to the basic principles underlying American capitalism. Employing the kind of buzz phrase that was made popular by Barry Goldwater and Ronald Reagan, the conservative English historian and journalist Paul Johnson said the Social Security Act "introduced a specific and permanent system of federal welfare."[17] Doctrinaire believers in the free market system regard the New Deal as the start of the federal government's ever greater control over our economic lives, to the detriment of growth. In this light, even the "little man" is hurt by the excessive burdens placed upon business by tax-happy, regulation-loving liberals in Congress. Conservatives maintain that liberal policies and programs deny U.S. citizens the *freedom* to spend their money as they see fit.

New Deal liberals would counter that if people cannot find steady work, they are not truly free. Only when they are able to acquire a good job and provide a degree of financial security for their families will they achieve this dream. In accord with this principle of economic liberalism, some of these jobs can be made available only through government programs. From this perspective, liberalism does not deny freedom, but guarantees it.

The FDR administration and the New Deal changed the meaning and purpose of American liberalism. To the free-market liberal Wendell Willkie, Roosevelt and his advisors offered a corrupt version of liberalism that placed the cherished ideals of freedom and progress with a new, nefarious, and illiberal institution he christened Big Government. Willkie ran for president on a platform to restore liberalism's good name and to save it from the usurpers. A proliberal critic from the right, Willkie's type is rare in American politics—few contemporary Republicans have anything positive to say about liberalism in the last four decades. Moreover, Willkie's criticisms did not sway many liberals in 1940—FDR was handily elected to a third term—and neither the GOP challenger nor his politics are much remembered today. It is the legacy of FDR's liberalism that endures: liberals and progressives will fight as hard to protect programs introduced during the New Deal, especially Social Security, as they will remnants of the New Frontier and Great Society.

The final five years of the Roosevelt presidency (FDR died in office on April 12, 1945) were devoted to fighting and winning World War II and working with Churchill and Stalin to devise the postwar map for Central and Eastern Europe. The Big Three—beginning at Casablanca in

January 1943 and continuing in Tehran later that year and, finally, at Yalta in February 1945—arrived at a series of agreements that left much of Eastern Europe under Soviet control. For many on the American right, Yalta became a symbol of liberal capitulation and cowardice in international affairs. They were especially bitter that FDR "sold out" Poland to the Soviets. It was not so simple. Over the past fifty years a number of historians have pointed out that "the most that can be said of the Yalta Conference was that it offers a striking study in misunderstanding, with Roosevelt in particular a victim of his own illusions. For by then Stalin hardly needed permission to do whatever he wished in Eastern Europe, as the British at least understood perfectly well."[18] Not until the liberation of Eastern Europe in 1989 and the end of the Soviet Union two years later was "Yalta" finally retired as a showpiece of antiliberal propaganda in American politics. There would soon be another war to fight, one that had no obvious connection to the Cold War between the United States and the Soviet Union.

Nonetheless, Yalta had a significant impact on domestic politics in the history of postwar American liberalism. The repercussions of the conference served as an early talking point for right-wing conservatives seeking to exploit Soviet-American tensions for their own political purposes. Forget the reality on the ground; the Right knew what *really* happened at Yalta. And the fact that the American president at the time was a proud, unapologetic liberal allowed conservatives to link this foreign policy "disaster" to liberalism.

In retrospect, what is astonishing about the Right's success at demonizing liberals and their alleged capitulation to communists—foreign and domestic—is that it occurred so soon after the end of a war won by two liberal presidents, Franklin Roosevelt and Harry Truman. Liberals were an easier target after Vietnam. Beginning in the late 1970s there was a kind of twisted logic to the often inaccurate and biased arguments by conservatives that liberals in Congress and the White House had "lost" Vietnam. In this case, two liberal presidents, Kennedy and Johnson, did not develop a clear and coherent strategy for victory, and later, the New Left/liberal antiwar movement helped turn public opinion against the war. But that is not the case with World War II. After all, it was Truman who made the decision to drop the atom bomb on two Japanese cities. A number of historians and writers on the left have argued ever since that the president took this action as much to impress the Soviets as to put an end to the war in the Pacific.

It was bad luck for American liberalism, however, that the end of World War II also marked the beginning of the Cold War. Liberals were given no credit for leading the fight against Hitler and the Japanese empire. During the ensuing decade, 1945–55, American liberalism experienced one of the most stress-filled periods in its history. The events of that time can still traumatize liberals of any age, even after the failures of the past quarter century. Low points include: loyalty oaths, the loss of China, the Alger Hiss case, the outlawing of the Communist Party, the rise of Richard Nixon and Joe McCarthy, the outbreak of the Korean War, the detonation of a hydrogen bomb by the Soviet Union, and Adlai Stevenson's back-to-back defeats for the presidency. Liberals were either blamed for—or suffered the consequences from—each of these events. And whereas the New Deal had "saved" the United States, liberals were now accused of handing the country over to the enemy.

Although they were clearly on the defensive, some prominent liberals did not meekly accept their fate during this dark period. In January 1947, a group of them started an organization known as Americans for Democratic Action, or the ADA. The founders included Eleanor Roosevelt, Walter Ruether, Arthur Schlesinger Jr., Reinhold Niebuhr, Hubert Humphrey, and John Kenneth Galbraith. While social and economic issues constituted an important part of the ADA's agenda, the organization is best remembered for its staunch anticommunism, described in the following way by the economist and author Richard Parker: "For many of its members, one of the ADA's most important missions was to halt and reverse the influence of domestic communists and fellow traveling radicals on postwar American liberalism."[19]

Within a few years, Humphrey sponsored legislation in the United

States Senate to outlaw the Communist Party. The bill passed with only one dissenting vote. The founding of Americans for Democratic Action represents one of the pivotal moments in the history of an influential subset of liberalism, known as Cold War liberalism. Over the ensuing sixty years, Cold War liberalism has come to stand for those self-proclaimed liberals who believe the United States must be strong and decisive in foreign affairs and harbor no illusions about the nature and ambitions of our enemies—whoever and wherever they are. This version has outlasted the Cold War. Contemporary observers who believe that the Democratic Party is naive about the threats posed by militant Islam and international terrorism have argued for a return to Cold War liberalism.

Both the existence of the ADA, which was hardly a fringe group, and policies enacted by Harry Truman should have demonstrated to even hard-right conservatives that influential liberals were committed to the fight against communism. Writing four decades later, Paul Johnson offered the view that "Harry Truman proved to be one of the great American presidents."[20] Johnson was enamored of Truman's foreign policy, especially toward the Soviet Union, which the author contrasted favorably both with that of his predecessor and the Democratic commanders-in-chief who came later.

In March 1947, the president proposed what has come to be known as the Truman Doctrine: "I believe it must be the policy of the United States to support free peoples who are resisting attempted subjugation by armed minorities or by outside pressure." Proposed in response to an immediate crisis in Greece, and the corresponding fear that victory by communist insurgents could lead to a "domino effect" across the Middle East, the Truman Doctrine has been regarded by many as justifying (falsely or not) U.S. involvement in local conflicts around the globe, including Korea, Iran and Guatemala in the 1950s, Cuba and Vietnam in the 1960s, and Chile and Angola in the 1970s. A few months later, Congress approved the National Security Act, which created the CIA and the National Security Council (NSC). These actions, part of an evolving policy of containment toward the Soviet Union, established the foundations of the postwar American foreign policy state.

As a result of this stance, Truman, though a pro-labor liberal on domestic issues who was the architect of the Fair Deal and a proponent of universal health insurance, has been severely criticized by some on the left. For example, in a brief essay, first published in *The Nation*, commemorating the fortieth anniversary of the Truman Doctrine and the NSC, Gore Vidal wrote: "The fact that the Soviet Union was no military or economic threat to us was immaterial. It must be made to appear threatening so that the continuing plan could be set in motion in order to create that National Security State in which we have been living for the past forty years."[21]

On June 25, 1950, communist North Korea launched an invasion of South Korea. Within two days, Truman, acting under the auspices of the United Nations, pledged U.S. support to the beleaguered country. But it was not simply the fate of the South Korean people that concerned the Truman Administration. As Hugh Brogan wrote, "It was assumed that the North Koreans would never have dared to act without the express authorization of Stalin."[22] In the judgment of American policy-makers, the Korean war was never just about Korea but part of the struggle for worldwide supremacy between the United States and the Soviet Union. From Truman through Johnson, one of the hallmarks of Cold War liberalism is the consideration of local or regional conflicts in larger terms. For example, it would have been absurd to regard Ho Chi Minh alone as a grave threat to the United States, one of the world's two superpowers. But if Ho Chi Minh is portrayed as the tool of the Soviet Union and China, then the war in Vietnam takes on a different meaning. We must fight them there in order not to fight them here.

Still, Cold War liberals remained bona fide liberals on domestic issues. At the 1948 Democratic Convention, Minneapolis mayor Hubert Humphrey proposed a far-reaching civil rights platform that was to the left of even Truman. And yet six years later Humphrey, by then a senator from Minnesota, introduced his Senate bill to outlaw the Communist Party. This combination of an aggressive left-liberalism on domestic matters and a bellicose attitude toward communism distinguishes Cold War liberals from their foreign policy progeny, the neoconservatives of the 1970s and 1980s. The neocons, as they came to be known, openly abhorred components of the liberal agenda involving race and government assistance, specifically quotas and the Aid to Dependent Children Act. Their support for Ronald Reagan's presidential campaign in 1980 stemmed from Reagan's conservative positions on foreign policy *and* domestic issues. It was only several years later, after the Republican Party had been captured by the Christian right, that neoconservatives criticized liberals almost exclusively for their positions on foreign policy. Many of the leading neoconservatives were Jewish, and they were as uncomfortable as liberals were with antiabortion laws, prayer in schools, and edicts that condemned gay people to hell.

The combination of President Truman's foreign policy—he also presided over the founding of NATO—and the invention of Cold War liberalism should have given liberals unimpeachable credentials in the battle against world communism, even during the darkest days of the Cold War. Furthermore, liberals in the early and mid-1950s were willing to compromise their ideals if it meant being left alone. "Many liberals acquiesced in the suppression of dissent. Some were scared of being caught up in the mania themselves and joined the mob lest it turn on them. Others were concerned that the handful of Soviet sympathizers in America were a great enough menace to warrant extreme action."[23]

Looking back, the surrender of liberals over civil liberties issues is shameful, in part because it did absolutely nothing to impress the other side. Nixon, McCarthy, and like-minded conservatives were determined to equate liberals with Communism and treason, regardless of evidence offered to the contrary. If the Democrats moved to the right on issues of national security, their Republican antagonists would simply move further to the right. For example, not even masochistic, self-hating liberals joined McCarthy in his quest to prove that the U.S. Army was riddled with communist spies.

It is an axiom of American politics since the end of World War II that Democrats cannot win a patriotism contest against the GOP. Whether the enemy resides in Moscow, Beijing, or in caves somewhere along the border between Afghanistan and Pakistan, conservatives in this country are unrestrained on matters of national security. They have owned" patriotism since 1945, and they will say anything to prevent liberals— Cold War or antiwar—from claiming even one inch of Old Glory.

Nonetheless, Cold War liberalism and Truman's aggressive anticommunism enabled liberals to pursue a strong foreign policy without sacrificing their fundamental beliefs. Liberals are not communists, and there was nothing wrong with making that point abundantly clear to the American masses. Furthermore, Cold War liberalism permitted one to remain a liberal without harboring any warm and fuzzy illusions about the nature of the Soviet threat.

However, in the 1960s and 1970s, as liberalism moved further left, some of the early Cold War liberals staged a noisy exit from the Democratic Party. They came to the conclusion that their brand of liberalism was incompatible with the Gene McCarthy-George McGovern-Tom Hayden variant. The advent of black power, feminism, gay rights, and, most of all, a foreign policy that demanded an immediate withdrawal from Vietnam, that valued negotiation over confrontation and human rights over ideology, and that called for reductions in the defense budget, pushed Cold War liberals and their neoconservative offspring to quit the party of Roosevelt, Truman, and JFK and to join the GOP. They did not stop there. They accused the new liberals of rooting against America, a charge that is revived with every conflict. It is a measure of the U.S. failure in Iraq that for the first time since the 1972 McGovern campaign Democrats could run and win on an antiwar platform. Both the Democratic takeover of the House and Senate in 2006 and the 2008 Democratic presidential primary reflect the sense that there are political advantages in opposing "Bush's war."

Still, younger Democrats who know McGovern mainly as the guy who got clobbered by Nixon are calling for the return of Cold War liberalism. They worry about the party's enduring "peace now" image and its association with weakness and failure in international relations. They concede that Iraq is now a disaster—many of them originally supported the war—but they are concerned that liberals and progressives will draw the wrong conclusions for U.S. policy in the future. This debate will continue long after the troops have returned home.

. . .

Whether extolling the virtues of individualism or protecting our way of life from totalitarianism, liberal thinkers and liberal politicians since Locke have embraced the ideas of freedom and progress. By the same token, fealty to these ideas provides a standard for assessing the credibility and efficacy of liberalism at any particular period in history. When liberalism no longer represents freedom and progress—Wendell Willkie argued that the FDR version sacrificed the former—then it does not meet the test of liberalism in the American tradition. Given these criteria, one of the key questions to be examined in this book is whether the decline of liberalism since the late 1960s was principally the result of a self-inflicted wound. Did liberals lose faith in liberalism?

CHAPTER TWO

Which Way Did the '60s Go?

In 1947, when he was seven years old, Rick Tuttle, who decades later served as Los Angeles City Controller, rode on a train with his family from Memphis to Cincinnati—the first stage of a regular journey home to the East Coast. On this particular trip, the train experienced mechanical failure just outside Memphis, which caused a state of near panic among the passengers. The train's sorry condition raised the possibility that Rick, a younger sibling, his parents, and grandmother would be stranded in a cold, dark railroad car for the night. They appealed to the conductor of the functioning train up ahead to allow them to board but garnered no sympathy and no satisfaction. As the situation became more desperate, Rick recalls watching his father approach a Pullman car porter, pull him aside, and hand him a card. He will never forget what happened next: "We walked over and suddenly several Pullman car porters ushered us onto the [operating] train. I said, 'Daddy, what did you show him?' And you know what he showed him? His NAACP card. I got some political consciousness that day."

Rick retained that consciousness through the 1950s, the sleepy decade separating the remnants of the old left from the emergence of the New Left. In 1960, Rick entered Wesleyan University, where he became a liberal activist. His initial cause involved a question of freedom of religion, or to be more precise, freedom from religion. Tuttle's fraternity included a pledge of belief in Jesus Christ as a personal savior, which made it impossible for Jews, Muslims, Buddhists, and atheists to join. Rick recalled that he and a few others in the fraternity attempted to get the national chapter to eliminate that requirement, but to no avail. Refusing to accept the status quo, Rick said that the Wesleyan fraternity voted simply to "fire the national." The national was not placated or amused, and initiated a lengthy legal battle over ownership of the fraternity building, which eventually resulted in a settlement favoring the Wesleyan chapter.

The next destinations in the odyssey of this early-1960s liberal were Georgia and Mississippi in the deep South. Inspired by a professor named John Maguire who became a key figure in the civil rights movement and, later, the president of Claremont Graduate University, Wesleyan University contributed a significant number of young men and women to the ranks of both the Freedom Riders and the drive to register voters. In 1964, Martin Luther King Jr. delivered the commencement address at Wesleyan.

Tuttle spent the summer of 1963 registering voters in Georgia and Mississippi. Among his assigned tasks was infiltrating white supremacist meetings. "Me with my Yankee accent," said Tuttle in a June 2005 interview with me, treading lightly over an experience that must have been equal parts tense and thrilling. He also participated in civil rights and voting rights marches in Savannah, Georgia.

In the early 1960s, liberals such as Rick Tuttle did not debate ideological fine points, ponder the future of their movement, or agonize over what went wrong. These liberals did not hide from, or deny, their liberalism. They took action not in the name of liberalism per se, but for civil rights, equality, freedom, and human rights. And though they were not conscious of it at the time, the civil rights movement provided both the training and impetus to advocate on behalf of similar causes throughout the rest of 1960s and the early 1970s. Students such as Tuttle were redefining liberalism for their own generation, creating a new left and outpacing the older liberals occupying the White House. "I took the view that the Kennedy Administration was not doing all it should be doing to protect civil rights workers and African-Americans," Tuttle said. "I did not evaluate President Kennedy solely from the point of view of civil rights, but I was putting major emphasis on that."

But Washington—and much of the nation—would eventually pull even with the marchers: within four years of Tuttle's joining the civil rights movement, Martin Luther King had won the Nobel Peace Prize and President Johnson had signed into law two landmark civil rights bills. The British historian Godfrey Hodgson describes how at the height of the movement, in March 1965, during the famous Selma march, "LBJ went up to the Capitol and there pronounced, to a Joint Session of Congress, the strongest commitment an American President had ever made to the struggle for black equality."[1] In the period 1963–1966, Congress approved the Civil Rights Act, a permanent Food Stamp program, Medicare for everyone over sixty-five, Medicaid for the poor, a national foundation to aid the arts and humanities, and the Voting Rights Act. Other than recalcitrant southern whites and Barry Goldwater, seemingly everyone was a proud liberal at this time in our history.

But in another sense 1965 marked an end as much as a beginning. Every decade evolves, but few (if any) in U.S. history changed politics and culture as rapidly and radically as the 1960s. Even today, it is astonishing to realize that only five years separate "Johnny Angel" from "Purple Haze," or the Singing Nun from Janis Joplin. A mere five months after the Selma march, the Watts riots in Los Angeles showed millions of white viewers a different image of black people. On their television sets they watched blacks *perpetrate* mob violence against innocent whites, rather than the other way around. And unlike Alabama and Mississippi, the people of Watts did not appear to welcome the presence or assistance of white liberals. Rioters did not bother to learn the political affiliations of blond, blue-eyed "outsiders" before throwing rocks and bottles. In Watts in August 1965 Rick Tuttle would have been running from black people, not marching with them. For many white viewers, the beatings, looting, burning, and sniping that went on from 1965 to 1968 in Watts, Detroit, Newark, and Chicago overshadowed any legitimate grievances black residents held regarding police brutality, job discrimination, racism, and lack of basic services. This time white people were attacked because of the color of their skin.

In America, blacks have little room for mistakes. The positive image that Dr. King, the Reverend Ralph Abernathy, and brave, nonviolent civil rights marchers in the South had generated among many nonsouthern whites could suffer irreparable damage from media reporting of one ghetto riot. Whereas in the spring of 1965 liberals and the liberal-inclined spoke glowingly about the prospects for integration, after Watts certain phrases became more widespread, such as "black culture," "white culture," and, more famously after the release of the Kerner Report in 1968, "two separate societies." This sense of us and them, or in its more insidious form, us versus them, would damage liberalism's credibility on matters of race.

Just as liberals were applauded for their courageous determination to end Jim Crow laws, so they would later be excoriated for seeming to sympathize with or coddle urban "hoodlums" that in the view of terrified middle-class whites deserved nothing more than a crack over the head with a baton and a lengthy stint in prison. Fifteen months after Watts, Ronald Reagan was elected governor of California, which in time would prove to be the catalyst for the unprecedented rise of right-wing conservatism across the country from 1980 to 2006. This was not the revolution that black militants and left-wing radicals hoped for in the aftermath of Watts.

. . .

Marc Haefele arrived in New York from Jacksonville, Florida, in 1961 as a liberal Democrat, and ten years later, living in a rural section of New Jersey, he remained a liberal Democrat. A liberal in 1971 could list many more causes on his or her political résumé than was possible a decade earlier, such as the antiwar movement, women's liberation, and environmentalism. As a student at New York University, Haefele had not only escaped the South and what he regarded as its stifling redneck culture, but also joined the growing civil rights movement on campus in an attempt to change that same culture from afar. A large NYU contingent—Marc included—took the train from New York City to Washington, DC, to attend the famous "I Have a Dream" civil rights rally on August 28, 1963. "I had never seen so many people in one place before, and wouldn't again until Woodstock six years later," said Marc when I interviewed him in May 2005.

Marc recalls that he was one of the few non-Jews among the white students who formed an NYU chapter of the Congress of Racial Equality (CORE). Among its many causes was bringing more black entertainers on campus, in the interests of what would today be called diversity and to counter what seemed to be a monopoly held by white folksingers. The members of CORE contemplated making an offer to the comedian Dick Gregory to perform, but they reluctantly concluded he was too popular and therefore outside the boundaries of NYU's limited entertainment budget. Instead they settled on a young black comic named Bill Cosby.

In 1964 Congress passed the Civil Rights Act, which for Marc represented the glorious outcome of everything he had worked toward since arriving at NYU and everything he believed in since he had started trying to make sense of the world. Passage of the legislation signaled a major victory for liberalism—another reason to stay involved. One should never underestimate the role winning plays in determining which team to support, both in sports and politics. Americans are not good losers." I had a very strong sense of victory and a kind of personal elation," said Haefele. "All of a sudden my father's people were duckin' and runnin.' It was like watching the prison doors open in Jacksonville. All of a sudden black people could sit on the same park benches as whites or if they chose go to the same stores."

Marc spent the 1960s in New York, although he periodically traveled to Jacksonville to visit his parents and, as a sidelight, monitor the progress of civil rights in his former hometown. And though Marc still considered Jacksonville retrograde and hostile on issues of race, he recalls with a mix of admiration and surprise that many residents were prescient about Vietnam—that is until the peace movement turned them into antihippy patriots. "One reason I decided the war was wrong," said Marc, "was my sense that in Jacksonville—which was in many ways a garrison town with a big naval base and naval air base—the war was not popular. This was between 1963 and 1966. After all, the Navy wasn't losing a whole lot of people, and it was the [liberal] Democrats who started the war. I saw even less patriotic fervor in Jacksonville than I saw in parts of suburban communities in Greater New York."

Uncle Sam would have liked Marc to go to Vietnam in a uniform, carry a gun, and experience the war firsthand. But Marc's strong preference was to spend the 1960s thousands of miles from Saigon, Da Nang, and the DMZ. Still, he did join a reserve unit and he kept in regular contact with Selective Service. Ironically, it was a man in Jacksonville who offered him a way out. "I remember my draft board guy—who talked just like Lyndon Johnson and looked a great deal like him—telling me, 'Now, you know, Marc, if you don't want to go to this war, you don't hafta.' And I said, 'OK, well, between you and me, I'd rather go back to New York and pick up my [publishing] career.'"

The prospect of military service behind him, Marc took a job at Random House, in the publicity department, and then subsequently landed an editor position at Doubleday, where he remained for five years. Now immersed in the Manhattan publishing world, Marc gravitated toward what looked suspiciously like the liberal elite, although the term wasn't widely used back then. He even left behind photographic evidence: in 1971, the magazine *GQ* ran a picture of Marc with long hair but no beard, wearing a dark blue suit and holding a fancy cigarette—an ornament that no liberal would dare to openly display today. Marc's professional triumphs included editing the science fiction writer Philip K. Dick and a young Stephen King. When he wasn't reading and editing manuscripts or attending business lunches and parties, Marc went to protests, primarily in New York and Washington, DC. "During this period the Vietnam War was everywhere, and we always marched," said Marc. "We—people my age, people in publishing—were all against the war. We called ourselves 'trendsetters' at the time."

The reasons for America's retreat from Vietnam still constitute a heated topic. Explanations include the impact of the antiwar movement on domestic politics, that the United States was losing, that Walter Cronkite had had enough, that Democrats in Congress had had enough, or all of the above. Eventually the once fiercely anticommunist Republican president Richard Nixon presided over the gradual withdrawal of American forces from Southeast Asia following his election in 1968. Nixon pursued a strategy that makes today's propeace/prowar Democratic senators seem like models of consistency.

Alternately a peacemaker and a warmonger, Nixon brought troops home, invaded Cambodia, approved secret bombings of Laos and Cambodia, abolished the draft, and ordered the mining of Haiphong Harbor in the spring of 1972 and the fierce bombing of North Vietnam at Christmas that same year. The president bundled these disparate acts into a tidy package he stamped Peace with Honor. By the spring of 1973, early in what would turn out to be Nixon's shortened second term as president, the last American ground troops returned to the United States. Although Marc and his cotrendsetters continued to loath the president, Nixon's actions did give them a belated sense of triumph. In the liberals' account, the antiwar movement had forced Johnson to declare on March 31, 1968, that he would not serve another term as president and stopped Nixon from escalating until victory was achieved. If there were any Americans who "won" the Vietnam War, it was the liberals and radicals who so vehemently and successfully opposed it. Occurring within a decade after passage of the Civil Rights Act and the Voting Rights Act, the Vietnam experience gave the Left a valid if ultimately false sense of its own power to effect major changes in American society.

Rosa Parks, Martin Luther King, the Reverend Ralph Abernathy, and the Freedom Riders had spawned political and social movements that extended well beyond the Mason-Dixon Line and black people. The same month as the Selma march, 216 faculty members at the University of Michigan signed an ad in the school newspaper stating that they were "deeply worried about the war in Vietnam."[2] One of the organizers of a subsequent teach-in at the Michigan campus got the idea from an earlier boycott of schools in the Boston area, an act clearly influenced by the civil rights movement. Though not consciously, the movement encouraged a succession of newly empowered groups to look at their own condition in America and ask hard questions about equality, dignity, and justice. Laura Pulido, who has written about people of color and their relationship with the left, notes, "The civil rights movement also politicized non-black people of color."[3]

In the West during the latter part of the 1960s young Mexican American activists renamed themselves Chicanos—not long after young Negroes renamed themselves blacks—and began demonstrating for improved schools, bilingual education, and school courses more reflective of their own experience, and against the Vietnam War, in which a disproportionate number of young men from their community were being drafted and killed. Pulido notes, "The political landscape of Chicana/o activism shifted in the mid-sixties in response to the Vietnam War, growing ethnic consciousness, the influence of Black Power, and frustration with Mexican-Americans' social and economic marginalization."[4]

. . .

New York played a pivotal role in the rise of women's liberation and, later, the gay rights movement. Marc Haefele gravitated toward feminism as a direct result of his job in publishing. "It was either late 1969 or early 1970 that a woman with a college graduate degree none of us had ever heard of came into the Doubleday offices on 277 Park Avenue, tenth floor, and sat in the outer office and said she had a book about feminism," Marc said. "And everyone gasped, because no one ever did this [came in off the street with a complete manuscript] except the crazy guys with shopping carts or whatever was the equivalent at the time." Still, a woman editor—one of the few on staff—took the manuscript home to read and came back to the office insisting that Doubleday must publish the book. And thus *Sexual Politics*, by Kate Millet, found an audience. "The book opened up a channel," said Marc. "Doubleday became for two or three years the fountainhead of modern feminism."

Marc was drafted by management to go out and recruit other feminist writers to the Doubleday family. As it happened, he was naturally sympathetic to the goals and attitudes of the women's movement, as a result of his personal experiences in the sexual jungle. "I was used to being one of these guys who watched the ugly, misbehaving men get the girls," said Marc. "And I thought, 'Up yours, you ugly, misbehaving assholes. Now you're getting yours.'" Angry white males can be liberals as well as right-wing conservatives.

Now, instead of marching up and down the streets of Manhattan and Washington, DC, Haefele practiced a kind of sedentary liberalism, sitting through numerous feminist conferences and attending sisterhood rallies for political and professional reasons. He felt comfortable in this role, despite his lonely presence in what could be a hostile environment for men, otherwise known as "the enemy." But Marc felt no compulsion to speak up for patriarchal society, which in many ways embarrassed and appalled him. For a number of years, in fact, Marc had noticed that many of his male allies in the civil rights and antiwar movements treated their female colleagues with disrespect and even contempt. Women were assigned to secondary roles and their views were often discounted. Marc believes that it these negative experiences did as much as *The Feminine Mystique*, *Sexual Politics*, and stereotypical gender roles to prompt younger women to transfer their own anger and humiliation into a movement by and for women.

The women's movement, which began toward the end of the 1960s, stemmed in part from women's identification with the condition of black people in America, as well as admiration at the success of the civil rights movement. "The prestige of the black movement and this concept of consciousness-raising explain a great deal that is otherwise puzzling about these movements," wrote Hodgson. "A favorite argument among some of the leaders of the women's movement made this comparison explicit. Gloria Steinem, for example, liked to say that women were niggers."[5]

In a similar vein to Steinem, John Lennon and Yoko Ono released a song entitled "Woman Is the Nigger of the World" on their *Some Time in New York City* album. Choosing a title intended to provoke white liberals as much as enlighten them—and hopeful that blacks would see the irony—John and Yoko implied that women and black people share a common history of being oppressed. The struggles of women, particularly rich white women, are in some sense validated when their circumstances are favorably compared with the group considered to have had it worse than any other in America. And just as black people needed the civil rights movement to make them free, so too did women need their own movement.

Gay liberationists also posited a link between their movement and the growing political consciousness of black people in the South—and North—during the 1960s. In his article "A Gay Manifesto (1969–1970)," Carl Wittman makes the following point: "In the past year there has been an awakening of gay liberation ideas and energy. How it began we don't know; maybe we were inspired by black people and their freedom movement."[6] More recently, proponents of gay marriage have linked their cause to the efforts of thirty and forty years earlier to erase laws against interracial marriage.

But it was one thing for participants in these later causes to claim to be inspired by the civil rights movement, and another to attempt to draw an exact analogy between the circumstances applicable to each of them. When feminists or gay activists pushed the analogy too far, they risked offending and alienating liberals who were otherwise in their corner. As an example, John and Yoko's assertion that "Woman Is the Nigger of the World" raised questions of historical accuracy that divided liberal movements and causes from one another. If woman is truly the "nigger of the world," then who plays the role of the Ku Klux Klansman or the racist southern sheriff? Sexist employers or oppressive husbands are bad, but not that bad.

Unlike gay activism or women's liberation, the environmental movement did not attempt to logically follow from the events of Greensboro, Selma, and Birmingham. Polluted streams or strip-mined mountainsides could never be thought of as an oppressed group of people, and saving Planet Earth was a task so big and momentous that it was beyond the scope of even Dr. King's dream. This explains why ecologists did not receive the immediate and unqualified support of liberals and radicals, and certainly not of organized labor, which in some cases regarded their tactics and goals as a threat comparable to the one posed by Big Business. I. F. Stone, one of the greatest journalists of the left in American history but now largely forgotten, disparaged the first showcase event of the environmental movement—Earth Day in 1970—as a dangerous distraction from more pressing concerns: "Two days before the Earth Day rally, Secretary of Defense Melvin Laird had made a speech to the Associated Press which can only be read as a deliberate effort to sabotage the S.A.L.T. talks, but here we were talking as if we had nothing to worry about but our drains."[7]

Haefele saw things differently. In 1971 he left Manhattan to live in rural New Jersey, a fledgling environmentalist returning to the land. Over the course of a decade he had participated to varying degrees in many of the movements that continue to guide American liberalism: civil rights, peace, gender equality, and now the environment. Unlike Stone, Haefele didn't regard left-wing multitasking as counterproductive. On the contrary, being a liberal at the end of the 1960s meant that one willingly traveled across an ever-expanding political universe. A plethora of issues, causes, and ideas were evidence of liberalism's vibrancy and society's needs. There was no such thing as a '60s liberal with too many causes. It was perfectly possible to oppose leaded gasoline, male chauvinism, and Nixon's Vietnam policy with equal fervor.

The environmental movement had the added attraction of bipartisan appeal. It was beyond the creative powers of most right-wing political consultants to wage a campaign around demonizing ecologists. Blacks, gays, and feminists were much better targets.

Ever since the Watts riot, liberalism had been increasingly perceived by mid-America as moving further away from the mainstream. The consensus that formed around the civil rights and voting rights acts began to deteriorate in the political maelstrom of 1965–75. By the time of the 1968 Democratic presidential primary, most young liberals were backing the antiwar candidacies of Eugene McCarthy and Robert Kennedy, while most New Deal liberals supported President Johnson and (once Johnson dropped out of the race) Vice President Hubert Humphrey.

As this conflict was splitting apart the Democratic Party, Republicans and even some Democrats were looking anew at hard-right conservatism, which had been discredited by the overwhelming defeat of Barry Goldwater in 1964. This reexamination culminated in the 1980 election of Ronald Reagan, who was regarded as the heir to Goldwater. In the 1980 presidential campaign, a liberal Republican, Illinois congressman John Anderson, felt compelled to run as a third-party candidate. In the general election Anderson picked up votes from Democrats who felt President Jimmy Carter was insufficiently liberal on key issues. Today, hardly any one recalls liberal Republicans.

In the aftermath of Earth Day, President Nixon created the Environmental Protection Agency, which is often cited by liberals in the twenty-first century—including George McGovern—as one of the main reasons why Richard Nixon was a better president than George W. Bush. Cynics say the EPA was Nixon's way of appeasing liberals while he continued his destructive policies elsewhere, but even if this were the case, can you imagine Reagan's disciples proposing this kind of compromise?

From his hideaway in New Jersey, surrounded by pro-Nixon neighbors, Marc Haefele nevertheless believed that the ecologists "would win no matter who was president." The environmental movement had the support of key Republicans and did not seek to change the rules of male-female relations, to abolish the death penalty, or to radically redefine American foreign policy. Even conservatives wanted to preserve their pristine oceanfront views. Happy thoughts of a greener and cleaner future helped sustain Marc in the aftermath of McGovern's landslide loss to Nixon in 1972.

CHAPTER THREE

Unhappy Together

During the period 1962–72, Marc Haefele gravitated from the civil rights movement to the antiwar movement to women's liberation to environmentalism, and all while holding a full-time job. What may have looked to outsiders like "issue-hopping," immaturity, or impatience were for Haefele and his colleagues practical and essential steps to remaking American society. For liberals it was like splashing bright paints on a huge canvas, and though they didn't know what the painting would look like in the end, they were certain it would be beautiful. Liberals celebrated local victories—Tuttle and friends changing the regulations on religion at their Wesleyan fraternity and Derek Shearer, who later served as an advisor to President Clinton, leading a successful movement at Yale in the mid-1960s to eliminate the requirement that students had to wear coats and ties to class—and victories of major historical import, such as ending desegregation in the South.

Liberalism in this period acquired a logic of its own. Why shouldn't the liberation of women follow naturally from the "liberation" of blacks in the South, and with a similar happy outcome? Like a corporate behemoth, liberalism kept adding various cultural and social movements to its existing economic and civil rights base. By the early 1970s, the typical liberal supported black studies centers and affirmative action; an immediate withdrawal of American troops from Vietnam; feminism, including tearing down the vestiges of patriarchal society; and, stringent regulations to reduce air and water pollution. Other than black studies centers and getting out of Vietnam, which are particular to a certain time and place, the typical liberal today—if such a person exists—would still believe in these things.

By the mid-1960s, many liberals and radicals switched from folk music to rock, which was characteristic of the movement's openness to change. At the end of the decade rock was only fifteen years old: unless your parents were open-minded, accepting, and curious, they probably demanded that you play the Beatles, the Rolling Stones, or the Who either when they were not home or at a low volume and with the door closed. To those under the age of twenty-five, rock still possessed the attraction and power of being ridiculed, misunderstood, or violently opposed by the old and uptight . It would be at least another two decades before kids had that awful experience of watching their parents boogie to the oldies at some house party in suburbia. The music you liked in the late 1960s defined your politics and the level of your commitment to the revolution." We hated SDS [Students for a Democratic Society], I mean, not hated them, we admired them for their nerve, but they weren't any- thing like us," recalled John Sinclair, cofounder in 1968 of the White Panther Party, a radical support group to the Black Panther Party, in a 2006 interview. "They didn't even listen to the Beatles. They listened to folk music."[1]

. . .

Though his first foray into politics—at the age of ten—involved placing (John) Kennedy bumper stickers on automobiles during the 1960 pres- idential campaign, Richard Katz recalls that his first overtly political act was booking the hard rock group Steppenwolf for a concert at University High School in west Los Angeles in 1968. In a June 2005 interview with me, Katz said Steppenwolf was "the first long-hair group to ever perform at our school." Students watched the band play the hits

"Born to Be Wild" and "Magic Carpet Ride" while teachers and administrators roamed among the crowd, some of them no doubt making a display of grimacing and putting their hands over their ears.

Within a year Katz signed on as an active member of the antiwar movement, even getting the opportunity in 1970—along with a small group of like-minded fellow San Diego State University students—to receive a briefing on Vietnam at the Santa Monica–based think tank, the Rand Corporation. One of the participants was Daniel Ellsberg, who just a year or so later would become world famous as the man who released the Pentagon Papers to the *New York Times.* "To us, he was a hawk on the war," recalled Katz, "although certainly there were conflicts going on inside him. But we didn't know any of that."

In his own choices, Katz epitomized the distinction between radical and liberal, left and New Left, and revolutionaries and reformers, all of which characterized youth politics at the end of the '60s. "I was never somebody who was into violence or storming buildings," said Katz, "that seemed counter-productive to me. But I did agree with picketing and protesting and making speeches. I was always vested in the political process, and I always believed in the political process."

Viewed from the outside, however, there was not a significant difference between liberals and radicals, which in the short and long term created profound political problems for the former. Reagan and Nixon grouped them together, under such memorable headings as "long-haired protestors," "agitators," and "anarchists." At the 1968 Chicago Democratic Convention, the police did not stop to ask one's political ideology before swinging their batons.

Katz relates a personal story that captures the mistrust, suspicion, and political tensions of the time. In the late summer of 1970, a few months after the Ohio National Guard shot and killed four students during a protest at Kent State University, Katz placed a bumper sticker on his dad's aged Rambler that read, "They shoot students, don't they?" a takeoff on the popular fatalistic film at that time called *They Shoot Horses, Don't They?* A few weeks later, as Katz drove around the familiar environs of west Los Angeles, he was stopped by the police. The officers told Katz that a guy named Richard Katz had some outstanding warrants and he just might be that guy. They put him in the squad car and took him down to the local station. "The cops were clearly reacting to the bumper sticker," said Katz. "I remember it so well: one officer saying to me that 'because we like you, we are not going to handcuff you.' I sat at the station for two-and-a-half hours while these guys are flipping through the porn catch of the day. Finally this guy comes up and says; 'oh, I guess it's not you.' I told them at the beginning the birthdates didn't match. But they clearly thought it would be fun to make me sweat for two-and-a-half hours because of the bumper sticker."

The concurrent rise of Goldwater-Reagan conservatism and the New Left in the period 1966–68 threatened liberalism on two fronts. One of these political movements argued that liberalism had gone too far; the other argued that it had not gone far enough. The far left obsessed over liberalism's supposed failures, while the Right harped (and still harps) on its actual or exaggerated triumphs. The assaults of these two forces marked the beginning of a sustained project to demean, denigrate, and destroy liberalism in the United States.

A major development in the right-wing war against liberalism occurred in 1966—the year of *Revolver* and "Good Vibrations"—when Ronald Reagan ran for governor of California. The Republican candidate hammered away at the notion that this new wave of left-wing radicalism was synonymous with liberalism by combining all acts of protest and manifestations of the counterculture into one big threat. This oversimplification—Reagan's trademark—appealed to an increasingly confused and worried middle class. And like any seductive concept, there was just enough truth to persuade those who were inclined to be persuaded. Reagan made sense of what they were seeing on television and reading in the papers.

When Californians went to the polls in November 1966, they voted overwhelmingly for Reagan against the incumbent governor, Pat Brown, who to this day is regarded as one of the purest and most effective liberals in post–World War II American politics. Reagan was able to convey that campus protestors and black militants were the fault of his opponent, even though Brown probably felt no more sympathy for these "troublemakers" than Reagan. Brown was a man of the left—but the old left. This distinction vanished during the campaign. As Ethan Rarick describes in his biography of Brown: "Ahead of his advisers, Reagan realized that Berkeley was a source of deep resentment for working Californians. Voters said the antics of Berkeley students posed a greater problem than unemployment, pollution, or transportation."[2] Change "Berkeley students" to "feminists," "gay activists," or "secular humanists" and you have the prototype of the contemporary right-wing political campaign, as well as the source of despair emanating from liberals when these campaigns succeed.

The irony is that during Reagan's first term California was practically overrun with violent protests, including the May 1969 People's Park confrontation in Berkeley, in which one man was killed and scores injured. The late 1960s also marked the emergence of the Black Panthers in Oakland. And yet few voters blamed these threats from the left on the current governor, as they had on Pat Brown. If anything, it made them love Reagan more. He had said there would be trouble, and he was right. Imagine how much worse shape we would be in if Brown was still governor? Apparently if politicians talk tough it doesn't much matter what happens on their watch, especially if they are conservatives—such as President George W. Bush and the War on Terror. In 1970, Reagan easily won reelection.

The threat posed to liberals and indeed all Democrats by Reagan's tactics in the late 1960s—"revolution" was still in the distance—did not prompt liberals and radicals to establish a united front. In fact, the New Left derived much of its strength from condemning liberalism as ineffectual or even as in cahoots with the enemy. In his history of the New Left, Todd Gitlin paraphrases their attitude thus: "Liberals! The very word has become the New Left's curse." Gitlin notes elsewhere that "we [the New Left] had built a politics on the accusation that liberals were hypocritical."[3] Robert Reich, Secretary of Labor under Bill Clinton, wrote a book full of pragmatic advice to liberals living under George W. Bush, and yet he too had unkind things to say about liberals at this time: "In the sixties (a period that in political and cultural terms actually ran from about 1964 to 1972), the New Left was the source of most of the political passions and intensity in America. Liberals were considered wimps, wishy-washy, bourgeois."[4]

Reich might have added "excessively polite" or "much too kind" to the list. In 1968, Abbie Hoffman, founder of the Youth International Party (Yippies), a group closely aligned with the New Left, wrote an article titled "White Niggers." Of all racial epithets this one was the ugliest to liberals, especially given its common usage by southern whites. It was inconceivable to liberals that any white person on the left could use that word—even ironically. This usage didn't bother Abbie Hoffman. He wanted to provoke and offend in order to highlight the differences between his self-consciously fearless politics and the legions of quaint, prissy liberals. The New Left posed the question: Given a seemingly interminable war in Southeast Asia, riots in ghettos across America, and sex, drugs, and rock and roll, what was the more appropriate stance? "White Nigger" was Hoffman's declaration of independence, and the title of his article made it easier for John and Yoko to record "Woman Is the Nigger of the World" a few years later.

. . .

The challenges from the left and right notwithstanding there was little evidence to imply that liberalism belonged to yesterday. And yet the lack of a strong campaign from liberals reveals much about liberalism's subsequent decline.

The first and in many respects most devastating blow—devastating because largely unanswered—was the rise of black power in the middle of the 1960s, which resulted in whites being essentially kicked out of the movement for racial equality. At one level, it was understandable that black people would want total control over their own political futures, especially considering slavery and its legacy of subservience. It was also understandable—particularly given the cult of youth that was so much part of the political, social, and cultural environment of the 1960s— that the generation of black leaders immediately following Martin Luther King would want to do things its own way. Excluding whites and refusing to rule out violence were two obvious departures from the King model.

White people had to understand that they were expendable simply because they were white. According to this view, preaching liberalism and tolerance did not absolve whites of responsibility for the fate of black people in the South, Watts, Harlem, Newark, or anywhere else. The white race was the problem, and therefore it could no longer be considered part of the solution. The emergent leader of the Black Power movement, Stokely Carmichael, expressed this view in language that would become increasingly common during the next several years: "The white man is irrelevant to blacks, except as an oppressive force."[5]

The first part of this statement was demonstrably false: whites had been tremendously important contributors to the success of the civil rights movement, in the field as well as in Congress, the White House, and state legislatures around the nation. Carmichael could hardly claim historical amnesia because this had transpired over the preceding five or so years. He was deliberately falsifying the record for his own militant purposes. Carmichael is entitled to his opinion, as any liberal would say. Still, that does not make the statement true, or any less despicable.

To the detriment of liberalism and the cause of civil rights, white liberals acquiesced to the desires of the new regime. As a consequence, the successful biracial liberal civil-rights coalition unraveled. Liberals simply walked away, in a manner more patronizing than accommodating, with the implication that radicalism was a phase that black people had to go through. Meanwhile, the relentless Carmichael called integration a "subterfuge for the maintenance of white supremacy," in an article published in June 1966 in the *New York Review of Books*, thereby guaranteeing that it would be seen by young Jewish liberals and their parents, both of whom had been active participants in the civil rights movement.[6] The sheer gall and ingratitude of Carmichael and other black leaders at the contributions of their white brothers and sisters bruised feelings that have not healed with the passage of time.

In the not-too-distant future issues such as quotas and affirmative action further divided the races and convinced previously accommodating whites that they were better off switching to the Republicans. But by the 1960s the damage was done. Had liberals stood firm in the wake of assaults from Carmichael, H. Rap Brown, and others and echoed the antiwar chant "Hell, no, we won't go," it would have been in the best tradition of their movement: an act of bravery, courage, and defiance. Instead, they walked away.

Liberals' inability to do the right thing showed them to be weak and afraid of confronting their "friends" under any circumstances. Whether accurate or not, the perception that liberals allow minority groups to get away with anything for no other reason than that they are minority groups has severely harmed liberalism's credibility. Liberals' passivity repels voters who demand action and reinforces the notion of liberals as cowardly and co-opted. At the same time, it has enabled conservatives and a few iconoclastic Democrats to strut like tough guys when they take a contrary—or hostile—position on issues regarding race, gender, or sexuality. This stance goes over well with Middle America.

The failure of liberals to aggressively confront their detractors on the left and right exposed another defect that would resonate through the decades. By 1966–67, liberalism was for all practical purposes a leaderless movement. Over the preceding five years, Presidents Kennedy and Johnson had indicated their support for the goals (if not the tactics) of the civil rights movement. Passage of the Civil Rights Act and the Voting Rights Act was primarily due to the extraordinary organizing skills of Martin Luther King and the political skills of LBJ. Their partnership—and its breakup over the Vietnam War—is one of the great stories of the 1960s, worthy of an extended off-Broadway treatment or a two-hour cable movie.

Once liberals switched from the civil rights movement to the antiwar movement their connection to Johnson was severed. He was now the villain chiefly responsible for escalating and prolonging an immoral war. What he had accomplished earlier in his administration on behalf of civil rights and the "Negro people" no longer sufficed. "I was skeptical of Johnson during the 1964 campaign, but he did say he was going to pass the civil rights bill as a legacy to President Kennedy," recalled Derek Shearer, Yale class of 1968, and later a close political advisor to President Clinton. "He also said he wasn't going to send American boys to Vietnam. And then I remember the winter of my freshman year, after Goldwater was defeated, and he [Johnson] started the bombing of North Vietnam. We felt like he had been lying to us."[7]

Vietnam all but destroyed any favorable impressions of the Johnson presidency among young liberals. With rare exceptions liberals offer only lukewarm praise for LBJ's presidency. Among historians and commentators Johnson's reputation suffered more from Vietnam than Reagan's from Iran-Contra, Clinton's from the Lewinsky affair, and maybe even Nixon's from Watergate, perhaps because Nixon did not have as far to fall.

Having rejected Johnson, liberals needed another leader to represent their newfound interests. As I will soon describe, the role was filled for a short time in 1968 by Eugene McCarthy and then by Robert Kennedy. In the 1972 presidential campaign, Democratic presidential nominee George McGovern emerged as the leader of the new liberalism, which by this time included support for gay rights and legalized abortion. McGovern's landslide loss that year ended his brief reign. Since then, liberalism has lacked a strong leader and advocate, which has been a contributing factor in its demise.

Johnson might have been capable of effectively answering the attacks on liberalism from the left and right in the mid-1960s, but, increasingly preoccupied with Vietnam, he possessed neither the will nor the political respect to play the part. Even if he had assumed this role, it is not clear that liberals would have been mollified or grateful. It was not the threat posed by conservatives that forced LBJ to withdraw from the 1968 presidential campaign, but the anti-Johnson sentiment on the left, stoked by the abject failure of his Vietnam policy.

CHAPTER FOUR

1968 in America

Zev Yaroslavsky, now a member of the Los Angeles County Board of Supervisors, supported Eugene McCarthy in the 1968 California Democratic primary. Too young to vote at nineteen but old enough to fight in Vietnam, Yaroslavsky embraced McCarthy's antiwar candidacy even before the Minnesota senator achieved his stunning second-place finish to President Johnson in the New Hampshire primary that March. Yaroslavsky grew up in a liberal family—pro-labor, pro–civil rights, and anticommunist. President Franklin Roosevelt was next to God, and President Truman was just a few rungs below. Lyndon Johnson and Hubert Humphrey came out of that same tradition: uncompromising liberals on domestic issues, and Cold War liberals on foreign policy. Yaroslavsky's father supported Johnson and Humphrey and the war in Vietnam. He neither countenanced nor acknowledged the concept of an *antiwar liberal*—especially when the enemy was communist. But for his son, opposition to the war was the issue. And by that measure, Johnson and Humphrey had betrayed liberalism and betrayed the country. During the spring of 1968 dinners at the Yaroslavsky home featured heated debates over the right course of action in Vietnam, a microcosm of the battle over the future of liberalism and the Democratic Party that had begun in earnest throughout the United States.

No one, except for Lyndon Johnson, suffered as much political damage from the war as Vice President Hubert Humphrey. In many ways Humphrey's situation was more tragic because he was not the decision-maker. But he was inextricably linked to the Johnson Administration's failed policies, and he would not or could not come out unequivocally against the war in 1968. He was a Johnson man, even though the president treated him with indifference throughout most of the campaign. Humphrey would (in late September) go only so far as to endorse, according to the war correspondent Stanley Karnow, "a total bombing halt and the de-Americanization of the war as 'an acceptable risk for peace.'"[1] "I was a big fan of Hubert Humphrey's," said Michael Dukakis, former governor of Massachusetts and the Democratic nominee for president in 1988, when I met with him in January 2006. "I just thought he let himself get tied to LBJ too closely; he had to break away. But he had a difficult time with that."

Dukakis had opposed the war since 1965, and voted for antiwar resolutions as a member of the Massachusetts legislature. Although a politician, and therefore more inclined to support official government policy, Dukakis eventually concluded that the usual rules did not apply to Vietnam. During the year when McCarthy, Robert Kennedy, and McGovern waged antiwar campaigns and Walter Cronkite, the anchorman of *CBS Evening News*, questioned American policy, Humphrey seemed cowardly or even immoral to the millions of Americans who advocated "Peace Now!" "We were left high and dry with Humphrey, who to me was a sad figure—somebody who had once been promising but had become a puppet of LBJ's and did not have the courage to stand up [to the president]," recalled Derek Shearer.

There was also profound resentment among Kennedy and McCarthy supporters that this symbol of the old Democratic Party and pre-Vietnam liberalism had won the nomination. As three British reporters observed in their seminal book on the 1968 presidential campaign, "The plain truth was that he [Humphrey] had come out of the convention in Chicago literally hated by one large and active fraction of the party—

the wing of it, what was more, to which he had always appealed in the past. And he was suspected, if not despised, by plenty of people in less liberal sections of the party."[2] Not a strong position from which to run for president, even if your opponent was Richard Nixon.

A mere five and a half months earlier, when New York senator Robert Kennedy formally entered the race, it appeared as if the Democrats were on the verge of a historic transformation. As Jeff Shesol describes in his account of the RFK/LBJ feud, "Bobby Kennedy's hair was almost perpetually shaggy; but, more important, he was young, direct, and dynamic; and he evoked the anger, irony, and moral stridency of the New Politics."[3] It was young versus old, the Beatles versus Montavani, new liberals versus New Deal liberals—and the class of '68 appeared to be winning. On March 31, 1968, President Johnson stunned the nation by announcing during a nationally televised broadcast that he would not seek or accept the Democratic nomination for president, a development for which the McCarthy and Kennedy campaigns and the antiwar movement all claimed credit. As the historian Alan Brinkley wrote in a 2006 review of a biography of LBJ, "Beleaguered by the war, repudiated by many of his onetime admirers, despised and ridiculed throughout the nation and the world . . . he began speaking to his family and close associates about stepping down. This time, almost no one tried to dissuade him."[4] Over the next nine weeks the Democratic primaries were a contest between two candidates who wanted the United States to get out of Vietnam.

But when Kennedy was assassinated on June 5, 1968, and McCarthy lost the will to fight for the top prize, Humphrey went on to secure the nomination. The '68 campaign has been haunted by "what ifs?" ever since. A common fantasy posits Kennedy winning the Democratic nomination and defeating Nixon in November. In this version, Kennedy would become the perfect liberal president suggested by his campaign: compassionate toward Chicanos, blacks, and the poor, a fighter against corruption in government, a crusader for equal rights and economic justice, and fully intent on removing American forces from Vietnam well before 1972.

Invited to attend a personal screening of the 2006 film *Bobby*, SDS founder Tom Hayden, one of the most vocal promoters of the RFK-as-president fantasy, told the *Los Angeles Times*: "We would have won in '64 [JFK]. We would have won in '68. I think you would have had a succession of Kennedy presidencies, which would have raised expectations and activated social movements."[5] One could argue that plenty of social movements were "activated" during that era, even given the tragic and untimely deaths of the Kennedy brothers.

In contrast to Hayden, not all of Bobby's supporters believe he would have received the nomination in August. "I don't think he [Senator Kennedy] would have gotten the nomination," said George McGovern in a 2005 interview. "I think Vice President Humphrey had an overwhelming majority of the delegates nailed down. Bobby was campaigning through the last primary, and most of the delegates then had already been picked."[6] Given McGovern's political experience, one is inclined to trust his assessment over those of baby boomers who never tire of saying that at twenty-two they were "out to change the world." But the Myth of Bobby, which endures to this day, has had the paradoxical effect of making many of his supporters seem irresponsible and self-absorbed. They have personalized the tragedy of his death (as they did the murder of John Lennon in 1980) and offered it as a metaphor for what has gone horribly wrong in America since the end of the 1960s. If only Sirhan Sirhan had not made it to the kitchen pantry of the Ambassador Hotel the night of the California primary, America would be a wonderful country and we would all be happy. To extend the Haydenesque interpretation of history: Robert Kennedy would have won in 1968 and been reelected in 1972, with perhaps eight years of Edward Kennedy to follow. I vividly recall a history professor of mine at Pitzer College in Claremont, California, shaking his head and telling our American studies class in 1976 in a tone both mournful and defeatist: "Politics has never been the same since Bobby died." My immediate impression was of a person who would spend the rest of his life essentially disengaged from campaigns and causes. I wondered at the time—and still wonder—

how many others like him were scattered across America: well-educated, intelligent liberals born between 1940 and 1950 who had been inspired by JFK and RFK but were unwilling to maintain a similar level of commitment after the summer of 1968.

Through charisma, cult of personality, and, in the case of Bobby, a combination of new politics and nostalgia for the New Frontier, the Kennedys—in life but even more in death—engendered the kind of adulation that made it seem an act of betrayal to transfer one's loyalty to other politicians, even if they held similar views to the brothers. Otherwise ardent believers in the concept of "people's history," in the case of John and Bobby liberals cling to the traditional "Great Man" theory.

It was not only disillusioned Kennedyites who joined the antiwar protestors, dogging Hubert Humphrey's campaign in the weeks following the Chicago convention. Given what we know today, it is hard to fathom that in 1968 Humphrey was hounded by demonstrations as much or more than Richard Nixon. Although the invasion of Cambodia, the secret bombing in Laos, the break-in at the office of Daniel Ellsberg's psychiatrist, and Watergate were in Nixon's future, the public was well aware of the Alger Hiss affair, the Checkers speech, the vicious 1950 Senate campaign against Helen Gahagan Douglas, and anticommunist saber rattling. And it does say something about the credibility of the man that less than six years after his "retirement" (in the aftermath of his humiliating defeat to Pat Brown in the California governor's race, prompting the famous jibe at the Los Angeles press conference that "you won't have Nixon to kick around anymore") the former vice president was not only back, but running for president.

Nixon was regarded as something of an afterthought to many non-Republicans in '68, especially given everything else going on. Compared with the Tet Offensive, assassinations, riots, anarchy, and the pending revolution, who cared about the potential threat of President Nixon? The former vice president had the good luck to be out of power during the tumultuous years of the 1960s, and could therefore not be held accountable for Watts, Newark, Detroit, campus upheavals, the counterculture, inflation and, above all, Vietnam. And as opposed to Barry Goldwater and that rising star Ronald Reagan, Nixon did not represent the worst of his own party—in the view of Democrats, of course. Other than the fact that he happened to be the Republican nominee for president in 1968, Nixon seemed to belong to another era. He was a face and a name from the previous decade. Why waste energy and squander resources disrupting his appearances?

On the other hand, Humphrey represented a direct link to policies that were causing needless death and destruction at that very moment. He might not have listened to the Beatles or read *Rolling Stone*, but the vice president was a key participant in the high drama of the 1960s. LBJ decided not to run for reelection in 1968 partly because he did not have the fortitude to confront an electorate outraged over Vietnam. In his place, Humphrey absorbed the blows. "We could not possibly have endorsed President Johnson if he had sought re-election, regardless of whom the Republicans might have nominated," wrote the *Nation* in an editorial published on the eve of the 1968 election. "Nor can we endorse Vice President Humphrey, even though Richard Nixon is his principal opponent. . . . We have never thought of the Vice President as merely a loyal lieutenant serving a general of whose policies he disapproved. On the contrary, we have always assumed that the Vice President agreed with the President's policies, including the decision to escalate the war."[7]

Many others on the left held similar feelings. As reported in the classic account of the 1968 campaign, *American Melodrama:* "On Monday, September 9, Humphrey began his formal campaign with two appearances, one in Philadelphia and one in Denver. In Philadelphia, the police commissioner, Frank Rizzo, a zealous satrap of Democratic mayor Tate, insisted with absurd loyalty that a hundred thousand people were there to hear Humphrey speak. There were, probably, anything between seven and ten thousand. There were chants and jeers and slogans, and sometimes they almost drowned out the feeble cheers of the city employees and their families who had been dragooned out as a claque.

"In Denver, it was worse. Because of bad advance work, the candi-

date's motorcade coincided with suppertime and drove through depress-
ingly empty streets. Hecklers with peace banners made up half the
crowd of three thousand that met Humphrey outside the Union
Convention Hall where he was due to speak. They greeted him with
shouts of '*Sieg biel!*' and 'Dump the Hump.'"8 Humphrey was the first
high-profile victim of the then unfolding liberal civil war. The people
screaming at him may well have chafed at being called liberals, and with
their campaign trail demeanor did not fit the standard definition, but
their anger encapsulated the sense of betrayal and all-consuming desire
for change that motivated RFK-McCarthy-McGovern supporters. In a
phrase that has been repeated endlessly by liberals (feminists in particular) over the past several decades, Humphrey simply "didn't get it." As
one of the few remaining Cold War liberals with presidential aspirations, he was a prime target for the emergent antiwar movement, which
desperately desired to force his kind from power—even if doing so
meant victory for Richard Nixon.

Four years later another Cold War liberal, Washington senator Henry
"Scoop" Jackson, made a brief and unsuccessful run for the Democratic
nomination. His defeat—and Humphrey's in 1968 and 1972—marked
the end of any serious effort to lead the nation by Democrats whose political consciousness was formed at the height of Soviet-American tensions
in the 1950s. But many of Jackson's and Humphrey's key followers,
seething at the triumph of McGovernism and the constant abuse heaped
on them for their beliefs, would become part of a new and disproportionately influential movement in American politics known as neocon-
servativism. In due course the neocons emerged as some of the most
trenchant and vocal critics of the new liberalism.

For example, one of Humphrey's aides during the 1968 race was
Jeane Kirkpatrick, who later served as United States Ambassador to the
United Nations under Ronald Reagan. At the 1984 Republican convention, Kirkpatrick, who died in December 2006, gave a rousing speech in
which she gleefully assailed "San Francisco Democrats"—the city where
the other party held its convention in 1984—for supporting a cowardly

and naive "blame America first" foreign policy. Kirkpatrick and another ex-Humphrey advisor, Ben Wattenberg, had by this point assumed leading roles in the neoconservative movement, which included ex-Democrats, many of them Jewish, who switched to the Republicans primarily over foreign policy, the growth of the welfare state, and the imposition of race- and gender-based quotas in government hiring practices. As Sidney Blumenthal puts it in his account of the neocon movement, "The neoconservatives generally read the [1972 Democratic] primary results through Old Left lenses as a victory for fellow-traveling. Opposition to the Vietnam War, after all, 'objectively' placed McGovern on the same side as the Soviets."[9]

In the 1950s and 1960s, Humphrey epitomized the courageous, ambitious, post–World War II liberal. Minus the long hair and disruptive behavior, he was every bit as much an advocate for change as the demonstrators stalking his campaign appearances in 1968. In 1948, Humphrey, the mayor of Minneapolis, made a speech at the Democratic Convention in favor of a minority plank on civil rights, which passed by sixty-nine votes. In volume three of his biography of Johnson, Robert Caro assesses the speech's importance thus: "At the time, there were not a few comparisons between Humphrey's speech and what has been described as—'the only convention speech that ever had a greater impact on the deliberation of the delegates'—William Jennings Bryan's 'Cross of Gold' oration of half a century before."[10] Adoption of the plank was a key factor in persuading many more black voters to leave the Republicans and join the Democrats, and in causing the opposite, the defection of southern whites to the GOP, which was the most significant political realignment of the postwar era. Democrats to this day can thank Humphrey and Johnson—among a select group of white politicians—for the fact that blacks consistently vote 80 to 90 percent in support of the Democratic candidate for president.

During his earlier years in the U.S. Senate, Humphrey contradicted his later image as an out-of-touch square by demonstrating his opposition to segregation with the kinds of provocative acts that were common in the civil rights and antiwar movements of the 1960s. Caro describes one example: "He showed up at the Senate Dining Room one day with a black member of his staff, Cyril King, and when the headwaiter, himself a black man, told them they could not be served (one can only cringe at the thought of one black man forced to tell another that because of his color he was not welcome as a guest), Humphrey first softly, and then loudly and angrily, kept insisting that he and King were going to eat together, until at last they were allowed to do so."[11] In their classic book *A Pocket History of the United States*, the historians Henry Steele Commager and Allan Nevins called Humphrey "the darling of the Northern liberals" when LBJ selected him to be his running mate in 1964.[12]

In a sense, then, Humphrey and his Democratic antagonists had more in common than either side would have been able or willing to acknowledge in the heat of the '68 campaign. But since Humphrey stood for a disastrous policy in Vietnam, the antiwar demonstrators could not be bothered hearing twenty-year-old tales of the courageous acts that he had undertaken in the 1940s on behalf of black people. That battle had been won: by 1968 black people in the South could legally vote for president, drink from the same water fountains as whites, and go to the best colleges. Now it was all about the war. The doves were liberals and the liberals were doves; hawks or quasi hawks were anything and everything to the right of that. The doves argued for the United States to withdraw immediately from Vietnam; the hawks wanted either to keep fighting until the enemy was defeated or, in Richard Nixon's phrase, to achieve "Peace with Honor." Though nobody was quite sure what *Peace with Honor* meant, perhaps including Nixon himself, those three words sounded patriotic, even triumphant. Given the situation on the ground by late 1968, this notion was enough to satisfy many onetime backers of the war who were nevertheless resigned to an outcome short of victory.

· · ·

Zev Yaroslavsky was one of those young activists who saw his personal "dream" of a viable antiwar candidacy disintegrate in the time between the New Hampshire primary and the Chicago convention—an event he missed while traveling in the Soviet Union. "The year 1968 didn't turn out very well if you were of my persuasion: student, antiwar activist, progressive," he said in a 2004 interview with me. To his later regret, Yaroslavsky played his own part in what he regards as the unfortunate conclusion to the 1968 presidential election. Embittered by Humphrey's triumph at the convention, and still smoldering over the political disagreements with his father, Yaroslavsky, like millions of other disillusioned young Democrats, stayed out of the general election campaign until the final week. Though too young to vote, it was his own frustration and sense of betrayal that stopped him from making calls and walking precincts. But with just a few seconds left on the electoral clock, Yaroslavsky came to a terrifying realization: America was on the verge of electing Richard Nixon! Other anti-Humphrey liberals and radicals had the same thought at the same time. "People of my age group hated Nixon," recalled Yaroslavsky. "After all, we knew something about Nixon in this state [California]." The frantic last-minute effort to keep Nixon from capturing the White House helped transform an anticipated landslide into a close race—along with the success of third-party challenger George Wallace at taking votes from the Republican nominee in the South. But it was too late for Humphrey. Some thirty-five years later, Yaroslavsky's views (especially in the area of foreign policy) are by his own admission more in line with those of Humphrey than either Gene McCarthy or George McGovern, whom he backed in 1972. This makes it even harder for the supervisor to accept today that he abandoned Humphrey, especially given the close finish. As for the *Nation*, I do not recall if its editors ever expressed misgivings over opting for "none of the above," even after Nixon expanded the war, approved domestic spying, and got involved in the Watergate cover-up.

Following the bitter end to the 1968 election, one could understand Hubert Humphrey feeling a sense of intense anger and betrayal toward progressive liberals, especially those under the age of thirty. In the year in which Humphrey appeared on the ballot with a right-wing Republican and a racist, the "kids" chose to undermine the campaign of the very person who should have been their obvious choice for president—Vietnam or not. When a candidate runs against Nixon and Wallace, he needs to have done some terrible things—by any Democrat's objective standards—to be considered nothing more than the lesser of three evils. But not all Democrats were thinking rationally in 1968. As a result, the Humphrey campaign's final days assumed a tragic aura, which paradoxically served to boost the candidate's postelection standing. No longer Johnson's lackey on Vietnam, he was now the hard-luck candidate in a presidential year unlike any other. Still, an enhanced public image didn't make the vice president feel better about losing to Nixon. Humphrey's defeat provided young Democrats and new liberals with the opportunity to influence the presidential nominating process and push ahead with one or more of their own candidates for 1972. Anti-Humphrey Democrats argued that there was something inherently wrong with a process or system that enabled Johnson's toady to receive the nomination in '68. Four years later these criticisms would assign much more importance to primaries in selecting delegates. Provided Nixon's "secret plan" to withdraw honorably from Vietnam was nothing more than a campaign ruse, antiwar liberals would get another chance at the Big Prize in '72.

CHAPTER FIVE

Curious about George

Now a Los Angeles city councilman, Bill Rosendahl joined George McGovern's presidential campaign in 1971, long before the stunning primary victories and media hype. He was present before the creation. After several months of performing a variety of roles, Rosendahl was promoted to chief fund-raiser for Illinois. "I was given a computer print-out of some five hundred contributors in Illinois," Rosendahl recalled in a 2004 interview with me. "I got off the plane with that computer print-out. That was it—a one-way ticket. I was in charge of the state."

"I raised money from wealthy people who could give as much money as they wanted to," said Rosendahl. "We had disclosure in those days, but no [spending] limits." Post-Watergate reforms would neutralize the skills of a person such as Bill Rosendahl, who used wit, charm, flattery, and access to raise large amounts of money from individual donors. By the time of the 1976 presidential election, federal election laws had severely restricted the amount of money that individuals could contribute to political campaigns. Stuffed envelopes replaced bulging suitcases as the method of delivery. The 1972 campaign marked the last presidential race in American history when a wealthy donor—properly identified on disclosure forms—could legally deposit a satchel crammed with one-hundred dollar bills at the headquarters of his favorite candidate. One could argue that substituting Political Action Committees (PACs) for fat cats has robbed presidential campaigns of their verve, personality, swagger, and even romance. It is much more fun to make villains out of fabulously wealthy, well-known major contributors than some amorphous committee consisting of thousands of anonymous middle-class contributors who may be otherwise lovely people.

In the early stages of the 1972 race, when McGovern lived dangerously from primary to primary, Rosendahl raised money in Illinois that was shipped to New Hampshire and other key early states. Rosendahl's technique improved and his geographic responsibilities broadened as McGovern closed in on the nomination and advanced to the general election.

Donors do not contribute to politicians as much as they invest in them. "I personally spent April through September crisscrossing the nation raising money for George," said Rosendahl. "I raised almost three million dollars personally for McGovern, more money than any other individual in America in 1972. It was basically [from] rich people, who would give or get me twenty-five thousand dollars or more. . . . I had a very close relationship with George where I could go into a person's home, call George on the phone and put them together. George would say something about the person or about the issues, and then I would walk away with a big check."

And what were those issues? Take your pick: Vietnam, the Vietnam War, the war, the war in Southeast Asia. McGovern in 1972 had a range of views on the economy, race, crime, and other domestic matters, but few people remember them, except perhaps as re-defined through the gross distortions of the Nixon campaign. Those contemporary columnists and commentators who invoke McGovern's legacy to rally the Right and terrorize the Left ignore all of the senator's positions except Give Peace a Chance. "If there wasn't the cause of the Vietnam War he wouldn't have gotten anywhere," acknowledged Rosendahl. "He just didn't have the charisma and the natural stature."

Terry Friedman, now a Los Angeles County Superior Court Judge, came out for McGovern in 1971, long before it was the popular thing to do at UCLA, from which Friedman graduated in June of that year. "We wanted someone who by virtue of their long-standing commitment we could trust to be against the war," he recalled in a 2004 interview with me. "I thought McGovern was exactly what we were looking for: an electoral vehicle to accomplish the important objective of ending the war in Vietnam. The only way that could happen would be through the election of a new president." McGovern arrived at this position in the mid-1960s, before Eugene McCarthy, Robert Kennedy, and most students on college campuses across the nation. In an entry in his diary *The Sixties*, the great critic Edmund Wilson records that he attended a Vietnam symposium in early 1966 in which participants included "an apparently intelligent young senator from South Dakota [George McGovern]. Though a Democrat, he was opposed to [President] Johnson's policy."[1]

Obviously, an antiwar candidate needs a war. McGovern knew this, and so did Nixon, who by the early 1970s (the middle of his first term) took concrete steps to reduce and eventually terminate American military involvement, albeit at a measured pace so as not to appear to be a full-fledged surrender. In October 1970, Nixon offered a plan for a cease fire in place, which, in the words of Stanley Karnow, "earned instant praise in Congress, where even such anti-war stalwarts as McGovern, [Mark] Hatfield, and [J. William] Fulbright lent their names to a resolution of approval."[2] In an election year, the president did not want "Johnson's war" to become known as "Nixon's war," although the invasion of Cambodia two years earlier was among Nixon's unique contributions to the U.S. effort.

In 1972, few Americans still believed that the country could win in Vietnam. For Nixon and McGovern, the relevant election-year question was how to go about losing the war—honorably of course. If elected, McGovern pledged to halt the bombing immediately and remove U.S. troops within three months after his inauguration. Rosendahl, Friedman, and millions of other McGovern supporters insisted on nothing less. But this withdrawal was too drastic to sell to the silent majority. The preferred Republican alternative was not to cut and run but to cut and jog. As Karnow writes: "By early 1972, Nixon could justly claim that he was fulfilling his pledge to reduce the U.S. combat role in Vietnam. He had withdrawn more than four hundred thousand GIs since he entered office, and American battle deaths were down to fewer than ten a week."[3]

No huge difference separated the Nixon plan and the McGovern proposal for dealing with Vietnam in 1972, but subsequent right-wing propaganda portrayed the Democrats as preparing to hand over everything west of the Mississippi to a North Vietnamese delegation. By 1972 many people argued for withdrawing U.S. forces from Southeast Asia, although our boys were a long way from what George W. Bush would call "Mission Accomplished" in a later war that drew unfavorable comparisons to Vietnam. This was not the equivalent of McGovern urging that the United States exit World War II prior to June 6, 1944. He took a position on Vietnam that for its time could be considered reasonably close to the mainstream. Conservatives and liberals just wanted to be done with this war. Pointing fingers, spreading blame, and outing the villains would come later. Seven years after LBJ drastically escalated U.S. involvement, here is what the country had to show for it: more than fifty thousand dead Americans and the Army of the Republic of Vietnam and Vietcong on track to unify the country under communist rule. The 1972 presidential race did not include a single serious candidate who had a plan to outright *win* the war.

But over the past thirty-five years, as America moved farther to the right, the McGovern campaign moved farther to the left—on paper. Although in the early 1970s there was no revolt in the Republican Party when President Nixon and Henry Kissinger embarked on efforts to negotiate a peace agreement with the enemy, Ronald Reagan's 1980 landslide victory over Jimmy Carter emboldened conservatives to openly revisit Vietnam. In his biography, *President Reagan: The Role of a Lifetime*, Lou Cannon quotes Reagan during the 1976 and 1980 campaigns as calling Vietnam " a noble cause" and a war the government was "afraid to win." In 1983, Norman Podhoretz, the editor of *Commentary*, published *Why We Were in Vietnam*. It's an odd book in that Podhoretz, usually not known for his reserve in political matters, never provides an illuminating explanation. Nearly a decade after the end of the war, the reader should have expected more than this: "Why, then, were we in Vietnam? To say it once again; because we were trying to save the Southern half of that country from the evils of communism."[4] Immediately following that per-functory pair of sentences, which could have been offered by many intel-lectual or working-class defenders of the war between 1956 and 1970, Podhoretz harshly criticizes an obscure antiwar activist from the sixties who held a different view. In fact much of the book attacks critics of America's policy in Vietnam—including McGovern, though not exten-sively—and the Nixon-Kissinger negotiations with North Vietnam. One gets the strong suspicion that the author was either unwilling to do the hard work of justifying the war over the course of an entire book or more likely harbored his own doubts as to why we were in Vietnam.

In subsequent years American conservatives, more powerful than ever and determined to discredit the theory and practice of 1960s lib-eralism, arrived at their own strategic position on the morality and prosecution of that war. "Conservatives had been as shaken as anyone by America's humiliation in Vietnam," wrote British journalists John Micklethwait and Adrian Wooldridge in describing the mind-set of the foreign-policy team gathered around President George W. Bush. "But they had drawn the opposite conclusion from their liberal counter-parts—not that America had plunged blindly into an unwinnable war but that it had failed to push hard enough for victory."[5] As the situation deteriorated in Iraq in 2005, 2006, and 2007, and a Democratic-led Congress in the spring of 2007 voted to end funding for the war by a certain date, President George W. Bush and his congressional Repub-lican allies accused them of wanting to "cut and run." They wisely didn't cite Vietnam as a historical example, but voters were free to make that connection.

In the opinion of most conservatives, who is to blame for the Vietnam debacle? A lengthy list: John F. Kennedy, Lyndon Johnson, Robert McNamara, liberals in Congress, the antiwar movement, the media, the intellectual elite, and, to a certain extent, Richard Nixon and Henry Kissinger. But special place is reserved for George McGovern, a mere South Dakota senator during the war and far removed from its day-to-day prosecution. This indisputable fact of history, however, has done nothing to curb or halt the anger and ridicule directed at McGovern from the right. After all, McGovern had the temerity to wage an avowedly antiwar campaign while America was still at war. There is an unwritten rule in American politics that candidates—especially liberal candidates—are supposed to keep their antiwar feelings to themselves while our troops are engaged in combat. This holds whether the war is immoral or moral, legal or illegal, superbly managed or poorly run. The candidate who flouts this tradition is predictably accused by conservatives of undermining the morale of our men and women in uniform, sending the wrong signal to our enemy, or both. In other words, one must only oppose a war when there is no war to oppose. It would have been acceptable for McGovern to campaign against Vietnam in 1985, and for Howard Dean to do the same over Iraq only in 2012, or maybe 2016.

The counter argument to flag-waving militarism—"peace is patriotic"—while intermittently effective, has not changed the prevailing attitude. To be in love with America is to be in love with America's military prowess. Since Democrats for the past half century have been perceived as the political party more inclined toward seeking peaceful solutions, they are at a disadvantage during periods of foreign conflict, real or manufactured. And they do not placate either detractors or supporters by adopting a prowar and propeace stance, as was the case with many Democrats during the run-up to and prosecution of the war in Iraq. Those who believe in peace must be as fervent and passionate about their position as those who believe in going to war—avowed liberals accept nothing less. As a result, post-Reagan conservatives have designated McGovern as the perfect symbol for a political party they seek to portray as weak on defense and hesitant to fight anywhere at any time.

The Democratic Party is regarded for the most part by its detractors as cowardly rather than isolationist—with the latter being the preferred term for extremists on the right who believe the United States should stay out of international affairs.

McGovern's own strategic decision to make unconditional opposition to the war central to his 1972 campaign, which was crucial to securing the nomination, also had the unintended or unforeseen effect of turning him into fodder for critics of the antiwar movement and subsequent antiwar movements. The younger conservatives who denigrate and demean McGovern were Little Leaguers, Girl Scouts, or not yet born during the war in Vietnam. The trashing of McGovern also points out the downside of campaigning on a single issue, or having garnered the reputation of campaigning on a single issue, which in the end amounts to the same thing. If people know one thing about George McGovern it is that he was the presidential nominee that best embodied the hopes, dreams, and philosophy of the antiwar movement. The stance that attracted Bill Rosendahl and many others to McGovern's candidacy in 1972 continues to repel conservatives and neoconservatives today.

. . .

As a student at UCLA in the late 1960s and early 1970s, Terry Friedman may not have thought of himself as a liberal, but there seems to be no better ideological term to describe a person in the highly politicized environment of a UC campus at the time of Vietnam who wholeheartedly believed in working for change within the system. "It was often a tough spot to be in, because on campus the radicals didn't think much of us, and on the outside people who had different views lumped us together with the radicals, because like them we opposed the war," Friedman said during an interview for this book. Pensive and soft-spoken in middle age, it is hard to envision Friedman during his undergraduate days even whispering the phrase "off the pigs." The differences between radicalism and liberalism in the 1960s were expressed not only in ideology and tactics, but in personality types as well. Friedman believed in achieving change through conciliation and consensus. "Throughout 1969, '70 and '71, I tried to steer student anger about the war into antiwar electoral politics," Friedman said. "I saw the McGovern campaign as a way of doing that at the highest level."

Like Bill Rosendahl, Friedman had earlier worked on Robert Kennedy's 1968 presidential campaign, which served as a kind of training school for the McGovern team four years later. At first shocked and then deflated in the weeks after RFK's assassination, Friedman had felt a sense of gratitude that McGovern stepped in at the eleventh hour to give the Kennedy people an alternative to the languid Gene McCarthy and the unacceptable Hubert Humphrey. "It was the first I'd heard of him," said Friedman. "He seemed like a sincere man, strongly against the war in Vietnam. And he seemed to be picking up the mantle of John and Robert Kennedy, who at the time were my heroes in politics."

Despite his own profound disappointment at the turn of events in 1968, and the continuous feelings of depression and unease he felt with Nixon as president, Friedman never considered retreating to the sidelines, if even to reassess his options. With thoughts of a career in politics, Friedman adopted a self-sustaining pragmatism, reassuring himself that under the American system the best person does not always win. Following the 1968 election, Friedman continued his association with the California Federation of Young Democrats and was elected president of the organization in 1970. When McGovern announced his candidacy in January 1971, Friedman quickly made contact with the senator's nascent California operation. Though the election was almost two years away and many potential Democratic candidates had not made their final decisions, once Friedman learned of McGovern's plans, there was nothing more to know.

During its initial stages, any long shot political campaign consists almost exclusively of true believers; wannabes, sycophants, and converts sign on as the candidate's prospects dramatically improve. Nobody gave McGovern much of a chance in early 1971, although he had made a late run for the nomination only thirty months earlier. Many establishment (i.e., powerful) Democrats preferred Maine senator Edmund Muskie to any other potential or announced candidates. Muskie had been Humphrey's vice presidential choice in 1968, and he had proved to be such a skilled campaigner that toward the end of that race some Democrats openly expressed their disappointment that the ticket did not in fact read "Muskie-Humphrey." But most important, Muskie was perceived to be the Democratic challenger with the best chance to defeat the despised Richard Nixon.

Until 2004 it would have been difficult to convey to people born after 1960 just how desperately the New Left, traditional liberals, and Democratic Party regulars wanted Nixon to lose in 1972. History tell us, after all, that Nixon brought most of the troops home from Vietnam; took the first and most important step to end the West's isolation of China; maintained good relations with the Soviets; and created the Environmental Protection Agency. And by the standards of early twenty-first-century conservatism, Nixon was a moderate-to-liberal Republican. While it would be going too far to say he is truly missed by Democrats, they are more inclined than in the past to find some good in him.

Still, it is one thing to live after Nixon and another to live under Nixon. Given that if Nixon triumphed he would be serving his second term, and no longer answerable to the voters, there was great concern over what this now obviously vindictive, paranoid, perhaps irrational man would be capable of doing without the constraint of another election. In January 1973, the journalist Peter Knobler wrote in the rock–pop culture magazine *Crawdaddy:* "I'm a young man, but I'll be thirty before Nixon is out office and I'm running scared. The presidential election was a choice between mass murder and the tentative rounding of corners, and the American people chose public execution."[6] Even allowing for counterculture excess, Knobler was expressing a genuine fear: would Nixon unleash his pent-up hatred of the Left and the media in an orgy of repressive and secret executive decisions? Would he now decide that America could win in Vietnam and change his policy from "Peace with Honor" to total victory? As for domestic politics, would he spy on

Americans or attempt to fix elections? Having in his own mind been "kicked around" throughout his twenty-five-year political career, what would happen when Nixon could kick back hard and not worry about political repercussions?

In recent American history, only the prospect that President George W. Bush would be reelected in 2004 generated a similar level of angst and fear among Democrats. The sudden success of Senator John Kerry during the early caucuses and primaries in 2004—achieved largely at the expense of Vermont governor Howard Dean—was widely attributed to a collective sense among Democrats that Kerry had the better chance of defeating Bush in November. In the case of Kerry and Muskie, and lesser contenders from both parties through the years, the belief is that strength of candidacy increases in proportion to proximity to the center of the political spectrum. (Even Bush softened his Christian conservatism during election season.) When compared to Dean, Kerry qualified as a centrist, at least on the Iraq war, while compared to McGovern, Muskie qualified as a centrist, at least on the war in Vietnam.

In order for a centrist or center-left candidates to achieve victory in competitive primaries, they need the votes of a certain percentage of liberals, even though they may not be an ideal political match. For these voters, pragmatism trumps idealism, usually because the alternative in the general election—for example, Richard Nixon—is feared and reviled. A former member of the California Assembly, Terry Friedman understands well that voters from time to time adopt pragmatic tactics. He may have even done so a few times in subsequent political life, but not in 1972. "I knew he [McGovern] was a dark horse, but when you are twenty-one years old, you are much more idealistic than when you are older," he explained. Backing Muskie would have compromised his goal of ending the war now. Instead, he supported McGovern and worked like hell to confound the experts and get his candidate nominated.

In its early days, the 1972 McGovern campaign ran on enthusiasm, hammers, nails, and maybe a few telephones and a borrowed copy machine. "I remember a couple of us standing on a ladder and putting

up a sign at McGovern headquarters," said Friedman. "We thought that
if we fell off the ladder that would put an end to the McGovern campaign in California." Nobody fell, and in time, the California operation
would come to resemble the proverbial well-oiled machine. In fact,
there are personal (if not political) advantages to building a campaign
with next to nothing in reserve. For a volunteer with higher ambitions,
it can be depressing to join the team only to discover that the key positions have already been filled.

The McGovern campaign's aura of informality—especially in the
early days—was also a sign of its integrity. By 1971–72, there were
already disturbing indications that the "revolution" was being taken over
by the mainstream. The Carpenters were one of the top-selling recording groups in America; Elvis Presley was a hit in Vegas; Led Zeppelin,
the last of the hippie bands, flaunted its hedonistic lifestyle; the success
of *All in the Family* on television and *The Godfather* in theaters revealed
a fondness for simpler times; and even people over thirty were wearing
their hair long. Who could have guessed a few years earlier that corporate America would attempt to take over the counterculture, and that the
attempt just might succeed? America was starting down the long road to
Starbucks, the Gap, casual Fridays, and other familiar manifestations of
Liberalism, Inc.

For antiwar liberals who opted to stick with the system, there was the
nagging concern that their friends and colleagues would consider them
sellouts, or worse, traitors to the cause. If you're not with us in the
streets, then you're against us—that sort of thing. Image counted for
much within the counterculture. Short hair, suits and ties, and classic
country music were symbols of the oppressors, and therefore expressly
forbidden. You couldn't be clean-shaven and enjoy post-1965 Beatles
music, or so it was believed. In time, such views were revealed to be sim-
plistic, even false. But back then, they established the line of demarca-
tion between the counterculture and everyone else.

The McGovern campaign sought a conventional outcome through
seemingly unconventional methods, which was comforting to those

enlistees worried about appearing too cozy with tradition or friendly with the establishment. The significant roles played by people such as Terry Friedman, Bill Rosendahl, and Barbra Streisand—who all worked to elect McGovern—confirmed that this was not your typical campaign. "They had me licking envelopes, going door to door raising money, and handing out brochures," recalls Stephen Vittoria in a 2005 interview for this book, and who was seventeen when he worked on the McGovern campaign in New Jersey. "It was the bottom of the barrel. But it was also one of those campaigns where everyone was made to feel that he had a position." Unlike Humphrey four years before, labor bosses and grizzled operatives did not for the most part play leading roles in this effort. For the first time, the various strains of late-'60s liberalism had achieved a political breakthrough. No more was their power and influence confined to ultraliberal congressional districts, private colleges in Massachusetts and New York, and public universities in Berkeley, Michigan, and Wisconsin.

. . .

Most voters have never fully accepted the idea of the perpetual presidential campaign, which was already in evidence in 1972. For nonparticipants it is like watching the rehearsal of a play months before the final production opens. The lead tries to learn his or her lines, the director constantly makes changes to the script, and the supporting players adapt to their ever-shifting roles. By the time it gets to Broadway, all of these details will presumably have been worked out. Now and then the reviewers, here known as political journalists, provide a progress report, including predictions, which in part reflect their not-so-secret desire to anoint the next king or queen ahead of the competition.

During the initial months and if possible on into the formal primary season, the candidate actively seeks money and endorsements, both of which lend credibility to a campaign. It is, however, a paradox of electoral politics that neither of these can be easily secured unless the campaign has credibility. There are few things more embarrassing to a politician than publicly endorsing the candidate who finishes second or below. As an example, in the 2004 campaign Al Gore held a well-attended press conference to announce he was supporting Howard Dean for president. Not more than a few weeks later, the governor started his swift descent. After the debacle of the 2000 election, the last thing Gore needed was another example of his political irrelevance.

Voters do not have as much to lose by declaring early, but they too like to hold back on making their selection until it is apparent who is favored to win. In that regard, people such as Terry Friedman are the exceptions. In January 1972, a year or so after Friedman stood on that wobbly ladder, McGovern campaign officials assigned him the task of organizing voters in Manchester, New Hampshire, just prior to the state's all-important primary. Friedman's inexperience and that of the other young staff was not apparent in their primary election successes. As the maverick journalist and author Hunter S. Thompson recalled: "McGovern's organization ran a classic operation in Manchester, canvassing almost every precinct two times, and winning ethnic sections that no one believed they could capture. The McGovern organization was superior in both numbers and fervor. The McGovern people canvassed the city so thoroughly that by election night they were able to predict the vote in most Manchester wards with deadly accuracy."[7]

When McGovern garnered 37 percent of the vote in New Hampshire, second only to 46 percent for the designated front-runner Ed Muskie, it provided a huge boost to his quest for national "legitimacy"— the signal for the media to pay close attention to the candidate, just as the New Hampshire result had boosted McCarthy four years earlier. At that point the campaign asked Friedman to organize voters in Racine, Wisconsin, after New Hampshire. His hot streak continued: McGovern won a majority—26 percent—of the vote in a crowded field, which, according to the rules, meant he captured the entire Wisconsin delegation. Various accounts of the 1972 primary maintain that the Wisconsin results made McGovern the preemptive favorite to win the nomination.

. . .

In New Hampshire and Racine, Terry Friedman and thousands of other members of what would come to be known as "McGovern's Army" had the assignment of convincing skeptical Democrats that their candidate was no wild-eyed radical, but the only person in the race with the courage and determination to put an immediate end to the madness of Vietnam. As Todd Gitlin, a veteran of the New Left and among the foremost scholars of youth politics of the 1960s, wrote: "The New Left's affirmative commitments were murky then, but one thing was not, the passion to end the war. This was the position of many young people who joined the McGovern campaign."[8]

By 1972, many Americans wanted the war over, and soon. "Surveys showed that increasing numbers of Americans wanted a firm deadline for a U.S. troop withdrawal from Southeast Asia, whatever the risks for the Saigon government," notes Karnow in summing up the nation's mood over Vietnam.[9] Losing was an option. Not even McGovern could say that getting out of Vietnam was a good thing, only that it was the right thing. And in a field of antiwar candidates, McGovern stood apart. He represented those Democrats who regarded "Peace Now" as a viable policy, and not merely as a phrase to chant at demonstrations. The problem for McGovern was not that he was a wild-eyed radical but that wild-eyed radicals were a visible part of his organization.

Gary Hart, who served as McGovern's campaign manager in '72, wrote a book about the experience titled *Right from the Start: A Chronicle of the McGovern Campaign*. The book includes a photo of approximately twenty-five volunteers assigned to the New Hampshire primary. None of them resemble Haight-Ashbury panhandlers or demonstrators who would yell "F——k the police"! On the other hand, some of the guys in the picture wear their hair long, and while the comparatively few young women appeared to be perfectly presentable, who knows what activities they were engaging in after a hard day of phone banking and precinct walking? To those with limited knowledge of the New Left or exposure to the counterculture, the difference of a couple of inches of hair on the men or whether or not the women wore bras meant something significant. Those who were partly jealous and partly disgusted condemned the morals, habits, and politics of young activists on the basis of often questionable evidence. In similar fashion, McGovern backers derided the image of the cigar-chomping union boss who supposedly represented the old Democratic Party.

Still, McGovern assiduously courted the groups, movements, and causes that had come to dominate the New Left during the previous five to seven years. As Hart wrote: "We were constructing a McGovern coalition of the Kennedy-McCarthy activists, the young, minority groups, anti-war organizations, women and others whose commitments to the principles of the Democratic Party generally outweighed the voice they had exerted in its affairs. This was a movement already in progress, seeking leadership after assassinations and rejections, and looking for someone with the kind of vision and courage necessary to question entrenched institutional assumptions."[10] With a bevy of conservative Democrats such as Henry "Scoop" Jackson, Hubert Humphrey, Edmund Muskie, and George Wallace in the race, McGovern wisely decided to seek support outside the party establishment. This strategy gave his candidacy the imprimatur of a lawful, peace-loving insurgency—not the worst PR at the end of a violent decade—but it also meant he had a lot of explaining to do to the American people. After all, millions of voters were not clear regarding the evolving agenda (or agendas) of women, minority groups, antiwar organizations, and so on. It would be up to McGovern to define it for them.

After the triumph in Wisconsin the campaign transferred Friedman to Northern California, where he had the responsibility of organizing college students ahead of that state's June primary. Sixteen months earlier Friedman declared for McGovern, expecting at the very least to send a message that America had to withdraw from Vietnam immediately. Friedman had made a moral decision to support the South Dakota senator, just as he felt compelled in 1968 to support the candidacy of

Bobby Kennedy. But now McGovern was closing in on the nomination, with former vice president Hubert Humphrey the only serious challenger. California could provide the necessary delegates to bring that once unlikely goal to fruition. Friedman was among the select group that was expected to deliver California for McGovern on the first Tuesday in June. By this point he was every bit the political operative, even if his reasons for supporting the campaign remained pure.

The 1972 presidential election marked the first time every student (other than prodigies admitted prior to their eighteenth birthdays) on campus could legally cast a ballot. Was it not obvious that Democrats would be the prime beneficiaries of the Twenty-sixth Amendment to the Constitution? Anyone who watched television or listened to the radio in the 1960s and early 1970s knew that the vast majority of young people had liberal or left inclinations. They were overrepresented in the civil rights movement, participated in massive demonstrations against the war in Vietnam, bought million of copies of *Sgt. Pepper's Lonely Hearts Club Band*, and gathered by the hundreds of thousands at Woodstock and Altamont. Every thing they did changed the world—or so it was said. And in November 1972 they would add George McGovern's victory to that list.

But conservatives—young and old—displayed no outward signs of regret at their exclusion from this ongoing party. Many of them even reveled in playing the role of the outsider. Let hippies have their Woodstock; we have John Wayne, Merle Haggard, *Dirty Harry*, and the Carpenters (who performed for Nixon and guests at the White House). Nixon delighted in pointing out the clean-cut, polite, classically Middle American young men and women who attended his rallies in '68 and '72. As we learned later, however, not all these kids were immune to the charms of the Rolling Stones, just as young conservatives since the early 1980s have been known to hangout in punk clubs. The myth of a cultural Berlin Wall, with the liberals on one side and the conservatives on the other, has been sustained by both camps for their own purposes.

Like Dick Clark on *American Bandstand* in the late 1950s, Nixon sought to assuage and exploit the fears of middle-class parents during a period of cultural ferment. Clark was the anti-Elvis and Nixon ran a campaign free of freaks; as opposed to that other party, which coveted their support, especially with McGovern as the nominee.

. . .

In 1972, Hubert Humphrey would have his revenge on the left. They would pay for harassing and undermining his campaign four years earlier. More specifically, George McGovern would pay because he had emerged as the leader of the left wing of the Democratic Party. Midway through the primary season, Humphrey became by default the candidate of the ABM (Anyone But McGovern) movement, which sought to deny the nomination to a person considered too far to the left, and, therefore, unacceptable and unelectable. Given McGovern's commanding lead in the delegate count, the Humphrey forces needed to hit hard and strike fast. Since Vietnam was unpopular, they could not expect to gain much traction by simply attacking McGovern's position. And besides, doing so would only remind voters that Humphrey served as vice president during the massive escalation of the war effort from 1965 to 1968. Instead, they launched perhaps the first nationwide counter-counterculture campaign, which has since been refined and expanded by conservative candidates running at all levels of government. Humphrey sought the votes of those people who hated and feared the political and cultural changes wrought by the 1960s. He was, in fact, the Democratic candidate for the silent majority. As Gary Hart recalled: "Humphrey supporters had begun a concerted campaign, largely through brochures and newspaper ads, to misrepresent McGovern's views on the so-called 'three a's'— abortion, amnesty, and acid." Hart went on to say that "McGovern definitely felt, four days before the [California] vote, that he was being hurt by these attacks."[11]

Rather than keep the focus on President Nixon's conduct of the war, McGovern had to switch into defensive mode and clarify his views on drugs, the military, and sexual freedom, which were the issues not-sosubtly suggested by acid, amnesty, and abortion. More than three decades later, he still could neither accept nor understand this line of attack from Humphrey, a man McGovern had considered one of his best friends in the Senate. Speaking in November 2005 at the Beverly Hills premiere of *One Bright Shining Moment*, a sympathetic account of McGovern's 1972 campaign, the aged senator (eighty-three at the time) covered each of these charges before an audience that loved him in 1972 and still loves him today. He maintained that the states should have the final word on abortion—precisely the position the Kerry-Edwards team took on gay marriage in 2004. He didn't talk about acid, specifically, but he said that he believed possession of pot should be a misdemeanor. And he would never consider amnesty while American troops were still fighting in Vietnam.

The acid and abortion part of this formulation was actually aimed more at the supposed lifestyle of McGovern's supporters than their political opinions. It is not only that they believed in acid and abortion, but that they most likely put these beliefs into practice. The person who remained monogamous but endorsed reproductive rights was not an especially helpful example of counterculture immorality. But when support for abortion was combined with heightened sexual activity (actual or assumed) you got a "true" picture of this era. The same applied to drug use.

The supposedly private life of an entire generation was open for inspection. In another decade or so the religious right would expand this strategy into a wholesale attack on liberalism and its contempt for so-called traditional values. In the short term, the "3 A's" were an unexpected gift to Nixon's people, who expended considerable energy and time in the first half of 1972 plotting Watergate and other "dirty tricks" to guarantee that Nixon won a second term.

Humphrey ran against the perceptions of McGovernism more than he did against the actual candidate. In a televised debate a few days before the California primary, the former vice president claimed his opponent's proposed defense budget would make the United States frighteningly vulnerable in a hostile world. He illustrated the point with a highly theatrical "sweeping away" of toy soldiers positioned on a map. Humphrey and then Nixon sought to transform McGovern from a reasonable liberal to a dangerous radical. They would save America from the monster whose political profile they were in the process of creating.

In the aftermath of the California primary, which McGovern won, Humphrey waged a bitter and ultimately unsuccessful challenge against the winner-take-all rules governing that state's delegates. The subsequent interparty battle cost McGovern several weeks in his effort to go beyond the primary and focus on defeating President Nixon.

On a national level, Humphrey's attacks damaged the front-runner well before the Democratic convention in Miami. The June 19, 1972, edition of *Newsweek* magazine showed George and his wife, Eleanor, smiling under the heading "Can He Put the Party Together?" "There are a number of guesses why McGovern's lead [in California] eroded so badly. But the explanation that counted, since so many party professionals believed it, was that the Humphrey campaign had finally begun showing McGovern as a furry-minded radical and that the voters had been frightened away in droves."[12] And this was in a state where liberalism and radicalism—the Black Panthers, Berkeley, the Chicano movement—had flourished over the previous decade. The article identified a related problem that would plague the McGovern campaign in the coming weeks and months and haunt the Democratic Party for many years. "Many regulars look forward to a Democratic convention dominated by McGovern delegates chosen under McGovern reform rules with all the enthusiasm Rome felt for the onslaught of the barbarian hordes."[13] Even Hunter S. Thompson, who despised Humphrey and openly rooted for McGovern, acknowledged his preferred candidate had taken some significant hits: "Hubert Humphrey managed to get McGovern tangled up in his own economic proposals from time to time during their TV debates in California—despite the fact that toward the end of that campaign Humphrey's senile condition was so obvious that even I began feeling sorry for him."[14]

• • •

In a faded manila folder, Terry Friedman has for all these years preserved the original typewritten sheets listing the names, ages, occupations, and ethnicities of the McGovern delegates and alternates from California. If not for the fact that one's gender is usually recognizable by one's first name—"Sadie Gorbet" and "Deborah L. Rossi" must be women, "Ralph Hurtado" has to be a man—you would expect that category to be included as well. Today's delegates could conceivably also be listed on paper by their sexuality—at least the ones who chose to define themselves as straight, gay, bi, or transsexual—but back in 1972 liberalism and society had not yet reached the point where those labels were officially recognized by the establishment. The McGovern delegates identified according to ethnicity went by the titles approved for use in the late 1960s and 1970s: black not African American, Chicano not Latino, and Asian not Asian-Pacific Islander. Even more than the rigid, jet-black letters characteristic of a mid-twentieth-century typewriter, the ethnic or racial classification of the delegates brands this document as a relic from an increasingly distant past in American history.

Yet the list is also very much of the present. In 1972, the Democratic Party for the first time mandated that delegations be representative of the composition of the general population, with a higher percentage of minorities, women, and youth. According to *Time*, close to 40 percent of the Democratic delegates were women in 1972, a huge increase over the 13 percent in 1968.[15] This change resulted from the work of the McGovern-Fraser Commission on Party Structures and Delegate Selection, formed in the aftermath of the 1968 Chicago convention. As I scanned the names on Friedman's list, "Black," "Chicano," Asian," and "other" (probably a euphemism for "white"), it occurred to me that I was witnessing one of the first transformative changes imposed by liberalism over the past three-plus decades. Conservatives call it quotas; liberals prefer affirmative action. Conservatives argue that under this system, if somebody wins, someone else must lose. Liberals believe that under this system, society wins and therefore everyone wins, including white males. During election season, conservatives have been more successful at exploiting the negatives of affirmative action than liberals have been at promoting the positives.

The 1972 Democratic convention was the first visible step in an inexorable process that by the early part of the twenty-first century has led to African Americans, Latinos, Asians, women, gays, and lesbians holding key positions in business and politics. Yes, *we* could do better—liberals and their core constituencies have this strange aversion to declaring victory—but society has improved since the days of the McGovern campaign.

The insistence—primarily on the part of conservatives—of recalling McGovern's campaign in terms of its "soft" foreign policy obscures the other more profound changes occurring within liberalism at the time. As we have seen, President Nixon was already taking significant steps to end America's involvement in Vietnam by 1972. What McGovern would have accomplished in weeks Nixon accomplished in the few months after being sworn in for a second time: on January 27, 1973, the Americans and North Vietnamese signed cease-fire agreements, and on March 29, 1973, the last American combat troops departed Vietnam. But the Republican Party most assuredly did not institute its own system of proportional representation at the 1972 convention, unless you count Sammy Davis Jr. famously hugging the president at a rally.

Discussions over affirmative action and quotas have lost none of their edge with the passage of time: not even Vietnam generates as much passion and anger anymore. During a trip to Washington, DC, with a business group in 1996, I listened to a happy hour discussion on this issue between two middle-aged women. Mothers with teenage sons, they expressed concern and anger that their boys would not be judged fairly by the system—college, law school, and corporate America. At that moment, it hit me: motherhood is more powerful than sisterhood. These moms were explaining their strong support for a pending California initiative that would curb affirmative action in college admissions. A quarter century of liberalism had not turned them into full-fledged supporters of the cause. In fact, the opposite was true.

While a typical liberal would seek to understand their pain, he or she would nevertheless consider their position to be woefully misguided and harmful to the nonnegotiable goal of equal opportunity. Didn't the women realize that affirmative action, quotas, and preferential treatment exist for them? One might wonder (as I did) whether they had at some point in their careers benefited from programs designed to promote women. Yet it didn't matter to them. The issue was whether their white male sons were being targeted for exclusion. Sometimes when the personal becomes political, feminism is the loser.

. . .

In the early summer of 1972, a few weeks before the Democratic National Convention, Terry Friedman played a significant role in the effort to oust Chicago mayor Richard Daley's loyalists from the Illinois delegation and replace them with so-called reform delegates. Like Hubert Humphrey, Friedman and a majority of the Credentials Committee were intent on avenging events of 1968. In this case, the catalyst was the beatings they and their friends received from Chicago cops. They were preoccupied with getting back at Daley for encouraging attacks on hippies, radicals, peaceniks, liberals, and seemingly anyone else in the streets of his city in late August 1968. It was Daley's misfortune to be a law-and-order Democrat rather than a law-and-order Republican, which would have made him invulnerable to any changes sought by the McGovern campaign.

Humiliating the mayor was not the sole purpose of this bold and controversial move. The ultimately successful effort to replace Daley loyalists with reform delegates was an early and highly public example of the quota system in action. "At the time, it was very exciting," recalled Friedman. "After all, we won!"

Notice the phrase "at the time." Angry and bitter about their fate, the Daley people, and their supporters around the country, kept their distance from or actively worked against the McGovern campaign—not unlike the behavior of the antiwar left four years before. Some of them probably voted for Nixon, like AFL-CIO head George Meany. Even worse from the standpoint of the reformers, the shunned delegates became a symbol of those millions of once proud and dedicated Democrats who felt alienated, ridiculed, and humiliated by McGovern's army and everything it represented.

Friedman is proud of the campaign's legacy, and he believes that what took place within the Democratic Party in 1972 brought about necessary changes in society, based in no small part on the core values of the new liberalism. And yet, as a student of political campaigns he has to account for McGovern's massive defeat at the polls. To the question "Where did we go wrong?" Friedman returns to the scene of his greatest triumph: getting rid of the Daley people. Thirty years later, this historic act doesn't seem quite so thrilling, necessary, or wise. "This was probably not the way to deal with the excesses of 1968 if you wanted to win the general election," he said. "But there wasn't a lot of mature judgment at the top of the campaign. The kids acted like kids, and the adults did, too."

CHAPTER SIX

Modern Times

When she was five years old and living in Montgomery, Alabama, Donzaleigh Abernathy believed that "death was imminent." As the daughter of the Reverend Ralph Abernathy, one of the leaders of the civil rights movement during the 1950s and 1960s who succeeded Martin Luther King as head of the Southern Christian Leadership Conference after King's assassination, Donzaleigh grew up with an acute awareness of violence and hate, even as her father and the man she still calls "Uncle Martin" practiced and preached precisely the opposite. A year before Donzaleigh's birth, the Abernathy family home was bombed. "There was a photograph that my mom put on the wall of our home that had been bombed," she said in an interview with me in April 2006. "She wanted us to be aware, and to know that it was not necessarily safe out there."

In 1963, the year Donzaleigh turned five, a horrific bombing at a church in Birmingham, Alabama, killed four black schoolgirls. "It had a devastating effect on me," she said. "I remember urinating on myself every day of nursery school after naptime. I was afraid that if I went to the bathroom a bomb would go off, and I was going to die. The teacher was always prepared with fresh clothes and a wash cloth to clean me off."

But Donzaleigh also cherishes exciting memories of literally watching history being made, as well as feelings of immense pride that her father, Dr. King, and the civil rights movement embarked on a noble, courageous, and ultimately triumphant journey to end segregation in the Old South. Despite the obvious danger and her young age, Donzaleigh recalls desperately wanting to participate. A wide-eyed daughter who idolized her strong and brave father, she learned through his example the values of human rights and individual freedom. However, there were not a lot of opportunities for elementary school children to participate, regardless of their lineage. Yet one time Donzaleigh almost got the chance.

She was at the Atlanta airport with her family and the King children, waiting for the two fathers to arrive before the civil rights leaders were to change planes and fly to their next destination. "I stayed with Uncle Martin and my daddy when they met the press," recalled Donzaleigh. "The boys were running around like crazy, with their shirttails out, and I learned they were going to go on this tiny plane. I asked if I could go, and my daddy said, 'No, Donzaleigh, you can't because you're a girl.' I was crushed."

Her dad's view about the proper role of women did not change over time. Many years later, long after King had been murdered and when the civil rights movement was in disarray, Donzaleigh approached her aging father and told him gently that she planned to keep her surname after she got married. Influenced by feminism and the struggle for women's equality in the mid-1970s, Donzaleigh regarded her decision as an act of both solidarity and empowerment.

But her father would not be swayed. "He kept telling me before he died [in 1990] that I needed to take the name of my husband, because that's what a woman does. And I said, 'No, I'm keeping my name. I should keep my name—my husband is not giving up his name.'" Gloria Steinem once admiringly told Donzaleigh that the women's movement "rose out of the civil rights movement." The Reverend Ralph Abernathy (and perhaps Dr. King, had he lived) would not necessarily have regarded this as a compliment. "Uncle Martin and daddy were huge chauvinists," said Donzaleigh.

. . .

In 1972, the Democratic Platform Committee included for the first time a statement on reproductive rights in its minority report. The report quietly states its case, without the ringing testimonials to human rights, civil liberties, or individual dignity that typify liberal rhetoric. Indeed, liberals developed the habit over thirty years of incorporating words or phrases that indicate support for abortion without ever using the word abortion: "choice," "a woman's right to choose," "a woman's right to her own body," and so on. While not exactly a case of "I'm for it, but I'm also against it" on abortion, liberals have been known in the last decade to fudge and dodge, their response to the thundering of the religious right. But the toned-down language and nuanced positions do not change the fact that in the end, liberals (including liberal Republicans) support abortion rights. As the 1972 platform statement declared, "In matters relating to human reproduction, each person's right to privacy, freedom of choice and individual conscience should be fully respected, consistent with relevant Supreme Court decisions."

The minority report "Rights, Power, and Social Justice" can be found on page MR 7 of the 1972 Democratic Platform Committee report. On page MR 8, as an addition to the subsection titled "The Right to Be Different," are several bullet points relating to sexual orientation, which was the first time the issue had been explicitly addressed in a political party's platform. The title suggests the opposite of what was intended: Aside from sexual preference, which according to the tenets of liberalism is biologically determined, aren't gay people pretty much like everyone else? Is that not the justification for gay rights in the first place? Or did liberals want to have it both ways? Gay people are free to express themselves as gay people, but apart from that "right," they are deserving of "normal" societal roles in what today has become an ever-expanding universe—that is, gay parenthood and same-sex marriage.

Years before the Village People and decades before *Will and Grace*, a minority plank in the Democratic platform took an unequivocal stand in favor of gay rights. The opening sentences in this section read like a classic manifesto of the times: "Millions of gay women and men in this country are subject to severe social, economic and legal oppression because of their sexual orientation. We affirm the right of all persons to define and express their own sensibility, emotionality and sexuality, and to choose their own lifestyle, so long as they do not infringe on the rights of others."[1] The words *severe* and *oppression* mark this passage as a production of the New Left.

Today the plight of the "gay poor" is not a top priority with homosexual rights organizations around the country; the movement has been oriented much more over the past two decades toward resolving issues of personal freedom. This decision has been detrimental to the wider success—and relevance—of liberalism. After all, reference to economic oppression provides a solid link between gay people and women, blacks, Chicanos, and the other guiding lights of the liberal constellation. It is a reminder that the poor, or to be more precise, the economically oppressed, exist within every tribe.

Given the fissures created later by the rise of identity politics, it is unfortunate that liberals and gay groups essentially abandoned this unifying message. Today gay rights organizations strain to find similarities between the effort to legalize gay marriage and the civil rights movement of the 1960s, both to enlist African American support and to establish historic continuity among liberal causes.

On the other hand, the second sentence should sound familiar to a contemporary audience. Employing language typically associated with pop psychology, the document asks that any comprehensive position on gay rights take into account a person's emotionality and sensibility. Given the difficulty in measuring success or failure, one presumes that the inclusion of these words is a concession to the influence of the counterculture and its obsession with improving the "inner-being." Somehow I can't imagine Roosevelt, Truman, Kennedy, or Johnson considering *emotionality* and *sensibility* when making policy. To be fair, these are not the words of McGovern, but of new voices in the Democratic

Party. And yet two decades later America elected a president—the director of McGovern's Texas operation in 1972—who told the American people "I feel your pain." The wife of this president, herself elected to the U.S. Senate in New York in 2000 and reelected six years later, embraced a New Idea called the politics of meaning.

Then there is the official endorsement in the document of the ever-popular "do your own thing" philosophy, here phrased in slightly more serious language as the right to "choose one's own lifestyle." Though this idea found its way into the minority report on sexual orientation, it can be applied to a bigger constituency: straight couples who live together without getting married, football players with long hair, and anyone else who adopted the freedoms of the 1960s. The Democratic Party—and liberalism—was now on record as providing intellectual and legislative support for various lifestyles, albeit with the well-worn caveat that these choices shouldn't infringe on the rights of others. Subsequent decades would demonstrate that the Democratic Party rarely met a lifestyle that it didn't understand.

This seemingly limitless tolerance has been taken to extremes in the category of sexual identity, and by 2006 the original notion of gay rights had expanded to gay/bi/lesbian/transgendered rights, and even a group known as the "intersex population." (I asked a couple of gay friends to define for me "the intersex" and none of them could provide a clear answer.) These subdivisions not only invite ridicule, by seeming to account for all manners and categories of sexuality, but they falsely presume a commonality of interests. Anyone who knows the least bit about the history of gay men and lesbians, for example, knows that they disagree as much or more than they agree. Not unlike heterosexual men and women.

Reading the section on sexual orientation in the 1972 Democratic Platform Committee's Minority Report, the question occurs as to why it could not have simply started and ended with the first bullet point: "Urge repeal of all laws, federal and state, regarding voluntary sex acts involving consenting persons in private, laws regulating attire, and laws used as a shield for police harassment." The statement is everything you would want in a highly partisan pamphlet: unambiguous, forceful, and succinct. It is also very much within the liberal tradition of legislating freedom. But instead of keeping the focus on civil rights, the references to "lifestyle" and so forth sow confusion and detract from the main point. Liberals were now being asked not only to protect a way of life, but to accept that way of life as well.

· · ·

At the 1972 convention, McGovern delivered one of the most misunderstood and most vilified acceptance speeches of the past half century. Beginning after 3:00 A.M. Eastern Standard Time, when the great majority of voters in the United States had gone to bed, his speech has garnered more attention and controversy through the years than it did when first broadcast. You hear almost nothing about the acceptance speeches of Jimmy Carter in 1976 and 1980, Walter Mondale in 1984, Michael Dukakis in 1988, or Al Gore in 2000, but McGovern's has never been forgotten.

McGovern's speech is one of the main reasons the campaign has experienced such a long afterlife. Commonly known as "Come Home, America"—a phrase that's introduced and repeated only in the final few paragraphs—the speech encompassed most of the major themes of the campaign. Not surprisingly, conservatives have seized ever since on those three words as proof above all of the Left's ignorance and naïveté in international affairs. They interpret "Come Home, America" as code for "Run Away, America"—that is, allow dangerous states and competing powers to do whatever they want, whenever they want, and wherever they want. In retrospect, that phrase may not have been wise given the other side's history of seizing on the flimsiest evidence to challenge the patriotism of Democrats. The present opponent, Richard Nixon, had few peers in waging precisely that kind of campaign.

Nonetheless, the content of the speech stands as a basic affirmation of liberal values, circa 1972. A key paragraph at the end succinctly wraps several issues around a single theme: "From secrecy and deception in high places, come home America. From military spending so wasteful that it weakens our nations, come home America. From the entrenchment of special privilege and tax favoritism, from the waste of idle hands to the joy of useful labor, from the prejudice based on race and sex, from the loneliness of the aging poor and the despair of the neglected sick, come home America."

McGovern obviously had the Nixon administration in mind as he recited the above list of horrors, but he could well have been thinking of Johnson and Kennedy too. After all, it was JFK who, during the 1960 campaign, talked repeatedly about the so-called missile gap, which led to calls for increased military spending and a warning from the departing President Eisenhower about the dangers of the military-industrial complex. And what was Vietnam but a classic and tragic example of "secrecy and deception in high places." McGovern was repudiating recent American political history, particularly the establishment of an imperial presidency—the title of an influential book by Arthur Schlesinger Jr. published a year after the speech.

But there was a problem. On the one hand, McGovern called for the return of a more decent, compassionate, and caring politics. With Richard Nixon occupying the White House, a man whose policies and personality evoked precisely the opposite impressions, that message established a contrast that was highly favorable to the challenger. So far, so good, if one was a Democrat of any persuasion. Yet there were millions of people who supported McGovern, and worked hard for McGovern, who had neither the desire to go back nor come home. With its nostalgic tone and seeming embrace of a simpler time, "Come Home, America" represented a kind of conservative manifesto for the new liberalism. This was not the hard-charging liberalism of Kennedy's inaugural address or Johnson's speeches on civil rights—no overt references to building something "new" or "great." Instead, McGovern's remarks implied a kind of weariness with the pace and events of recent history and a reaction to the accumulation of bad news. You know the list: assassinations, Vietnam, riots, urban crime, inflation, corruption. The candidate was prepared to tackle the big problems, but not under the auspices of a liberal master plan. If the era of big government was not yet over, as Clinton declared two-and-a-half decades later, it was under review.

In this regard, the theme of the speech did not accurately reflect the attitudes of everyone in its intended audience. If anything, feminists, gay rights activists, and Chicano power proponents were poised to build a greater Great Society, one that accounted for their emergent constituencies, which had been seemingly ignored or even dismissed by liberalism in the recent past. What did FDR, Truman, or LBJ ever do for the cause of legal abortion or the integration of gay people into "normal" society? For that matter, what was McGovern's level of commitment on these issues? Inspired by the idea of the McGovern campaign as much as by its substance, this new generation of liberals acted as if it was the dawn of another great era for liberalism.

The candidate may not have been fully aware of his own impact, although it certainly could not have displeased him. A new liberal coalition was being formed under his leadership. "McGovern was riding a horse; the antiwar movement, plus every disenfranchised constituency in the country," observed Zev Yaroslavsky. In its convention issue, *Time* declared that "the McGovern drive has convincingly demonstrated that people outside organized politics can band together and take over a national party."[2]

. . .

The vice-presidential selection process occupies that otherwise dull period between the end of the primaries and the party convention. For political reporters it offers a chance at redemption following the inaccurate predictions they made in the previous months about which candidates were up or down, in or out. In an arena where manipulation, control, and spin are part of everyday life, to know in advance the actual VP choice counts as a bona fide scoop. Note the word *actual*: in 2004 the *New York Post* proclaimed in a screaming headline that John Kerry had picked Missouri congressman Dick Gephardt as his running mate. I'm not sure who was more upset by the gaffe—the *Post*, Kerry, Gephardt, or North Carolina senator John Edwards, whom the nominee subsequently named to the ticket.

In round one of the process, several possible choices are proffered through the media: minorities, women, and perhaps a midwestern or southern white male on the Democratic side, perhaps a minority and at least one woman on the Republican side. In round two, the list is winnowed down to three to five people, each of whom is called to the candidate's home (usually) for a prescreening interview. The media meanwhile assume the role of a human resources department, looking into the past of everyone on the short list with as much or maybe even more gusto than the presidential nominee's own staff. The race to be first with something controversial—sexual, political, medical, ethical—drives the pursuit much more than does any cherished concept of the public's right to know.

The time and effort invested in selecting a vice-presidential candidate today represents another offshoot of the 1972 campaign. Along with holding the record for the worst electoral defeat in American presidential history, George McGovern has the unfortunate distinction of presiding over the single worst vice-presidential selection process in American history. Employing the phrase "presiding over" may be too generous; to this day, no one associated with the campaign has come out and said that he was the one who failed to adequately vet the background of Missouri senator Thomas Eagleton.

The cover of the July 24, 1972, edition of *Time* magazine shows McGovern and Eagleton, hands clasped at the podium in the traditional convention closing-night pose, optimistically smiling while looking out at the delegates. The headline reads: "In Quest of a Second Miracle." Nobody doubted the difficulty of defeating Richard Nixon, least of all the national media, which has a professional interest in hyping political races. And yet coming out of the convention McGovern had to be thankful that he was running against this incumbent. Nixon had almost done the impossible—blowing the 1968 campaign against Hubert Humphrey—and in 1962 had suffered a huge defeat in the California governor's race. On top of mediocre campaign skills, Nixon possessed a truly erratic and at times frighteningly bizarre personality, which now and then eluded the best efforts of the reelection campaign to keep it out of public view. The McGovern campaign may have attracted more than its share of freaks, but McGovern himself seemed normal next to Nixon. And though in a presidential election personality is not everything, in this case the comparison clearly favored the challenger.

But ten days later, the McGovern campaign was in shambles, and in need of a miracle just to compete. The Eagleton Affair, as it has been known ever since, severely damaged McGovern's well-earned reputation as a different sort of politician: straightforward, on the level, in but not of Washington. This reputation was based more on policy than politics. McGovern's plan to end American involvement in Vietnam, his call for a thirty-two-billion defense budget cutback spread over three years, and his controversial proposal to "abolish welfare payments and substitute minimum income grants with a maximum of about one thousand dollars per person annually" went further than his Democratic opponents—a mixed blessing for the campaign.[3] Still, no one could deny McGovern meant what he said. Indeed, the Republicans were counting on it.

Almost immediately after the convention it was revealed that Eagleton, who died in 2007, had been hospitalized three times in the 1960s for "nervous exhaustion and fatigue," and that his treatments included electroshock therapy. Should Vice President Eagleton become President Eagleton, his personal medical history would raise questions about his fitness in times of international crises. Would this guy be too willing to push the button, or not willing enough?

McGovern initially proclaimed he was behind his nominee "1,000 percent"—one of those regrettable utterances that later makes you wonder what he could have been thinking at the time. As the revelations continued over several days, and the campaign floundered, Eagleton resigned from the ticket less than two weeks after he had been nominated. Forced to shop for a new vice-presidential candidate, McGovern eventually gave the job to a Kennedy by marriage, R. Sargent Shriver, but only after five other potential victims had refused. Other than Nixon supporters, of course, no one was happy. As Gary Hart remarked in his memoir, "In overwhelming numbers the voters felt that McGovern had either 'acted like a politician' in getting rid of Eagleton, had somehow personally wronged Eagleton himself, or had handled the matter badly by first keeping Eagleton and then removing him. Many believed a combination of all three."[4]

Conservatives would like to think that the Eagleton Affair played no part in the final tally, because that assessment confirms their oft-expressed opinion that the McGovern wing of the Democratic Party is too far left for America, whether one is talking about 1972 or 2008. A smooth VP selection process would not have changed a thing, or so they maintain. On the other hand, Gary Hart blames the size (if not the fact) of McGovern's defeat on what he termed the "Eagleton matter." Hart offers polling data to substantiate his theory: in mid-August, right after Eagleton departed the ticket, the Harris poll showed Nixon at 57 percent, with 34 percent supporting McGovern and 9 percent undecided. A month later, Harris had Nixon at 63 percent, McGovern at 29 percent, and 8 percent undecided. The rout was on.

. . .

Raised by politically active women, Linda Griego left New Mexico in 1966 at the age of eighteen to go to Washington and work for local congressman Tom Morris, a loyal ally of President Johnson who supported the Great Society and the war in Vietnam. Neither hawk nor dove when she arrived on the Hill, Griego within two years became a staunch opponent of the war. The reason was not Morris—for whom Griego had tremendous respect, despite their differences on the issue—but her work assisting her boss on the House Armed Services Committee. "I read all the letters that came into the office dealing with the military," she said in an interview with me in February 2006.

"Mothers saying, 'My son is wounded, and I want him home.' And then you look at the ages of the people who were dying—Frank Gonzalez, eighteen . . . they were my age. It really begins to affect you."

Starting in early 1968, Griego and other Morris staff members who held similar views on the war left the office in the evenings to join protests or attend campaign rallies for Eugene McCarthy. If Morris was aware of their after-hour activities, he did not allow them to interfere with the day-to-day running of the office. "He was a straight arrow, and all work," said Griego, adding, "I respected him for his views, but we didn't think alike. I went to my rallies and felt perfectly fine supporting someone who was the opposite of him."

Later that year, Morris lost his reelection bid in a newly created district that Greigo says favored the GOP. Now out of work, she eventually landed a job in the office of a freshman senator from California named Alan Cranston, who openly opposed the war. Richard Nixon's victory in 1968 freed Cranston to speak out against U.S. policies in Vietnam without facing criticism for being a disloyal Democrat. An advisor to Cranston on veterans' affairs, this time Griego was an antiwar staffer in an antiwar office. In this environment, attending rallies and protests was practically a requirement of the job.

In 1972, Griego backed the presidential bid of George McGovern, a senator that Cranston "liked a lot." She performed the usual tasks of an energetic volunteer: stuffing envelopes, making phone calls, distributing bumper stickers and lawn signs. Working on the campaign with like-minded liberals, many of them young, politically astute, and well educated, Griego had the overwhelming sense that regardless of the outcome of the election McGovern represented the possibilities and the future of the Democratic Party. Then she went for a brief visit to her home in New Mexico. "I remember saying to people that I supported McGovern, and they said if he gets elected, we won't have jobs," recalled Griego. "They said he was a person who was 'too far out there' on issues of foreign relations . . . to care about whether people had food on the table." These were working-class Democrats who in some cases had supported the party since the New Deal. They never doubted until now that the party represented their interests above all, and that without Democrats in office they would be done for. But McGovern was different. His campaign attracted a disproportionate share of long-hair students, feminists, and intellectuals, all elitists who appeared to care about only the causes that affected their own privileged circle—including an immediate withdrawal of U.S. troops from Vietnam. A new kind of liberal seemed on the verge of taking over the party, with McGovern as the conduit. The traditional liberals—whom the new liberals regarded as old and irrelevant—were confused, hurt, and suspicious. *Their* party did not promote abortion, gay rights, and a seeming retrenchment of American power. Perhaps it was time to consider once unpalatable alternatives.

Hoping for a relaxing break from the intensity of the campaign, Griego wandered into the battlefield of a brewing Democratic Party civil war. It was her first strong indication that the people did not embrace or in some cases support the candidate that was supposedly for the people. Whether liberalism had gone off track or these New Mexico residents simply did not get it was beside the point. The Democrats—and liberals—were in trouble. "An image was now attached to liberals that somehow they're not in touch with the person on the street," said Griego.

. . .

Some argue that the results of the 1972 election marked the real end of the 1960s. According to this view, Nixon's landslide victory destroyed any illusions that the New Left and its sympathizers could achieve real political power in America. "There was still two years of momentum of youthful '60s idealism that pushed past 1970 into 1972, and then Nixon's victory stopped it dead," said Joel Bellman, who worked as a sixteen-year-old volunteer in McGovern's campaign, in a 2004 interview with me. "After that it was a total blowout. The '70s were a period of drift and complacency politically." Among other things, Nixon sought to further divide the black/white civil rights coalition. His race-based appeals in '68 and '72—including cynical support for affirmative action programs—were intended to turn working-class, pro-labor whites against blacks and the Democratic Party. Hammering the "law and order" theme, Nixon appealed to the seemingly millions of whites who watched with rage and fear as "ungrateful" blacks rioted and aggressively lobbied for quotas and affirmative action. Dr. King was a good man, but something happened between "I Have a Dream" in 1963 and black students brandishing guns at Cornell University in 1969.

Failed campaigns rarely have legacies, except as the negative example against which subsequent candidates develop their strategies and select their positions. One exception is the 1964 Goldwater campaign: true believers vowed to continue the fight, and to a remarkable extent kept their word. A second is Ronald Reagan's competitive but ultimately unsuccessful effort in 1976 to defeat President Gerald Ford for the Republican nomination. Both Goldwater and Reagan appealed to staunch conservatives, who in the last three decades have proven to be the most loyal and supremely confident bloc of voters in the American political system. Like communists of the 1930s, they believed—and still believe—in historical destiny. To paraphrase the most famous slogan of the 1964 Goldwater campaign: In their hearts, they knew he was right, and in their hearts, they knew *they* would eventually prevail. This unswerving faith in their cause and belief in happy political endings coexist with a worldview that is often pessimistic, cynical, and harsh. For liberals, the reverse holds: elections are blown and candidates screw up, but humankind can always be made better.

. . .

Bill Rosendahl spent election night 1972 in Sioux Falls, South Dakota, with McGovern. Not many people get to occupy the same room as a presidential candidate—winner or loser—on election night, when the end finally comes. In homes across the country that evening, millions of McGovern supporters, volunteers, and contributors would console each other, curse America, and fear the prospect of four more years under Nixon. Rosendahl could go through that process later. Tonight, he would be with McGovern. "I was in a hotel suite, and George had been taking a nap," said Rosendahl, recalling that evening thirty-two years after the fact. "George came out of the bedroom with his bathrobe on. I was in the room with one other person. George comes right out and says 'How did I do?' The other guy just cried and stormed out of the room. I told McGovern he'd lost. He then asked: 'How did I do in South Dakota?' Frankly, he had already lost South Dakota. I didn't have the heart to tell him, so I just said it's too close to call. 'But it looks like you won in Massachusetts!'"

"When I told him he lost, he wasn't crushed," noted Rosendahl. "He just wanted to know how bad it was. McGovern doesn't show his emotions much. He's a very private guy."

The next morning Rosendahl shared a final campaign breakfast in Sioux Falls with the actress Shirley MacLaine and other members of the inner circle. "We were sitting at a café," said Rosendahl, "and we knew we would never all be together again. What had brought everyone together was the energy of the moment, and the issue of the moment [Vietnam]."

McGovern would never again be a serious candidate for president— not given the size of his defeat, the presumed repudiation of his political philosophy, and his identification with getting out of Vietnam as quickly as possible. Liberals may back the underdog in society, but not in politics. Unlike Goldwater, who to this day is revered by conservatives despite (or perhaps because of) his landslide defeat in 1964, McGovern was for three decades gently but firmly asked to stay away by his "friends." But this cruel request has in no way banished the memory of '72 from electoral politics. It is referenced all the time, for example, by Frank Rich in a 2006 column for the *New York Times:* "A similar panic can be found among the wave of pundits, some of them self-proclaimed liberals, who apoplectically fret that Mr. (Ned of Connecticut) Lamont's victory signals the hijacking of the Democratic Party by the far left . . . and a prospective replay of its electoral apocalypse of 1972."[5]

Even staunch opponents of the Vietnam War would seek out new candidates and fresh ideas once the last U.S. troops had returned home. No politician in American history—except Lyndon Johnson—is as singularly identified with that war as George McGovern. You would be hard-pressed to find a hundred Americans who can name anything else of significance about McGovern's eighteen years in the U.S. Senate. Rosendahl has remained close to the senator over the years, raising money for a McGovern wing at a library in South Dakota, but he also described the campaign as a "moment"—and not a crusade, realignment, or movement. "Moments" by definition do not endure. They come and then they go, leaving bittersweet memories but no lasting legacy.

From the inside, McGovern's campaign must have seemed ephemeral. Several of the key people who worked for McGovern later found great success in politics: Bill Clinton, for one, would soon start down the long and ultimately golden road of Democratic centrism. Another prominent McGovern alumnus, Sandy Berger, served as Clinton's national security advisor. Several of them went to work for Jimmy Carter, who would be elected president in 1976, running to the right of McGovern on economic and foreign-policy issues.

On the morning after McGovern's loss, Rosendahl and others didn't convene for the purpose of continuing "McGovernism" by other means. They had had their chance, had bombed at the polls, and now it was time to move on to something or someone else—after a proper mourning period, of course.

. . .

But what if the McGovern campaign can be seen as the triumphant final act of the '60s rather than the end of an era? Arguing that position would require one to look past the election results, which seemed to repudiate everything that Jane Fonda, Tom Hayden, and Terry Friedman believed in. Yet I think that the campaign actually represents both a beginning and an end, which is why it is an essential starting point to assess the fate of liberalism.

After 1972, liberals felt betrayed by America. Any country that so overwhelmingly voted for Nixon had to be considered deeply flawed, perhaps beyond redemption. This attitude—which gained force with other events in the next three decades—eroded liberals' confidence and diminished their strength as they tried to contend with the conservative wave that engulfed the country for the next thirty-five years. The resigned liberal is as much a part of modern politics as either the disenchanted liberal or the former liberal. This depressed feeling contributes to the inability of liberals to mount a strong defense against belligerent, aggressive, and self-righteous conservatism. It has made liberals ashamed of who they are and, in some cases, of who they were.

Yet there is more to the story. The McGovern campaign served as the central address for several percolating movements and causes that would subsequently define liberalism and the political and cultural legacy of the late 1960s and the 1970s. Not even Bill Clinton in his reassessment of post-LBJ liberalism threw out the business about support for reproductive rights, gay rights, and affirmative action. The movements promoting these causes seek change, of course, but they also seek validation, especially from the mainstream. They hope in the long run to attain normal status (by their definition) within society. A woman who has an abortion wishes to get on with her life free from pity, scorn, or discrimination. The push for gay marriage in part reflects the desire on the part of same-sex couples to be viewed as "normal" Americans: raising kids, joining the PTA, moving to suburbia.

The McGovern campaign helped give voice to these causes, and as such represents a landmark event in the evolution of post–World War II American democracy. The contrast with Western Europe during the same period is striking. Speaking of the young leftists in France and other nations—the generation of 1968—the British historian Tony Judt writes: "The sense of exclusion, from decision-making and thus from power, reflected another dimension of the Sixties whose implications were not fully appreciated at the time. Thanks to the system of two-round legislative elections and presidential election by universal suffrage, political life in France had coalesced by the mid-Sixties into a stable system of electoral and parliamentary coalitions built around two political families: Communists and Socialists on the Left, centrists and Gaullists on the Right. By tacit agreement across the spectrum, smaller parties and fringe groups were either forced to merge with one of the other four big units or else be squeezed out of mainstream politics."[6]

But in America at the end of the 1960s and early 1970s feminists, gay-rights activists, the peace movement (above and beyond Vietnam), advocates for economic and social justice, and all-purpose lefties signed on to the McGovern campaign, and for the most part have stayed with the Democratic Party. Of course, traditional working-class, pro-labor Democrats—those faithful to FDR, Harry Truman, Tip O'Neill, and Hubert Humphrey—found off-putting and, at times, deplorable the newfound emphasis on personal and social issues that went under the name of liberalism, as well as the continuation of antiwar and anti-American (to some at least) attitudes.

On the other side, conservatives saw these changes as an opportunity to expand their appeal and base. The enemies of hard-working Americans were no longer merely "tax and spend" liberals, but "acid, amnesty, and abortion" as well. (One could add affirmative action and any word beginning with the letter "a" that signifies gay people.) Eventually this characterization would attract the strong support of evangelical Christians, who were not to that point predictably Republican. In fact, Jimmy Carter ran extremely well among evangelicals in 1976. But this rising constituency soon discovered that on social issues he was not with them. Four years later, evangelicals gave most of their support and a majority of their votes to an indifferent churchgoer on his second marriage—and from Hollywood no less—instead of the devout Georgian. Liberals in recent years have agonized over how these voters could so blatantly act against their own economic interests simply because conservatives adopt a hard-line position on gay rights and abortion.

The past thirty-five years in the history of liberalism can be viewed as both an extension of and a reaction to the McGovern campaign. "Remember '72" could serve as a rallying cry for proponents and opponents. But given that liberalism has experienced an appreciable decline during this period, it is the detractors who have the advantage.

CHAPTER SEVEN

I Am Woman, Say It Loud

In 1970, the hard rock–funk group Funkadelic released an album with the memorable title *Free Your Mind and Your Ass Will Follow*. Led by George Clinton, whose outrageous hair, insane clothes, and bona fide wit set him apart from other rock and funk stars, Funkadelic symbolized the ideals and promise of the 1960s as much as or more than any band playing in any style. At a time when popular music was divided along rigid racial lines—"black radio" and "funk" versus "FM rock" and "pop"—Clinton appealed to a universal audience. He did not just talk about freedom; he embraced it, deliberately challenging the ghettoization practiced by the music industry and radio. "But as black hippies, the radio and the record industry didn't know what to do with us," Clinton told *Mojo* magazine in 2006, "because we were basically too white for black folks and too black for white folks."[1]

The album title could also be regarded as an eight-word manifesto for the counterculture and the New Left. In that sense, its timing could not have been better. By 1970, liberalism had moved beyond freedom to liberation, the new buzzword. Youth did not want to be merely freed, but liberated, in mind, body, and spirit.

. . .

The Funkadelic album was one of the many instances of the increasingly close and supportive relationship between pop music and New Left–liberal politics. Before liberals seized control of Hollywood, they achieved disproportionate success on the *Billboard* charts.

During the late 1960s and 1970s soul music endorsed and cheered on the civil rights and later the black power movements. In late 1964, just before his untimely and tragic death, soul singer Sam Cooke released "A Change Is Gonna Come," which cracked the Top 40. Recorded in a smooth gospel style, the song functioned as a morale booster for civil-rights marchers and as a predictor of the future direction of the country. Given what would transpire throughout the United States over the next seven years, "A Change Is Gonna Come" could also be regarded as the definitive pop music statement about the entire era. There is nothing particularly compelling about the lyrics; the title says it all.

Almost four years later James Brown released "Say It Loud—I'm Black and I'm Proud." At that point—the fall of 1968—white people and the media were just starting to make the transition from "Negro" to "black." Reaching no. 10 on the pop charts, this single cleared up any lingering confusion over what to call "us." I lose count of how many times the title is repeated: Brown yells out "say it loud," and a chorus of what sounds like a roomful of feisty thirteen-year-olds responds with, "I'm black and I'm proud." Throughout the song Brown never forgets that he has a responsibility to provide the hard-funk sound—including a short, searing guitar riff—that typified his best material from 1966 to 1973.

These two songs were musical examples of combining the personal and the political—black performers singing about black stuff. When Motown discovered politics in and around late 1969, the label, in typical fashion, sought to appeal to a wider audience. Edwin Starr's "War" (no. 1 in 1970) was unmistakably about Vietnam, and therefore spoke directly to privileged white college students as well as to poor white, black, and Chicano kids who by that point composed a sizable portion of the draftees. Earlier that same summer Motown released "Ball of Confusion (That's What the World Is Today)" by the Temptations, which reached no. 3 in the charts. There is hardly a constituency in this vast, wide country whose pet issue is not at least referenced in the lyrics. Marvin Gaye's landmark album *What's Going On* from the spring of 1971 rivaled anything recorded by California-based singer-songwriters regarding the systematic destruction of Planet Earth.

The "Say It Loud" of feminism was Helen Reddy's "I Am Woman," with its memorable and oft-repeated phrase "Hear me roar." Released at the end of 1972, the song went all the way to no. 1 and provided an added pick-me-up for a movement then in its prime. More women delegates than ever before had attended the 1972 Democratic Convention; *Ms.* magazine had recently begun publication; and, within a month, while the song was still being played incessantly on the radio, the U.S. Supreme Court handed down its pro-choice decision in *Roe v. Wade*. And though none of us is truly "invincible," as the singer claims on behalf of her gender, who can blame women at that time for believing it? "'I Am Woman' was a statement of female pride and solidarity articulated with a directness that had never before reached the pop Top 10," wrote Gillian Gaar in her history of women in rock.[2]

Unlike black people, who were after all the founders of rock and roll and rhythm and blues, the mere presence of women in rock represented a breakthrough. At the time of "I Am Woman" females were woefully underrepresented in the genre, and the bias existed—and still exists to an extent—that due to some sort of biological deficiency women could neither play the drums nor play lead guitar. As is the case with today's increased number of female studio heads and film directors, the rise in all-girl bands during the 1980s, 1990s, and the 2000s signified progress.

The hits adopted by the gay community in the 1970s were more politically subtle than Helen Reddy's effort, but are remembered with pride by the people who were there. As David Ehrenstein put it in a book review for the *Los Angeles Times*, "With Sylvester, the black gay man whose rich falsetto made 'You Make Me Feel (Mighty Real)' the disco national anthem (until 'I Will Survive' came along), the form found its perfect blend. Add sex, drugs, and muscle worship and you've got quite a socio-sexual stew."[3] Neither of these songs contains overt references to gay people, but the titles alone project an attitude and mood that resonated with that segment of the audience. In the case of "I Will Survive," recorded by disco diva Gloria Gaynor, the words assumed added poignancy and drama with the onset of the AIDS crisis.

For young gay men in the 1970s and 1980s, disco was not only their own Woodstock, but also their own Selma. At least this is what we have been led to believe from numerous articles and books recalling the times and experiences. Ehrenstein's reference to the "socio-sexual stew" is from his review of a book entitled *Turn the Beat Around: The Secret History of Disco*, by the writer Peter Shapiro. The text might have been more appropriately called the (Open) Secret History of Disco. Today, anyone who pays attention to the 1970s is aware of the crucial role that discos and disco singles—the twelve-inch versions, if you please— played in the sexual awakening of gay people. And though one hears prodigious numbers of encounters (2,500, 3,000, 3,500) from those who were sweating on the dance floor every night to the music of Chic, Sister Sledge, and Donna Summer, the disco was never just about sex, or even primarily about sex., but about the intersection between freedom and pleasure. "Disco in a sense was liberalism's last hurrah, the final party before the neocon apocalypse," writes Ehrenstein, quoting from Shapiro's book.

In terms of the chronology, Shapiro is no doubt correct. The decline of disco in 1981–82 corresponds with the rise of Reagan, although the two events are not directly related. Like folk rock, acid rock, punk, postpunk, or any other once-trendy style, disco had by then become a victim of the ever-grinding American pop-music machine. You cannot have discos without disco music, but the major record labels were increasingly unwilling or unable to supply the latter. The last great disco release was probably "I'm Coming Out" by Diana Ross (could the title have been more obvious?), which hit the charts in the summer of 1980. Preparing to seize control of the R&B market was the reenergized funk of Rick James and Prince, and more importantly, something new and strange called rap music.

Shapiro links disco to liberalism, but it is liberalism with a difference. This was after-hours liberalism, liberalism packaged as hedonism: pleasure first and politics second. Only a few years earlier, gay men seeking conversation, sex, or a dance partner in gay-friendly clubs and bars had to constantly worry about getting swept up in a random raid by the local vice squad. Men and women who were nine-to-five heterosexuals, out of fear, necessity, or both, jeopardized their own carefully crafted reputations by going to these kinds of establishments. By the time disco arrived, however, the gay rights movement and a heightened level of sophistication throughout society about sexual realities—a legacy of the 1960s—had diminished both the consequences of exposure and the possibility of harassment. In this environment, attending Studio 54 or similar places was not so much an act of courage or even defiance but of self-expression. As the folk rock group the Turtles put it in a song from 1965 that you would not have heard at Studio 54: "I am what I am, and that's all I ever can be."

Discos, disco music, "I Am Woman," "War," films such as *Easy Rider* and *Alice's Restaurant,* and the visible support for McGovern from Warren Beatty, Barbra Streisand, and other celebrities contributed to the growing perception in the 1970s that Hollywood and the wider entertainment industry was a haven for liberals and liberal causes. In his examination of the Hollywood-Washington connection, Ronald Brownstein notes that "Beatty amassed more influence inside the McGovern campaign than any Hollywood figure had ever accumulated in a presidential campaign."[4] By the end of the 1960s, according to right-wing mythology, Hollywood was being overrun by pot-smokers, free-lovers and, above all, America-haters. It was no longer John Wayne's world.

CHAPTER EIGHT

Sexual Positions

Lillian T. grew up in the 1950s in Philadelphia, where her mother taught dance at the University of Pennsylvania and Temple University. When she was a little girl, Lillian's parents went through a bitter divorce. In a vengeful merging of the personal with the political, Lillian's father contacted the institutions that employed his ex-wife and asserted that she was a member of the Communist Party. Lillian recalls that Temple dropped her mother immediately, without hearing the other side of the story, but Penn refused to cave. Both her parents had been involved in various left-wing activities since the 1930s and certainly might have known and been friendly with communists. For the record, however, Lillian insists that they never actually joined the party.

Having seen politics used for such destructive purposes—and against her mother no less—it might be expected that in her teenage years Lillian would choose self-indulgence, gossip, and primping over engaging the world. Instead, as a student at the Philadelphia School for Girls, she wrote papers about relations between the United States and Cuba—this was during the time of the Bay of Pigs invasion and the Cuban Missile Crisis—and participated in sit-ins, marches, and demonstrations with like-minded colleagues. She deliberately ignored the girls who chatted about boys and fretted over what to wear on Friday night.

On occasion, Lillian and a group of black and white friends would attend rock and roll and rhythm and blues dances hosted by Jerry Blavat, a well-known Philadelphia DJ in the early 1960s. Openly defying the unstated prohibition against interracial couples on the dance floor, Lillian and the others would split up into mixed pairs and dance the Twist, the Watusi, and so forth, only to be immediately chased away by event coordinators. Refusing to be cowed, her group would congregate in a corner, wait several minutes, and head back to the dance floor, eliciting the same predictable response.

Adding to her political education, Lillian listened to Pete Seeger and the Weavers, whom she admired for their lyrics, their view of the world, and their pure folk sound. At the age of fifteen she traveled to the historic March on Washington (August 28, 1963), the details of which are still shared in classrooms across America, especially during Black History Month. For a young liberal in the 1960s, being present to hear Dr. Martin Luther King's "I Have a Dream" speech was a defining moment, along with participating in the antiwar March on the Pentagon in 1967, getting chased through the streets of Chicago during the 1968 Democratic Convention, and waking up to the sound of Jimi Hendrix performing the national anthem at Woodstock in 1969.

Lillian didn't make it to the last three. In 1967, at the age of nineteen, she had a child out of wedlock with a man who all but disappeared. She acquired a new title—single mother—at a time when organized day care did not exist, and when neither the people in power nor grassroots organizations accommodated the particular needs of women in her circumstances. Lillian formed an informal cooperative with two other single mothers living nearby. They assisted each other with babysitting duties, transportation, and mundane daily tasks that become much harder to perform when one is trying to raise a child on one's own. Unaware of Aid to Families of Dependent Children or other applicable welfare programs—not that she would have relied on the government as her sole source of income anyway—Lillian worked full time at a variety of manufacturing jobs.

The demands of (single) motherhood put a halt to Lillian's activism. She barely had time to follow the war in Vietnam on television, let alone devote several hours to joining a protest in front of an induction center or campus ROTC building. Similarly, she missed the opening years of the women's movement and other early manifestations of the "identity politics," which would become such an integral component of liberalism by the mid-1970s. And yet despite her temporary retirement from liberal activism, Lillian's decision to give birth was in a very real sense dictated by the social and political conditions of the time. If you were a feminist, Lillian's story proved why change was necessary.

Before Lillian had her first child and before the *Roe v. Wade* decision made the procedure legal, she had an abortion. Despite the medical risks and legal issues, Lillian felt she was much too young and frankly too busy—with politics and other things—to raise a child either alone or jointly. The man who impregnated her had no desire to be a parent either, and he referred Lillian to a woman in Philadelphia who performed abortions out of her own home. Lillian went to the location, where she recalled being comforted both by the abortionist's pleasant manner and by the fact that this woman did not lecture her on being responsible.

The rest of the day did not go as well. "The emotional and physical terror of it all . . ." said Lillian, still shuddering at the thought of that afternoon thirty-eight years ago. "It didn't happen right away; it happened after a while. They provoke it [the fetus] and you go through the whole 'expelling process.' It's just hideous—hideous and terrifying. Afterward I was terrified I had actually done something to myself."[1] The next time Lillian became pregnant, she knew that she simply could not go through that experience.

Several years later, after the Supreme Court ruled in *Roe v. Wade*, Lillian had another abortion. Recounting details of this procedure, she sounds more sanguine and at ease. "God, it was like a whole other experience [compared to the first abortion]." Abortion was now legal and safe, but not rare. In his account of the period between Nixon's resignation and the first Bush administration, James Patterson notes the following: "Between 1974 and 1977, 3.5 million legal abortions were performed in the United States—or nearly four for every ten live births. The number of abortions further increased in the early 1980s and remained high until the early 1990s, averaging over 1.5 million between 1980 and 1990."[2] In response, a national movement had begun to coalesce that regarded those who performed abortions and even those who have abortions as murderers. But Lillian did not feel like a murderer, and she was grateful that the procedure (post-*Roe*) did not threaten her own life. A few years earlier, liberals and radicals had on occasion screamed such epithets as "baby killers" and "murderers" at U.S. government officials and recently returned Vietnam veterans. Whether intentionally or not, antiabortion activists by the end of the 1970s were using this exact language to intimidate the pro-choice community, many of whom were liberals and many of whom had been involved in the antiwar movement.

. . .

The word few people use when discussing abortion is "sex." Proponents speak of a woman's right to her own body or a woman's right to choose; opponents fire back with the aforementioned insults or carefully selected phrases from the Bible. Newspaper headline writers and TV news producers do not complain; anytime you have an issue involving religion, death, and female empowerment, a receptive and large readership or viewing audience is all but guaranteed.

But imagine how much happier the media would feel if sex entered the debate. We live in a sex-drenched society, and yet here is one instance where its omission is a surprise. It cannot be mere coincidence that abortion was made legal at a time of heightened sexual activity. One did not need to devour the Kinsey Report or peruse more recent surveys of sexual behavior to know that more women were having more sex. In an essay regarding the change in the attitude of women toward their own sexual fulfillment, Kay S. Hymowitz wrote: "The creed of sexuality demands that the individual 'explore' or 'develop' her sexuality fully by experimenting with different partners, in different positions, at different times of the day, or in different rooms of the house or office."[3]

The "How many partners have you had?" question provided further evidence of the change, even though many women—no doubt still wary of society's double standard as it applies to female sexuality—were thought to purposely underestimate their number of conquests. In the entire history of sex in America, nothing shattered taboos and shocked elders like increased bed hopping among the female population between roughly 1965 and 1995. Previously, not only traditionalists—male and female—would have argued that in the sexual arena men and women were creatures from different planets. Men wanted and needed "it" all the time; women by comparison were far more circumspect and demure. But then the birth control pill, rock and roll, miniskirts, *Playboy*, *Penthouse*, sex on the screen, easily accessible porn, and a new kind of peer pressure among young women to explore their sexuality helped to blow away the second part of that theory. Today it barely registers when women in their teens and twenties stand in line to receive autographed copies of a book entitled *How to Make Love like a Porn Star*. We now know that when it comes to desiring sex, women and men have much in common, with existing differences attracting more attention than similarities.

Given this environment, it seems rather disingenuous to separate abortion from female sexuality. To put it bluntly, abortion is a form of birth control, and it was birth control of a different sort that got us into this mess in the first place. The women's movement and liberalism in general have been ambivalent on the issue of sexual freedom (more on that in a moment) but they cannot honestly deny that abortion can and should be considered within the context of changed attitudes about sex. Distancing abortion from the sexual act makes no more sense than distancing pregnancy from the sexual act. And no one can claim in this case that "it depends what you mean by sex."

The right wing has no compunction about bringing up the subject of sex—*The Starr Report* from 1998 is an especially egregious example of this—but for the most part it refrains from arguing that legal abortion is an invitation to promiscuity. Yet the mere fact that abortion provides another option for sexually active women would seem to make it that much more offensive to the protectors of family values. After all, the abstinence movement and other Christian-oriented regulators of sexual behavior are primarily concerned with preserving female virtue; male virtue is not a concept typically considered in a sexual context. You would think that the antiabortion camp would want to incorporate sex into its argument, especially when combined with the existing charge that abortion is murder.

On the other hand, the reluctance of pro-choice groups to connect abortion and sex further reveals a deep sense of unease among liberals about the effects and the aftereffects of the so-called sexual revolution. In a political environment where millions of conservative Republicans would probably be delighted if chastity and virginity were endorsed in their party's platform, liberals seemingly have no choice but to consider themselves on some level as "pro-sex." And yet liberals are confused and deeply divided over exactly how far they want to press the point. From a feminist perspective, the key question comes down to this: Is sexual freedom good for women, not so good for women, or bad for women? Sexual freedom by definition means that a woman can say "yes" without being judged, harassed, or discriminated against, but what are the consequences—for her and for all women—of that decision? How does it advance the greater cause for a woman to go to bed with some frat boy interested only in a one-night or a one-hour stand? Why does the option of engaging in sex without feelings of love or guilt mark an important step on the road to full gender equality?

A true liberal from the 1960s would argue that personal freedom assumes precedence over all else. If a woman eighteen or older wants to have sex then she should be able to do so without being scorned by society or her peers. As long as it is taken of her own free will, her decision is nobody's damn business. And if it happens that intercourse results in an unwanted pregnancy, she can always get a safe and legal abortion.

Whether one is a midlevel bureaucrat, the head of a movie studio, or a coed at a major university, saying "no" can be as empowering and in some sense as satisfying as saying "yes." As regards young women and sex, the right or even duty to turn down a proposition harked back to the moral climate of an earlier era, one which feminism was seemingly trying to eradicate. There is nothing more horrifying in feminist—and liberal—circles than the stereotypical picture of domestic life in the 1950s: dad working in some boring job, mom trapped in the kitchen, daughter doomed to repeat mom's experience. The very title of the television program *Father Knows Best*, which is considered a stylized but not wholly inaccurate depiction of that world, deeply offends the sensibilities of modern enlightened women and their modern enlightened male friends. Making fun of the social environment of the 1950s—including its prevailing views on sex—is practically a tradition in Hollywood. We are so cool, and they were so square.

Yet by the 1980s and 1990s, feminists had launched a counterattack against supposed current sexual attitudes that made the 1950s look liberal by comparison. This effort started with the best of intentions: addressing the problem of sexual violence against women. But in a manner not uncharacteristic of the New Left, it soon swelled into a universal theory that condemned the innocent along with the guilty. In this case, male heterosexuals rather than the white race were judged to be the oppressors. The shy and awkward computer nerd was no better than a football player under the influence of a twelve-pack of Coors. During the Clarence Thomas hearings in 1991, the boorish conduct of an obviously ill-qualified nominee was widely regarded as typical of too many men, conservative or liberal. Most disconcertingly for liberals who had not undergone their post-'60s reeducation, feminists such as the late Andrea Dworkin worked with law-and-order types in an effort to outlaw pornography.

By the 1990s, the sexual revolution had descended into inter- and intragenerational conflict. Media coverage of a young man taking advantage of a woman under the influence invariably suggested that only the party with the penis was at fault. Given the general level of suspicion, mistrust, and anger directed at male behavior, even intelligent folks could be excused for thinking that yes, it is true, all men really are beasts. As Fontana Biancamaria noted in a 2006 article in the *Times Literary Supplement:* "Besides presenting a distorted version of social reality, this kind of approach also has the consequence of considering any male sexuality or virility as necessarily offensive, threatening or violent."[4]

. . .

At the beginning, feminism not only seemed comfortable with sex but gave primacy to the female orgasm and was peripherally responsible for those encounter groups where women removed their clothes and got reacquainted with their privates. Jane DeLynn contributed this description in a cultural anthology of the 1970s: "The forty-two-year-old sexual guru of the Women's Movement . . . was making erotic paintings by day and going to A.A. meetings at night. She started doing Yoga in 1969, and in 1972 held her first workshops. In them, she teaches other women how to get along better with their bodies—in particular, to have bigger and better orgasms."[5]

If the bedroom was a battleground then feminists wanted women to have a well-stocked supply of weapons. In the late 1970s, coeds absorbed sexually explicit novels written by women for women, such as *Fear of Flying* and *Loose Change*, and perused nonfiction tomes on female sexual behavior and fantasies written by Shere Hite, Nancy Friday, and others. In conjunction with the ongoing change in attitudes, feminism helped to create an environment in which engaging in sex of various kinds was possible and desirable. Rare indeed was the mother who had had more sexual partners and experiences than her baby-boomer daughter.

But within a couple of decades some of the daughters of baby-boomer mothers complained that they had been raised around too much sex, whether engaged in or talked about. The editorial pages of the *Wall Street Journal* in particular welcomes pieces by these critics, who deplore a culture in which young men think they can score without much effort, and in which young women are apparently free to engage in casual sex without feelings of regret. A culture in which the peer and societal pressure for young women to have sex is as great or greater than was the pressure fifty and sixty years ago to remain a virgin until marriage. Many of these critics blame feminism for the disappearance of shame and chivalry, arguing that the presence of both exalted womanhood in the past.

But feminism had another side, which questioned and condemned the premises and impact on women of sexual liberation. Acknowledging that an environment of casual flings and one-night stands is less advantageous for women than it is for men, who have a head start in this department, feminists launched a crusade against male sexuality. These efforts were concentrated on college campuses and in the workplace, two arenas where women had made considerable strides since the early 1970s. Feminists had to be careful, however, not to recycle solutions that harked back to the days of dorms separated by gender and the imposition of strictly enforced visiting hours.

Instead, they operated under assumptions about men and their behavior that went well beyond traditional prudery. Men wanted to get inside your pants, that part was obvious. But did this also mean that all men were potential abusers and rapists? The sensitive male of the 1970s had been replaced by a nasty and brutish version, more Attila the Hun than Alan Alda. In less than a generation, young males had apparently regressed to behaving toward young females in ways that made the "sexist" 1950s seem enlightened by comparison. And the fault lay entirely with men—not feminism.

In the workplace, guidelines covering sexual harassment sought to address every possible scenario in which men could seek either to take advantage of their female coworkers or make them feel truly uncomfortable. As conceived, the regulations were clearly intended to deter predators, perverts, and creeps, but their wide scope seemed to include even those guys who just wanted to be friendly. No one—male or female—could offer a legitimate argument in opposition to rules preventing unwarranted advances in the workplace, or more importantly, supervisors demanding sexual favors in exchange for promotions and raises. These are classic examples of sex used for the purpose of harassment and as an instrument of power. But how should one regard provisions against hugging, patting, or the all-purpose "inappropriate touching?" Or for that matter, winking, staring, and leering, each of which is ripe for misinterpretation? (Question: How much time must elapse before mere looking turns into staring?) What was originally conceived as a valid and specific means of protecting women on the job had expanded to the proportions of Big Brother. And all the while liberals just stood and watched.

. . .

Beginning in the early 1990s, Rush Limbaugh applied the always-popular Nazi analogy to feminism, and his freewheeling use of the term "femi-Nazi" caught on with conservatives around the country. I first heard the expression in 1993 from a pair of young female staffers who worked for a Republican member of Congress from Alabama. More often accused of fascist tendencies or outright fascism, the Right in this case returned the compliment to their antagonists, albeit with a smirk: no one really believed that Gloria Steinem represented the second coming of Hitler. Still, no other group vying for space under liberalism's big tent—African Americans, gays and lesbians, Latinos—had "Nazi" affixed to its name.

Femi-Nazi constituted an extreme example of the backlash against feminism that originated around the midpoint of the Reagan administration. As the mouthpiece for a new, aggressive conservatism, Limbaugh detested just about everything feminists stood for, and he was more than happy to share his views with a daily audience of millions of adoring males. Just as many women watch *Oprah* or *Dr. Phil* to be entertained, enlightened, and reassured, men have gravitated to talk radio in part for the comfort of knowing others out there felt the same way. Whereas it might be a daunting prospect to complain directly to one's wife or girlfriend about the excesses of feminism, on talk radio men were encouraged to share their true feelings about the modern woman. To use a word conservatives despise, it was "therapeutic."

Other popular radio talk-show hosts like Howard Stern and Tom Leykis eschewed the political criticisms of feminism—both of them deplored George W. Bush and leaned to the left—but attacked its prurient nature under the guise of straight-sex talk for males. Stern, Leykis, and like-minded hosts told young men it was OK to want to get laid, and it was OK to get laid. You did not need to apologize for having these feelings; as a matter of fact, these feelings are inseparable from what it is to be a man. The antithesis of pretty boys, Stern and Leykis were ideal spokespersons for the adage that any man who plays it smart and cool has a decent chance of going to bed with a gorgeous woman. In another knock against feminism—and a blatant grab for higher ratings—these programs regularly featured as guests strippers and porn stars. Thanks to the free publicity, women in these professions had by the late 1990s achieved goddesslike status among men of a certain demographic.

In an irony that appalled feminists of Gloria Steinem's generation, porn actresses and strippers were regarded by some younger women as exemplars of the true spirit of feminism. These fans maintained that feminism is ultimately about giving women choices, and having sex on camera or wrapping oneself around a pole to stoke the fantasies of middle-aged businessmen represents a choice. Judged strictly as a career move, they had a point: porn stars and strippers were paid reasonably well and in some cases achieved fame. Furthermore, the changing cultural landscape in the United States meant that these women no longer had to feel embarrassed or ashamed at pursuing this particular line of work. And contrary to the stereotype that the adult-entertainment industry is stocked with abused, desperate, and economically under-privileged women in need of therapy, it was not unheard of for well-educated and happy women to enter the business, some of whom later wrote about their experiences with evident pride. By the early twenty-first century, female exhibitionism included getting naked over the Internet, photos not infrequently accompanied by text that for better or worse revealed the subject to be a student of creative writing with literary aspirations.

Since the late 1960s the United States has undergone a sexual revolution, a sexual counterrevolution—spurred by feminists, religious conservatives, and the stark reality of AIDS—and now is poised halfway between a sexual counterrevolution and a sexual counter-counterrevolution. These various phases are indicative of our nation's ambivalence toward sex and toward freedom. One of the major shifts in conservatism over the past forty-five years—Barry Goldwater to George W. Bush—involves a far greater desire on the part of the Right to monitor and control sexual behavior: legislatively, in the courts, or from the podium and pulpit. In the old days, conservatives were so preoccupied with protecting our freedoms from the communists that they hardly had time to worry about what happened behind closed or even partially closed doors, unless it involved national security. Various Christian anti-communist organizations that attracted thousands and thousands of followers throughout the country for the most part also adopted this laissez-faire approach.

Today nobody misses Goldwater more than Democrats, who look back fondly at a time when their chief antagonists were chain-smoking, scotch-drinking libertarians rather than televangelists eagerly awaiting the apocalypse. But the end of the Cold War, combined with the continuation of counterculture values, produced a strain of conservatism that is now so powerful it has quieted or converted people from both parties who should know better. The religious right believes in meddling in other people's lives when it concerns so-called sexual morality. If government is the most effective instrument through which to change "offensive" behavior, then they have no qualms about taking that road. In this sense the religious right is more pragmatic than their predecessors in the conservative movement, who on questions of the individual and the state listened more to Russell Kirk and William F. Buckley than the Bible. Liberals have had far more enthusiasm for challenging traditional conservatives than the angry Christians of the post-Reagan era. This has been a public relations and political disaster. There is no more evidence for the modern Democratic Party's cowardice than its refusal to fight fire and brimstone with fire.

Feminism and the movement for gay rights, however, also had a profound effect on the nature and character of liberalism. Both began by seeking traditionally liberal outcomes—ending discrimination in the workplace, equal opportunity, respect—but eventually crossed over into the less familiar and more treacherous terrain of sexual politics. The early rallying cry was sexual freedom, which is still basically true for gay people, although AIDS and the prevalence of other sexually transmitted diseases have obviously toned down rhetoric if not behavior. On the other hand, women have not reached anything close to consensus on what constitutes proper sexual conduct. The good girl/bad girl syndrome remains intact, although the goalposts have moved in accordance with changing mores.

With the exception of the adult-entertainment industry, which despite highfalutin verbiage about freedom of expression is motivated far more by money than politics, and certain semisecluded beaches, sex is a private act. It is also not a predictor of political affiliations because promiscuity and prudery exist in conservative and liberal circles. We should be no more shocked by right-wing ministers who commit adultery than by liberal activists who have not had sex in three years.

And yet the highly personal nature of sex, its hidden qualities, pleasures, terrors, and mysteries, is at odds with liberalism, which primarily seeks recognition, acceptance, justice, and public acknowledgement for groups that have been seemingly overlooked or held down by society. After all, the civil rights movement fought to make the invisible man become visible and the gay rights movement patented the term "coming out." In a somewhat different vein, antiwar protestors at the 1968 Democratic Convention in Chicago chanted "the whole world is watching."

Among the most powerful legacies of '60s liberalism is that it upgraded the status of and enhanced the opportunities for gays, blacks, women, and Latinos. According to this view, liberalism circa 1965–70 led the transition in the United States from the dark ages to the renaissance. Baby boomers cringe at the thought of what it must have been like to live as a closeted gay man in, say, 1954, or a lonely, unfulfilled (in every way) housewife in 1957, with nowhere to go and no one to talk to. It is no accident that liberals fighting to preserve this legacy invoke a terrifying past—back-alley abortions, gay men and lesbians forced to deny their true identities—as a way of motivating the faithful. When liberals from a certain generation cry "never again," they mean the Eisenhower era.

Given this all-encompassing, all-consuming desire to change the nature of social and political relations in the United States, it was inevitable that sex would at some point appear on the liberal agenda. What better way to wipe out the mentality of the 1950s than to advocate having more sex and actually to have more sex? Despite the sexual charge of James Dean, Elvis Presley, and Little Richard, there was apparently not much sexual activity in the 1950s. How could it be otherwise? Supposedly no one lived together before marriage or engaged in premarital sex. There was no easily available birth control, urban gay ghettos, or hotel clerks who checked in you and your partner without asking embarrassing questions. Mocking the sexual attitudes of the 1950s is practically a subdivision of the entertainment industry. I cannot recall the number of films, plays, comic books, and songs that ridicule the girl who won't go all the way, or the "lucky" boy who having finally found a willing girl fumbles and stumbles to a quick and unsatisfying—especially for her—climax. As for gay sex, it seemed to have not yet been invented.

By the 1970s, however, a consensus had formed within liberalism that a healthy society was free from sexual hang-ups. It was a wonderful thing that mature adults could attend a theatrical performance of *Oh! Calcutta!* or *The Boys in the Band*, purchase *The Joy of Sex* at a local bookstore, or catch a downtown matinee of *Deep Throat*. Popular films of the period such as *Easy Rider*, *Medium Cool*, and *M.A.S.H.* combined leftist politics with scenes of a sexually explicit nature, which left conservatives wondering what the hell had happened to Hollywood.

In a perfect liberal world, talking about sex could only lead to beneficial and satisfying sexual relationships, especially for women, who, according to legend, had been denied the right to express or act upon their desires for centuries. Along with abortion and gay rights, the freedom to openly discuss sex and to see honest depictions of sex were clear signs of progress. No more carting home a copy of *Playboy* wrapped in a brown paper bag or watching movies where the camera panned to birds in the sky as a cinematic euphemism for sexual activity. Where sex was concerned, from now on adults would be treated like adults.

But free-spirited liberals chose to either ignore or dismiss the potentially damaging repercussions stemming from their version of sexual tolerance. The successive triumphs of liberalism during the late 1960s and early 1970s no doubt spawned feelings of complacency and a strong sense that "we own the future." Yet could liberals have realistically expected that all the prudes out there would simply acquiesce to the ethos of "if it feels good, do it"? Sex sells, but so too does antisex. In a later chapter, I will discuss in detail how sexual liberalism helped to galvanize a new and powerful conservative voting bloc in American politics.

However, not everyone discomforted by the prospect of a sexually liberated America supported Richard Nixon and Ronald Reagan. Some believed fervently in a woman's right to choose and were proud to have as friends both gay men and lesbians. But feminists were not unwilling to sacrifice the fundamental liberal belief in freedom and progress in the quest to empower women. A prime example is the evolution of sexual harassment guidelines.

Even the religious right has never suggested that staring at a coworker should be grounds for dismissal. The efforts by feminists and their liberal supporters to punish a broad range of alleged sexual behaviors represented a new and potentially insidious threat to the classic liberal notion of the good life and personal freedom. For a society supposedly awash in irony, it was ironic indeed that the liberals keen on protecting women in this manner did not even acknowledge that they were undermining and weakening the greater cause. Extreme efforts to repress perceived sexual conduct blatantly contradicted the ideals of liberalism, and therefore made no sense. Still, it was a rare liberal—rarer still in the case of politicians—with the courage or wisdom to point this out on the record.

Though less threatening to civil liberties, the attempt to legalize same-sex marriage can in one sense also be viewed as a retrenchment from sexual liberalism as it evolved thirty to forty years earlier. One of the arguments put forth by the pro side maintained that allowing gay people to marry would curb promiscuity, particularly in the case of men. Like the ideal heterosexual married couple, married gay couples would settle down into nice, quiet, and healthy—in every sense—sexual lives. In fact, homosexual spouses would be even better behaved than their hetero neighbors, since it would probably take several years before you heard about cases of gay adultery and the existence of gay "mistresses."

Some gay activists challenged the marriage movement on the grounds that it represented a betrayal of hard-won freedoms, a complaint noted by Anemona Hartocollis in the *New York Times*: "As the fight for same-sex marriage rages across the country . . . the anti-gay marriage gay men and lesbians say they are feeling emboldened to speak out against what they view as the hijacking of gay civil rights by a distressingly conservative, politically correct part of the gay establishment."[6] If there was ever an identifiably liberal cause in modern American politics it was gay marriage, which received much of the blame for swinging the hotly contested 2004 presidential election to George W. Bush. And yet here were self-proclaimed sexual libertines arguing that although gay marriage was on the agenda of liberals, it reflected socially conservative attitudes in both intent and spirit. A house with a white picket fence is still a house with a white picket fence, whether the owners are named Adam and Eve or Adam and Steve.

. . .

Ironically, the rise of identity politics coincided with the beginnings of a retreat from McGovern-style liberalism among Democrats at the highest levels of the party. The presidential nominee that followed McGovern in 1976 was for a long time not even considered a liberal by many on the left and the right. But by the end of his term, he was despised by Republicans, abandoned by Democrats, and viewed by many in both camps as representative of the worst in post-'60s liberalism. Regardless of how either ex-liberals or reformed liberals defined their own politics, there were others out there who would never allow them to escape that liberal label.

CHAPTER NINE

Out of Time

Though he had voted in the Democratic presidential primary election for California governor Jerry Brown, in 1976 Stephen Vittoria decided to volunteer for the party's nominee, Georgia governor Jimmy Carter, in the fall campaign against President Gerald Ford. In the aftermath of McGovern's depressing defeat four years earlier, Vittoria had made a personal choice to get out of politics and gravitate toward theater and film, where unhappy endings are only temporary. But Jerry Brown seemed to offer a new, if rather quixotic, brand of liberalism, and Carter had a real shot at reclaiming the White House for the Democrats after eight years of GOP rule. If not exactly excited, Vittoria was sufficiently interested to volunteer in the same New Jersey town (West Orange) and for the same local Democratic Party organization where he had flourished in 1972.

But it was not the same. The North Vietnamese and Viet Cong had triumphed, the antiwar movement had disbanded, and Carter was running on a post-Watergate, ideologically neutral message of "I will never lie to you." Inside the Jersey headquarters, Vittoria found the mood businesslike, uptight, and curiously dispassionate; not at all like the free-spirited, communal feel and intense dedication and commitment of the local McGovern operation. "In 1972, there was a vibrancy and a sense of angst," explained Vittoria in a September 2005 interview with me. "By '76, that was pretty dead. And the people looked much more 'suburban.' It just bored the daylights out of me."

Before there were the New Democrats there were new Democrats who consciously separated themselves from the image and style of the McGovern campaign. It may have been a necessary makeover, but Vittoria was not impressed. He quit the Carter campaign in October and for the next twenty-five years deliberately stayed away from politics, liberalism, and the Democrats. And that is probably where he would have remained if not for George W. Bush, the Patriot Act, and the war in Iraq. Appropriately, Vittoria's reentry into politics involved making a documentary about the McGovern campaign. Now approaching middle age, the filmmaker found a way to unite the political passion of his youth with the career he chose as an alternative to politics.

In some ways, Vittoria would have been quite comfortable among Goldwater supporters. Like them, he did not believe that a single landslide defeat destroyed a political movement. Election results are no reason to abandon one's ideals. There are no term limits on the need for change. If supporting McGovern made sense in October 1972, it still made sense in December 1972, or for that matter December 1973.

But unfortunately for Vittoria and others like him, the Democrats did not have a candidate willing or able to do for the McGovern alumni what Reagan did in 1980 for the Goldwater faithful: align with the movement and through sheer confidence, charisma, and conviction lead it to victory. Even worse, most liberals after 1972 had no patience for McGovernism. In the words of journalist Jules Witcover, "the negative lesson of the candidacy of George McGovern was not lost on the liberal True Believers. Ideas and rhetoric to the left of mainstream American politics, they had learned painfully, inspire too few voters for success in a general election, and are too vulnerable to attack."[1] It is a myth—developed during this period of electoral failure—that liberals do not really want to win elections. They want to win terribly; so much, in fact, that they reassess after each debacle. The reelection of George W. Bush marked the first time that I heard the Left in significant numbers blame the American people for what transpired, and yet even that analysis did not prevent liberals from wondering what they needed to change for 2008.

In contrast to contemporary conservative propaganda, which consistently places Jimmy Carter and George McGovern in the same category, you could hardly have had two more different candidates from the same party within a single four-year span: the vibe Vittoria felt from the Carter campaign was no illusion. The candidates and candidacies reflected the differences between the Midwest and the new South; hippies and "reformed" hippies; Vietnam and post-Vietnam; counterculture and southern culture; 1960s liberalism and some new variant, as yet unnamed and undefined. Or was it liberalism at all? In his book, *The Real Jimmy Carter*, conservative author Steven F. Hayward describes how in the primary Carter ran on an anti-Washington platform that hardly deviated from standard GOP faire. Given how Carter's politics evolved, Hayward rather incredulously notes that a CBS/*New York Times* poll commissioned on the eve of the 1976 Democratic Convention reported that 52 percent of the American public thought the nominee "was a conservative."[2] No doubt he was being compared by respondents to the ticket offered by the Democrats four years before.

Carter won a close race in 1976 with the help of a bloc of voters that would soon turn hostile to him and his party. The social historian of religion David Hempton made this observation: "Although the proportion of white Evangelicals voting Republican fell temporarily in 1976 when Jimmy Carter was elected, it has increased steadily ever since."[3] The vote can be explained in part by regional pride: Carter was the first southern Democrat nominated for president in a hundred years. By the time of the 1980 election, however, evangelicals from that region of the country had had enough of Carter and his party. In his 2005 book *Our Endangered Values*, Carter writes about a crucial moment when he sensed that support from his brother and sister evangelicals was slipping away: "A few weeks before our hostages were seized in Iran [in November

1979], the newly elected president of the Southern Baptist Convention came to the Oval Office to visit me. . . . I congratulated him on his new position, and we spent a few minutes exchanging courtesies. As he and his wife were leaving, he said, 'We are praying Mr. President, that you will abandon secular humanism as your religion.' This was a shock to me. I considered myself to be a loyal and faithful Baptist, and had no idea what he meant."[4]

Carter had scrupulously separated his religious and political views—hence the feeling of "shock"—but not so an emergent bloc of conservative Christian voters. And certainly on social issues Carter was not with them, despite his Southern Baptist roots, but a man clearly in sympathy with the liberal perspective. He accepted *Roe v. Wade* and, in 1977, officials from his administration held a White House meeting with a delegation of gay and lesbian leaders. At a press conference after the event, Jean O'Leary, one of the attendees and the coexecutive director of the Gay and Lesbian Task Force, said: "This is the first time in the history of this country a president has seen fit to acknowledge the rights and needs of some 20 million Americans."[5] You can imagine how news of O'Leary's comments and the meeting were received in houses of worship below the Mason-Dixon Line.

In his first campaign for president, Carter had to overcome the doubts and prejudices of northern liberals who could not get past his accent. For all the talk of a new South, it had not been that long since Mississippi governor Ross Barnett fought against allowing James Meredith to attend "Ole Miss" and Alabama governor George Wallace stood in a schoolhouse doorway and pledged "segregation forever." And even though Carter's race-relations credentials seemed to be in order, there was a lot more to liberalism then eliminating "colored only" drinking fountains.

After the turmoil of the early part of the decade, it seemed in many ways as if the 1960s bypassed the South. Where were the antiwar demonstrations and feminist protests, and where was evidence of the counterculture? By 1966, the students who had traveled to Alabama and

Mississippi a few years earlier instead remained in Berkeley, Ann Arbor, and Cambridge, where there was plenty to keep them occupied. They were joined by incoming classes who regarded rock and roll rather than folk as the music of rebellion and change. And with the rise of black power, the tactics if not the goals of the civil rights movement were called into question from the left. By the time of his assassination in April 1968, Martin Luther King was one of several black leaders—self-appointed and otherwise—vying for attention in a rapidly changing political and social environment. This is how the social commentator Stanley Crouch summed up the change in black leadership: "The alienation of abstract facelessness that Martin Luther King and the civil rights workers had won so many battles against was given greater strength when black political talk became progressively anti-white, anti-capitalist, and made threats of overthrowing the system itself."[6] As George Wallace had proved in his presidential campaigns of 1968 and, until he was shot, of 1972, a southern politician could appeal to voters in the North. Like Carter and Reagan in subsequent elections, Wallace ran an anti-Washington campaign, albeit one infused with the racist taint of states' rights. In politics, you can never completely escape your past. But even with Wallace's surprising success, it did not seem possible that he could capture the Democratic Party nomination, which is partly why the governor chose to stand as an independent in 1968.

In contrast, Carter was always running as a Democrat so he had to come to terms with the post-1960s liberal agenda—feminism, gay rights, affirmative action, and a foreign policy that emphasized negotiation over aggression. The decline of Democratic political power in the South—in 1972, Nixon captured every state in the region, an unprecedented feat for a GOP presidential candidate—meant among other things that the party's beliefs and attitudes were being developed elsewhere. But Carter was able to adapt. By the end of his term, and during his active quarter century as an ex-president, you might have thought he started his political career as mayor of San Francisco. There was no more talk about this guy being conservative. Instead, according to

Steven Hayward, "Carter, perhaps, represents McGovernism redoubled by self-righteous arrogance, which is a pretty good description of modern liberalism as represented by the like of the Clintons, Al Gore, John Kerry, and Howard Dean."[7] Two of the people in this lineup are southerners; after four years of Carter, eight years of Clinton, and Gore's 2000 presidential bid, few distinguish anymore between liberals from up north and liberals from down south. As an insider, Stephen Vittoria could sense a profound difference in the style and passion of the Carter campaign and the McGovern campaign, but most of the rest of the world cared only about the perceived similarity of their politics.

. . .

How would George McGovern have handled the Iranian hostage crisis? As far as I know, the question was never asked, but the bitter and partisan attacks on Carter for allowing it to happen, bungling the rescue, and finally presiding over a seemingly endless stalemate with a bunch of Islamic gangsters were reminiscent of what McGovern experienced during his presidential bid eight years earlier. More than any other foreign policy disaster that occurred on his watch—including the Soviet invasion of Afghanistan—the Iranian hostage crisis defined Carter as both inept and dangerously naive in international affairs. It also probably cost him the election in 1980. Philip Jenkins, in his account of the forces that led to the rise of the political right, captures the mood: "The year 1980 was one of the most frightening in modern American history. The sense of national weakness and dissolution that had been gathering through the decade found a focus in massive international crisis, which reverberated in domestic politics. . . . The hostage crisis in Iran was bad enough by itself, highlighting American military weakness and portending oil shortages and gas lines, but it was aggravated by the memories that it inevitably conjured up: the fall of the U.S. embassy in Saigon, American prisoners in Vietnam."[8]

Had Reagan been president during the hostage crisis (which began in November 1979) we do not know if events would have unfolded differently. But we do know that under any circumstances he would have escaped much of the criticism, and that somehow in the end it would have been the liberals' fault, either for sapping the morale of the military, shackling the CIA, ridiculing America before the world, or any combination thereof. In the fall of 1983, Reagan received comparatively little condemnation for the bombing in Beirut that took the lives of 241 U.S. marines and led to the humiliating withdrawal of U.S. troops from the region within a few weeks, despite the fact that, according to Jenkins, the barracks attack caused by far the largest number of combat deaths of U.S. forces since the Vietnam War."[9] Yet little more than a year later, Reagan was elected in a record landslide over Walter Mondale. Reagan, as a staunch foe of liberalism and an unapologetic cold warrior, a man who thought we should have stayed the course in Vietnam until victory, had the proper credentials—regardless of events on the ground. According to the contemporary rules of American politics, a hard-right conservative with a Star-Spangled reputation cannot be held responsible for foreign policy catastrophes.

Carter's defeat in 1980 led neither to a purge nor even a profound reassessment of liberalism. Because of the Iranian hostage issue, the results were widely viewed as an anomaly, a referendum on the president's inept leadership in the face of a direct threat to the mighty United States from a crazed ayatollah and a gaggle of bearded students. We know Reagan's people were worried that Carter would find a way to resolve the crisis before the election; one of the stories coming out of the 1980 election was that the Republican campaign feared "an October surprise." And so despite Reagan asking the famous question, "Are you better off now than you were four years ago"—a knock on Carter and a swipe at liberalism—a firm resolution of the Iranian situation could have trumped memories of the "awful" Carter years, and just in time for the president to turn back a formidable challenge.

Given Reagan's two presidential victories and enduring popularity— aided unwittingly among Democrats by their total disgust at the policies and personality of George W. Bush—one can forget that he suffered a major political defeat during his eight years in the White House. In 1982, the Republicans were creamed in the midterm congressional elections, partly due to voter fears that Reagan, like Goldwater before him, wanted to tamper with Social Security. Only a Democratic-led Congress, it was argued, stood between the president and financial disaster for millions of senior citizens. Directed by Tip O'Neill, the crusty and wise Speaker of the House, that message resonated in districts across the country. As did this one, in the aftermath of the rout: the liberals are not dead yet. Not even close.

Two years later, Walter Mondale, vice president of the United States under Jimmy Carter, was the Democratic Party nominee against Ronald Reagan. Mondale's major challenger in the Democratic primary had been Gary Hart, then senator from Colorado and a former campaign manager for George McGovern. Hart's campaign, which gained momentum with as much speed as any in recent American history, proved that a McGovern veteran could mount a credible challenge to contemporary economic liberalism. The effect of Hart's campaign is noted by Lou Cannon in his biography of Reagan: "Some analysts would later say that the [1984] election had been decided when Gary Hart pressed Walter Mondale in Iowa and defeated him in New Hampshire, forcing Mondale into a protracted contest to win a nomination that might have stood a better chance if he had been able to achieve it more easily."[10] With his staunch support of free trade and intense opposition to protectionism, Hart was a Democratic Leadership Council Democrat before there was a DLC (founded in 1985). He shared the McGovern campaign's discomfort with labor, which adored Mondale anyway, and ran as if he really did not need or desire its support. Instead of hippies, Hart courted an emerging group known as yuppies. Some argued that yuppies were actually ex-hippies, but with shorter hair, a more responsible attitude toward career, and a Reaganesque view that the accumulation of wealth was good and the accumulation of more wealth even better.

By their actions and words, yuppies displayed an enthusiasm for capitalism and the free market that would have horrified New Deal liberals, and did horrify many Great Society liberals who were still active in politics. And yet by the standards of the time, yuppies met the definition of liberal if they believed in a woman's right to choose and that a qualified female (or any person of color) should be afforded every opportunity to advance as far as possible in the workplace; supported gay rights and were themselves gay-friendly; despised oil companies and loved Planet Earth; rejected the extremes of Reagan's anticommunism as both anachronistic and dangerous; agreed with maintaining an economic safety net (as long as it did not mean raising taxes too much); and considered it ridiculous when religious types castigated Hollywood for corrupting our children.

But in addition to these political and social beliefs, yuppies wanted the freedom to pay reasonable prices for an array of to-die-for products made outside of the United States, and that freedom was threatened under protectionist policies. The fact that those same policies were in place to keep American workers from losing their jobs was of little evident concern to pro–free trade Democrats, who when they bothered to consider that possibility argued that lower prices for foreign goods actually created jobs by stimulating the economy.

In the end, Hart did not secure the nomination, but his attacks on Mondale as a symbol of the old Democratic Party and a tool of labor continued to resonate with voters in the general election campaign. At a time when liberalism was either evolving or digressing—according to who was doing the analysis—Mondale stood for a different era in the history of liberalism and the history of the United States. He was either unable or unwilling to accept that the Reagan phenomenon had changed the ground rules of the debate between an ascendant right and a descendant left. In his nomination speech, Mondale pledged to reduce the ballooning federal deficit by raising taxes. Perhaps in the past liberals could say such things in public, but in 1984 Mondale received no credit for honesty, even from within his own party. In James Patterson's account, "this promise, which made little political sense, delighted Republicans, who branded Mondale a 'typical tax-and-spend, gloom-and-doom,' Democrat."[11]

Four years later, the Republican nominee, Vice President Bush, turned Mondale's promise around, proclaiming before an exuberant GOP convention that he would tell the Democrats in Congress, "Read my lips, no new taxes." Midway through his term the then-president quietly went back on his word, infuriating Newt Gingrich and other upstart conservatives, who idolized Reagan and were always suspicious of George H. W. Bush and his brand of go-along, get-along DC politics. Should one choose to rummage in the Bush family's attic, this was one of the events that no doubt pushed George W. Bush farther right. In his own mind, the son was the legitimate heir to the Reagan legacy.

If I may paraphrase Oscar Wilde: to lose one election to Ronald Reagan is a misfortune; to lose two must surely be carelessness. After Mondale's crushing defeat, certain key Democrats decided the party had been naive if not downright stupid to remain faithful to the tenets of New Deal liberalism. They assessed—correctly, as it turned out—that Reagan was no fluke, but the affable spearhead of a serious movement that had altered the views of millions of middle-class Americans regarding the proper role of government. In 1985, disaffected Democrats formed a nonprofit organization called the Democratic Leadership Council (DLC for short), which issued the following five-point plan for self-proclaimed New Democrats:

1. The private sector—not government—should be the primary engine for economic growth and opportunity.
2. The values that most Americans share—liberty of conscience, individual responsibility, work, faith, family, and community—should be embodied in the policies of our government.
3. America needs a new ethic of civic responsibility in which people who receive government assistance have an obligation to give something back to the country.
4. In foreign policy, America should lead other nations toward democracy and market economies.
5. As advocates of activist government, we need to reinvent government so that it is both more responsive to those it serves and more accountable to taxpayers who pay for it.

One should never underestimate the role that losing elections plays in reassessing and remaking ideology. Or at least this applies to the liberal side; conservatives, as we have seen, tend to stick to their fundamental views and wait for a majority of the country to catch up or, to be more precise, go back. But liberals and Democrats in general are by nature impatient and vaguely dissatisfied—with society, certainly, and probably with themselves as well. As a corollary, they believe that the plight of the individual and the course of human history can always be improved: cleaner air, more productive and responsive public schools, the end of war, no more racism, sexism, or homophobia. Above all, they are constantly on the lookout for problems to solve.

In the aftermath of the Mondale debacle, the problem to solve was simply this: What to do about the Democrats? For now, the course of human history would have to wait. As reflected in the five points, the DLC primarily saw liberalism's deficiencies in economic terms: too much reliance on the public sector; maintenance of a welfare system that handed out money and asked nothing in return; the implication that taxpayers—an economic unit by definition—were getting shortchanged by their government; and a foreign policy that did little to encourage the development of market economies. The list reads not unlike Reagan's criticisms of liberalism—minus the starring role assigned to the infamous "welfare queen"—which is why the DLC was routinely accused by unrepentant liberals of being Republican in everything but name.

In fact, the charge was at best only half true. Regarding the future direction of liberalism, the DLC plan was as significant for what it excluded as for what it included. Specifically, there was no mention of race, gender politics, or gay rights. The DLC's founders either did not recognize or deliberately dismissed the cultural issues that, much more than the economy, would soon define the differences between liberal and conservative and Democrat and Republican. On the other side, however, the religious right was already making preparations for the next war.

The closest the DLC came to addressing these issues is point two, which states that "the values that most Americans share . . . should be embodied in the policies of our government." As given, these values include work, faith, family, and community. Presented in such bland form, the point seems like a throwaway, a vague concession to recent political trends. Who can be against work, faith, family, and community? More important, what policies would discourage these values and what policies would encourage them? At least in the criticism of liberal economic policies, we know where things stand. In 1996, President Bill Clinton—who six years earlier had served as DLC chairman—signed a welfare reform measure that was based directly on point three. As Patterson wrote, "What was clear at that time was 'ending welfare as we know it' strengthened Clinton's political appeal to centrists—many of whom shared his sense that America's system of public assistance needed reforming—and to voters further on the right."[12]

During the twenty years between the formulation of the DLC and the reelection of George W. Bush, the Democrats lost three presidential elections, the House of Representatives, and the Senate. Although it would not be fair or accurate to blame this disaster entirely on the DLC, in light of the results, it is difficult to see how its reforms improved the party's fortunes—the prospect of which prompted the DLC to action in the first place. For one thing, Republicans simply act as if the DLC is irrelevant and continue to level the old charge that Democrats of any category are "tax-and-spend liberals." Democrats have only to propose a single tax increase, even on people making two hundred thousand dollars a year or more, in order to set off wild celebrating inside the headquarters of their GOP rivals. The opposition will reinterpret the proposal as an attack on the middle class and dare the Democrats to prove otherwise. Now on the defensive, the Democrats either back away from the original idea or get caught up in a numbers game they cannot win.

Competing against a party renowned for such stunts as producing candidates who sign a "no new taxes" pledge, Democrats can never move far enough to the right on this issue to placate their conservative critics. When the Clinton campaign in 1992 proclaimed, "It's the economy, stupid," they were referring to the supposed incompetence of the George H. W. Bush administration and not as much to its economic theories. After getting elected, Clinton discovered that after twelve years of Reagan-Bush the federal budget deficit was far greater than anybody knew. In response, he proposed a debt reduction (or economic stimulus) package that included a tax increase. The Democratic-led House of Representatives passed the proposal by one vote in 1993, and the U.S. economy attained historic levels of growth throughout the rest of the decade, which included federal budget surpluses that few thought were possible. As described by Louis Uchitelle for the *New York Times*, Clinton's "approach coincided with a period of economic prosperity, low unemployment, and falling deficits. Over time, this combination— called Rubinomics after the Clinton administration's treasury secretary Robert E. Rubin—became the Democratic establishment's accepted model for the future."[13]

During the Carter years, the Democrats suffered from the twin burdens of economic catastrophe (double-digit inflation, soaring interest rates) and the supposed failure of liberal policies. In 1980, Reagan ran a successful campaign against both. But Clinton cleaned up the Reagan-Bush economic mess, shattering in the process the notion—leftover from the Carter administration—that Democrats are by nature incapable of successfully managing the economy. He did this by emphasizing debt reduction, which had been a cornerstone of Barry Goldwater's agenda since the 1950s, and personal responsibility, embodied in the welfare reform measure approved by a GOP-led Congress in 1996.

And yet still conservatives regard Clinton as a liberal. Twenty years earlier, he might have been able to shake the label, when the distinction between left and right primarily came down to economics and the war in Vietnam. By the 1990s, however, the predominance of abortion and gay rights in political campaigns had altered the fundamental definition of liberal and conservative. In Goldwater's heyday, conservatives did not much care what you did in the bedroom, unless your partner spied for the communists. But today many of those who claim to be legitimate heirs to the Goldwater legacy, including people old enough to have worked on his 1964 campaign, take great interest in the sex lives of their fellow Americans. Big Government liberals are castigated by the Right for adopting a comparatively laissez-faire approach on coupling.

Since Clinton—and like-minded Democrats such as Al Gore—has remained to the left on cultural issues (notwithstanding such nuanced statements as abortion should be "safe, legal, and rare"), he is by modern standards a liberal. At the same time, he and the DLC essentially ignored aspects of liberalism that had tarnished the ideology and given the movement a bad name, such as political correctness, multiculturalism, and what might be termed pious secularism. Their halfhearted clean-up operation did not eliminate the problem of post-'60s liberalism. And as Clinton and his fellow centrist liberals should have learned from the 1988 presidential campaign, there is no compromising with the liberal-bashers.

. . .

I met Michael Dukakis, the man who headed the 1988 Democratic ticket, on a cloudy Tuesday afternoon in his small, sparse office at UCLA, where he teaches in the spring quarter. Given Dukakis's prominent role in the recent history of liberalism and his distinguished political career in Massachusetts, I expected a more grandiose setting: commendations on the wall, photos with historic figures (including a Kennedy or two), framed newspaper headlines, event programs. But there was no visible evidence that this faculty member was any different from the hundreds of others ensconced in tight, cozy quarters across the UCLA campus.

And where were the books? During the 1988 general election campaign, Vice President Bush and his team portrayed Dukakis as cerebral, remote, and prone to the use of big words. This was in contrast to the Republican candidate, who, though he grew up in Connecticut and still maintained a summer home in Kennebunkport, Maine, was packaged as a true Texan, that is, a Genuine Man. As a consequence, according to the campaign, George Herbert Walker Bush had the ability to relate to the concerns of real Americans in a way the intellectually elitist Democrat with the odd-sounding last name did not.

I thought that argument was ridiculous, but I did accept the notion of Dukakis as the politician content to curl up with a hefty white paper before going to bed. With that image in mind, I figured the bookshelves in his office would at least include volumes by Socrates, Locke, Hobbes, Rousseau, Jefferson, Madison, Emerson, Thoreau, Gandhi, and Galbraith, plus political biographies, history books (U.S. and world), and *Profiles in Courage*. If nothing else, surely the Republicans in '88 got that bit right. And besides, I was curious to learn what Michael Dukakis liked to read, without having to take up precious time during our interview.

Yet I do not recall seeing even a faculty manual or interdepartmental memo laying on the desk. Dukakis obviously did his reading elsewhere. The former governor of Massachusetts may have looked silly riding around in a tank, but his clean and orderly UCLA office had an undeniable military feel, as if he expected an unannounced visit from the company commander at any minute.

As I thought about it later, however, something about his spartan surroundings made sense. When he served as governor of Massachusetts, Dukakis had taken pride in playing the role of a fiscally responsible Democrat, instituting a welfare-to-work plan and, as he said, in an interview with me in January 2006, adopting the idea expressed by John Kennedy that "the best social program we have is full employment." "It wasn't that I thought you threw people out the window when they were temporarily in trouble, but I'm a big work guy," he added.

Before the DLC made it popular, Dukakis ran and governed as a Democrat opposed to waste and excess. After visiting his office, I was willing to believe that Dukakis took this approach in his private life as well. Then I remembered the most famous line Dukakis uttered during the presidential campaign, one which was turned against him when he experienced a sudden and drastic loss of support: "This election is not about ideology, it's about competence." At UCLA, Dukakis inhabited a *competent* office: a couple of chairs, a clean desk, a phone, and a computer. When it comes right down to it, what more does one need?

I had visited Dukakis to talk about ideology, specifically liberalism, his own, and its general condition today. I wished to speak to him because in my view the 1988 election represented one of the low points in the modern history of the liberal movement, on par with McGovern's landslide loss. When Dukakis went down that year, he took what remained of liberalism with him.

Bush had based much of his campaign on alternately assailing and mocking liberalism. His motives were fairly obvious from the beginning. Eight years earlier, in the Republican presidential primary, Bush had attacked Ronald Reagan and his supporters from the left, sounding very much like a liberal Republican or moderate Democrat. Bush was then pro-choice, and he gave the country the memorable phrase "voodoo economics" to describe the supply-side concoction Reagan was peddling. But when Reagan secured the nomination, and he offered Bush the second spot on the Republican ticket, you heard no more talk about voodoo economics—except from Democrats. The choice of Bush was presumably intended to assuage the fears of liberal Republicans and moderate Democrats that the ex-governor of California was a right-wing menace. A grateful Bush eagerly accepted the position, and he spent the next two terms playing the loyal company man in one of the most conservative administrations in U.S. history.

In 1988, Bush ran for president again, this time with a résumé that included having served as Reagan's VP. But while Bush had apparently moved to the right—no more disparaging remarks about Reagan's economic plan and now wanting to outlaw abortion except in the case of rape or incest or to save the life of the mother—the Republican Party had moved even farther right. This shift is recalled by Joan Didion in her collection of essays *Political Fictions:* "The Bush campaign was oriented to 'values,' and the values to which it referred were those not of a postwar but a prewar America."[14] This was the year that the televangelist Pat Robertson entered the GOP presidential primary, signifying, along with the Moral Majority and the Christian Coalition, the dramatic rise of the religious right in Republican politics. Evangelical voters loved Reagan even if he did not necessarily love them back, and they interpreted his success as a genuine opportunity to reverse the social liberalism that in their opinion was leading the United States to ruin.

Bush, however, remained suspect to some conservatives: had eight years in the Reagan White House really changed his thinking? Even Reagan's evolution from liberal to conservative evolved over a longer period than eight years. And Reagan had come from humble midwestern origins, as opposed to Bush, who despite having claimed a Texas address for decades could never really escape his blue-blood pedigree, including obvious pride at having attended Yale. His family and longtime friends did not call him "Poppy" for nothing.

There was also something slightly effeminate about Bush or, to put it more charitably, insufficiently masculine, which no doubt concerned his consultants at a time when the religious right was declaring war on homosexuality. Bush could ill afford to get swept up in the political equivalent of a vice squad raid. With a personal life that included a spouse, a large family, and as some alleged, a mistress, Bush was probably immune from whispering campaigns. But in an environment where the Reverend Jerry Falwell scared the hell out of Republicans, one could never be too careful.

To prove his toughness and burnish his nascent conservative credentials, Bush attacked liberalism—the ideology and that of his opponent—in the '88 race with a venom and zeal that exceeded even Reagan's during the tumultuous 1960s and early 1970s. Though Reagan had just been elected president twice by huge margins, and the emergence of the DLC was posing a significant challenge to the Democratic Party from the right, Bush ran as if liberals were everywhere in power. At the same time, Reagan left office having struck up an unlikely friendship and unlikelier political partnership with Soviet leader Mikhail Gorbachev, which diluted the sense of Cold War paranoia that had been so effective for Republican candidates over the previous four decades. As a result, Bush waged his presidential campaign above all on fear of liberalism.

This effort was planned and coordinated by Lee Atwater, a southern operative who understood that the civil rights movement had not succeeded in eliminating racism, and who also knew that his kind of people love the Stars and Stripes just about as much as they love the confederate flag. With Atwater's guidance, Bush made a household name out of Willie Horton, who was in Patterson's words, "a convicted first degree murderer, who on a weekend furlough had repeatedly beaten and stabbed a man and raped his fiancée."[15] Horton had been out of prison due to a brief furlough program in Massachusetts supported by Dukakis. The fact that Horton "happened" to be an African American and his victims "happened" to be white, made his the perfect crime for the Bush campaign. It's one thing for liberals to be portrayed as coddling criminals, but it's even better if the criminals they are supposedly coddling are black.

Among the vivid memories that those born in America after 1945 retain is the words of the Pledge of Allegiance, a consequence of having been required to recite the pledge at the beginning of each school day from at least kindergarten through sixth grade. In my school, every kid stood and spoke those lines out loud, no questions asked, whether he or she hailed from a family of socialists or a family of racists. I recall reciting the pledge as more of a chore than an assertion of patriotic pride, although the text being thankfully brief, it did not bother me one way or the other. Despite having a budding interest in politics, what I could not have imagined is that the Pledge of Allegiance would some twenty years later become one of the dominant issues in an American presidential campaign.

In 1977, long after I had graduated from the public school system, Massachusetts governor Michael Dukakis vetoed a law that would have required teachers to lead students in reciting the pledge. The governor had been advised that the law was probably unconstitutional, because it could have subjected these teachers to criminal prosecution. This was also the position of the American Civil Liberties Union (ACLU), which Dukakis joined as a student at Swarthmore in the early 1950s, during the height of the McCarthy era. "I was actively involved in the membership drive for the ACLU," recalled Dukakis during our interview, "which signed up about one-third of the student body and faculty as members in response to McCarthy."

Had Dukakis—like Bill Clinton—unofficially declared himself a candidate for president of the United States in his teens, perhaps he would have reconsidered joining the ACLU. Then again, who could have anticipated the 1988 Bush campaign? For Atwater and company, the combination of an opposition candidate who vetoed a pro–Pledge of Allegiance bill and was a member of the ACLU was a wonderful gift, on par with running against a candidate who supported a prison furlough program in which a black man raped a white woman. At seemingly each of his campaign stops, Bush dutifully led the crowd in the Pledge of Allegiance, arching his frame and tilting his head back in a pose halfway between presidential and physically challenged. Having stoked the patriotism of his audience, he would proceed to charge his opponent with being a "card-carrying member of the ACLU." Like people from the same race who address each other using a derogatory term, or from the same ethnic group who drop the occasional ethnic slur for strictly internal consumption, members of the ACLU have been known to identify each other using this archaic phase. In this context, *card-carrying member* sounds more ridiculous than anything else, even though millions of voters in 1988 apparently took it very seriously.

And yet the most enduring contribution of the Bush campaign to the American political lexicon was the "L-word," which (although appropriated a few years back by a cable television show about women who fancy other women) has one meaning of historical importance. It is tempting to interpret the phrase as additional evidence of the difficulties that both presidents Bush have with language, as if such a simple word as *liberalism*" or *liberal* could pose syntactical problems. But since I have heard George H. W. Bush (and his son) clearly enunciate "liberal" and "liberalism" on frequent occasions, it must be the case that the "L-word" was invented with a specific purpose in mind.

Until the "L-word," the only time I heard an expression of this kind was the "F-word"; as a society, we have since been introduced to the "N-word." All of which suggests that liberalism is now on the same level as a vulgar term for sexual intercourse and an ugly, racist word denoting a black person. It was unconscionable, though not surprising, that other-wise intelligent political reporters repeated the phrase in their own reports from the campaign trail, thereby giving it legitimacy. You still hear it used today, although not repeated incessantly as happened in the 1988 campaign. And, in fact, the "L-word" is an ideal fit for a society that is linguistically challenged and increasingly disdainful of critical thinking or deep political discussions. But more important, its deploy-ment has significantly contributed to the ridicule and disrespect that has been a central component of the attack on liberalism over the past thirty-five years.

. . .

Born in 1933, the year that Franklin Delano Roosevelt assumed the presidency, Michael Dukakis readily accepts the word *liberal* to describe his own political views. Or to be precise, he did so when we spoke within the quiet comfort of his UCLA office. If he had been as open during the 1988 campaign, it might have made a difference in the final results. This led me to wonder if behind closed doors Clinton, Gore, Kerry, and other reticent liberals conquer their fears and allow the truth to emerge. Maybe liberals are progressives only when they are out in public.

Along with his membership in the ACLU and strong support for civil liberties, Dukakis in the 1950s believed in universal health care, racial equality, and economic justice. Though he never accompanied civil rights marchers in the South, during the late 1950s and early 1960s Dukakis said he fought hard for fair housing legislation and school desegregation in Boston, Cambridge, Springfield and other Massachusetts cities. And despite being a native of President Kennedy's home state, Dukakis was among the young liberals who felt Kennedy lacked a sufficient commitment to the cause of civil rights: "He moved more slowly than I think a lot of us would have liked."

Dukakis was an opponent of the war in Vietnam from as early as 1965, although more out of a rough-hewn pragmatism than intellectual or moral conviction. Having served in the U.S. military in Korea for sixteen months, "it seemed to me that based on my own experiences, I couldn't see how you could fight a war without frontiers. You wouldn't know if the guy coming down the street is going to blow you up or not. It's the same thing we have in Iraq." As in the case of the civil rights movement, Dukakis did not join antiwar marches in the streets—although he attended the 1968 Democratic Convention in Chicago—but expressed his opposition through the legislative process. He voted for antiwar resolutions in the Massachusetts Legislature and endorsed Eugene McCarthy's presidential candidacy.

The passage of the civil rights and voting rights measures in 1964 and 1965, which severely weakened the Democratic Party in the South, and the internal split over the war in Vietnam that began in 1968, precipitated a kind of political identity crisis for liberals of Dukakis's generation and older. The electoral and political assumptions that had prevailed during their earlier years were no longer valid. Dukakis described feelings of ideological disorientation during the early 1970s: "Who are we, what are we for and against? What's going on?" Liberals thought they knew where they stood in relation to conservatives, but not in relation to each other. Dukakis noted the feelings of confusion increased for some with the advent of sexual politics and gay liberation. These additions raised questions and sought outcomes that not every liberal—or conservative, for that matter—felt was appropriately addressed in a political context. For a person such as Dukakis, who during our interview came across as reserved and straitlaced, the existence of the counterculture must have seemed disconcerting, even outright threatening. And yet the counterculture was an integral part of the new liberalism, at least in spirit. If Dukakis desired a successful career in politics, he would have to come terms with its prominent role.

By the time of the 1988 campaign, the Democratic Party during the previous sixteen years had nominated for president a New Left liberal (McGovern), a former Georgia governor representative of the New South (Jimmy Carter, twice), and a classic, pro-union liberal (Walter Mondale). The party lost three of those elections—1972, 1980, and 1984—and only triumphed in 1976 due to the fluke of Watergate. In Dukakis, the Democrats nominated a candidate both self-assured and composed, qualities that favorably compared with the confused state of mind of other liberals and the political insecurities of his Republican opponent. With Reagan no longer on the scene, there seemed to be no way we could screw it up this time.

But it was Dukakis's very self-assurance and composure that helped to sink his campaign. When Bush launched his preposterous attack on liberalism, and hammered away on the Pledge of Allegiance and Willie Horton, Dukakis figured no one would take these attacks seriously. Didn't the American public understand what liberalism had brought this country over the past fifty years, that is, Social Security, the GI Bill, civil rights for black people, equal rights for women and gays, protection in the workplace, cleaner air and water, Medicare, higher wages, the end of an immoral and illegal war in Southeast Asia? Given that record of achievement, which as a whole improved millions of lives, how could Bush get away with bullying liberals and trashing liberalism? Instead of recognizing that not only the success of his campaign but the future of liberalism as a force in American politics was at stake, Dukakis simply waited for common sense to win out.

Yet by huge margins American voters had elected (1980) and then reelected (1984) Ronald Reagan as president. The number of people tired of liberalism, and indifferent to its glorious past, apparently far exceeded the number of people who felt it was still the best hope for the future of the United States. Bush's campaign-trail theatrics represented the continuation of a decade-long trend in national politics. But Dukakis in our interview attributed Reagan's success to being a "likeable guy," and we know what he said back in 1988 about ideology versus competence. What did liberalism—good or bad—have to do with it?

Today Dukakis wishes he had answered the Bush charges about his record instantly—and then leveled some of his own. "I'm a guy that comes from metropolitan Boston, and he comes from metropolitan Houston. Both have about the same population. And yet the homicide rate is six times greater [in Houston] than it is in Boston. And I let the guy take the crime issue away from me. Maybe I deserved to lose. I should have kicked the living crap out of this guy.

"It was my fault. Willie Horton—hell. The most liberal furlough program in America was the Reagan-Bush furlough program in the federal prison system. They were furloughing people for forty-five days, folks were getting murdered."

One can understand and sympathize with his frustration. With the exception of Richard Nixon, if you lose the first general election for president of the United States, you are pretty well finished as a serious candidate. Ex-coaches and ex-candidates torture themselves over what they might have done to change the outcome all those years ago. But at the same time, Dukakis must know that a "tougher than thou" strategy is difficult for liberals to sell to the public, as John Kerry would discover in 2004, when he matched his record of military service in Vietnam against that of President George W. Bush in the Air National Guard.

Republicans have a sixty-year head start—beginning with Richard Nixon and Joe McCarthy during the earliest days of the Cold War—in the promotion of shameless patriotism. As for being tough on crime, it is politically safer for the party that rarely gets more than 10 percent of the black vote and castigates the ACLU to play the role of Dirty Harry. After all, it was Ronald Reagan who while serving as president borrowed one of Clint Eastwood's most famous lines: "Go ahead, make my day."

I cannot say with assurance that a Dukakis victory in 1988 would have been good for the United States, but I do know that it would have been good for liberalism. The '88 Bush campaign introduced a nastier and more preposterous form of liberal-bashing, which continues unabated to this day. It is ironic but not surprising that a Republican candidate regarded with suspicion by his party's right wing should have exceeded even many archconservatives in his antiliberal rhetoric. Because of the failure of Democrats to stand up to the 1988 Bush campaign, you can now get away with saying almost anything about liberals. The rise of Rush Limbaugh as a national figure, for example, occurred in the wake of Bush's election, when the talk-show host spurred an ultimately successful national protest against the Democratic-led Congress voting itself a pay increase.

Had Michael Dukakis, an unrepentant liberal from the old school, been able to grasp the significance of the Bush campaign's tactics and respond appropriately, it could have arrested or reversed liberalism's decline. Instead, the United States embarked upon probably the most extreme right-wing, antiliberal course in its history.

CHAPTER TEN

Yesterday's Gone

Its common name is the "malaise" speech. On July 15, 1979, President Jimmy Carter delivered a nationwide address officially titled: "Energy and the National Goals—A Crisis of Confidence." The first half of the speech did not focus on the energy situation in the United Sates per se—due in part to the Iranian revolution, gas prices had been rising precipitously and long lines to purchase gas were not uncommon around the country—but on what the president perceived to be a depressed spirit and feelings of hopelessness permeating the American psyche. As proof, he offered both his own opinions (based on listening to "men and women like you") and those of anonymous guests from all segments of society who had been invited to a private summit at Camp David for the express purpose of assessing the national mood.

The speech is recalled for several reasons. In the opening paragraph, Carter describes himself as a president who "feels your pain," a statement of questionable sincerity, containing more personal therapy than presidential politics and wrongly thought to have been invented by Bill Clinton. But it is something that a post-'60s liberal might say or believe. At several points the speech unabashedly references religion and spirituality. For example, Carter approvingly quotes a "religious leader" who told him: "No material shortage can touch the important things like

God's love for us or our love for one another." Describing a "crisis of confidence," Carter at key points in the speech invokes language and sentiment that you would hear on any Sunday morning in America: "It is a crisis that strikes at the very heart and soul and spirit of our national will. We can see this crisis in the growing doubt about the meaning of our own lives and the loss of a unity of purpose for our nation." A few paragraphs later, the president describes a country characterized among other things by "our faith in God," but in which too many citizens today "tend to worship self-indulgence and consumption." If we ever needed confirmation of Carter's deep and abiding Christian faith, this address provided it.

But the speech has not been recalled through the years as a classic example of the mingling of politics and religion. Instead, conservatives cite its pessimistic tone and overall glum mood to charge Carter in particular and liberals in general with harboring negative feelings about the United States and its possibilities. And, of course, they contrast the "malaise" speech with the personality and optimistic message of Ronald Reagan, Carter's 1980 opponent, who could not help but smile when he thought about our country and its promise.

The enduring perception that liberals are pessimists and conservatives are optimists—traceable in large part to Carter's speech and the Carter-Reagan campaign—represents a significant shift in American politics. Through the 1960s and much of the 1970s, liberals were consumed with the notion that they could make America the greatest nation on the face of the earth; a place free from racism, sexism, homophobia, discrimination, bigotry, excessive pollution, economic injustice, and the military-industrial complex. You cannot embrace such an ambitious agenda without feeling hopeful about the future. After all, President Kennedy had talked about a New Frontier; President Johnson set out to build a Great Society; and candidate Jimmy Carter wrote a book called *Why Not the Best?* which in four words summed up the spirit and dreams of liberalism.

By contrast, conservatives by definition were resistant to change, which also implied that they did not believe in the capacity of human beings to improve their condition, at least through the introduction of new programs. Even the always-optimistic Reagan set out to reverse the liberalism of the 1960s and 1970s. His belief in America and the American people was steeped in nostalgia and predicated on the notion that we could return to a better time. When Reagan asked the American people during his debate with Carter, "Are you better off than you were four years ago," he did not appear to be especially worried if the response was a resounding "no." Whatever the answer, Reagan would find a way out of the mess.

What liberalism had delivered—for good or for bad—conservatism could take away. Like Margaret Thatcher in Britain, Reagan ruled with the understanding that nothing is inevitable about politics or history. Given the proper leadership, the seemingly impregnable liberal state could be dismantled, the influence of unions curbed, affirmative action tamed, military power restored, taxes lowered, defeatism and pessimism banished. Antiliberalism required its own ambitious agenda.

In 1984, the Reagan reelection team ran a famous commercial that proclaimed, "It's morning again in America." Millions of people disagreed, particularly those negatively affected by what was being called "Reaganonmics," but apparently they stayed home the day of the election. The 1980s belonged to Reagan, just as the 1960s belonged to Kennedy and Johnson. The gap between the malaise speech and "It's morning again in America" was a mere five years, but in that short amount of time liberals had become resigned to the triumph of what was once unthinkable: Goldwater-Reagan conservatism. For liberals, Reagan's defeat of Carter marked the beginning of their own long national nightmare. But for the other side, it marked the start of a wonderful period in our nation's history. As Kim Phillips-Fein proclaimed in a review of a book on Reagan's presidency, "Among conservatives, it goes without saying that Reagan is the greatest American president of the 20th century; the man who vanquished Soviet Communism abroad and liberal politics at home."[1] Had liberalism's decline been concurrent with something other than the rise of Reagan—liberal Republicanism, say, or pragmatic centrism—it would not have been so historically significant. To take the most obvious example: if George H. W. Bush had defeated Reagan in the 1980 GOP primary and then defeated Carter in the general election, the country would have continued under policies and programs not radically different from the liberalism of the 1960s. Frustrated by its inability to get the White House to pay attention, the Christian right might have looked for a George Wallace–like figure to run as a third-party candidate. Leading GOP politicians such as Newt Gingrich, Tom DeLay, and George W. Bush might never have acquired power, or not by presenting themselves to the electorate as hard-right ideologues.

Reagan's success and stature above all gave conservatives the confidence not only to challenge liberalism, but to obliterate it with words and actions. And doubly sweet for conservatives, starting in the 1980s and increasingly over the next two decades, liberals crumbled. By the time of the first Bush administration, conservatives could say or write nearly anything about liberals and get away with it.

· · ·

In the aftermath of McGovern's defeat, those questioning the direction of liberalism now had some hard evidence with which to press their case for a different kind of reform. After years of moving farther and farther to the left, liberalism in their view had ceased to be an election-day asset for the Democratic Party, or a force for positive change in the lives of many Americans. One of the young activists who willingly accepted the challenge of rethinking and redirecting liberalism in the early 1970s was Morley Winograd, at the time a leading figure in the Michigan Democratic Party. But as Winograd quickly discovered, determining where and what to change could be a confusing and contentious process.

As a college student at the University of Michigan, Winograd had walked precincts, stuffed envelopes, and made phone calls for John F. Kennedy's presidential campaign. Eight years later, he supported John's younger brother for president. "I was there for [Robert] Kennedy both because of an emotional affiliation with the Kennedy name and the Kennedy family, and because [Eugene] McCarthy looked like an amateur politician to me," he said, in a June 2005 interview with me. Winograd added that he was aligned with the reform wing of the Oakland County Democratic Party, which was opposed to the war in Vietnam, as was Bobby Kennedy. His other overriding cause was changing the rules governing the state Democratic Party to allow for greater participation and influence from people who held similar beliefs. "By the terms used then, I was a liberal," said Winograd.

In September 1968, three months after Senator Kennedy's assassination, Winograd took a position with the Democratic Party in Oakland County, Michigan, registering new voters and developing innovative ways to increase voter turnout. By extension, his efforts benefited Vice President Hubert Humphrey, whose nomination had angered many backers of Kennedy and McCarthy. Winograd was not enamored of Humphrey either; he worked for the party strictly at the urging of his brother. "My brother, who was younger than me by eight years, was in the streets of Chicago in '68 rallying people for McGovern," said Winograd. "He came back from that experience convinced that political organizing was the solution, and he asked me to help him."

Following Humphrey's bitter and narrow defeat by Richard Nixon, Winograd resumed his quest to make the Oakland County Democratic Party more inclusive. He could not have picked a better—and worse—time for such a project. On the one hand, the party contained an uneasy mix of antiwar leftists, many of them from comparatively privileged backgrounds, and veteran union organizers. For the Democrats to succeed locally and nationally in 1972 and beyond, they would need to bring together these disparate and at times openly antagonistic groups. On the other hand, the party contained an uneasy mix of antiwar leftists, many of them from comparatively privileged backgrounds, and veteran union activists. How could anyone expect to unite two such disparate and at times openly antagonistic groups?

Another factor that complicated these efforts was the circumstances of the 1968 election. Michigan had been one of only two Midwest states to go for Humphrey (the vice president's home state of Minnesota was the other) and through the campaign labor had remained fiercely loyal to the Democratic nominee, condemning American Independent Party candidate George Wallace, who was picking up support from individual union members. "Humphrey was their political hero, the unions would do anything for him," said Winograd. Without the financial support and tireless involvement of labor across the country, Humphrey could never have come so close to defeating Nixon—in the final tally only five hundred thousand votes nationwide separated the candidates. Winograd said that in Michigan the United Auto Workers essentially delivered the state for Humphrey.

But as discussed earlier in this book, the antiwar movement despised Humphrey for not taking a strong stand against LBJ's Vietnam policy. Some of its members angrily demonstrated against Humphrey on the campaign trail, while others opted out of any participation in his campaign or signed on at only the last minute, when Nixon's lead was too big to overcome. An argument has been made ever since that their actions (or inactions) delivered the presidency to Nixon in 1968. It would be understandable if labor—in Michigan and around the country—had no interest in forging an alliance even for the sake of convenience with the antiwar faction in the Democratic Party. And yet in the belief that a political party divided against itself cannot stand, Winograd attempted to end the discord and establish a common bond.

He met strong resistance—but not, as it happened, from union members. "I realized that the guys on the reform side [antiwar wing of the party] were as interested in taking power as the guys on the other side. But their desire to stack and pack everything so they would always win was particularly off-putting." As a result, Winograd changed his mind. He would now work to rescue the Democratic Party from the new liberals. "I remember being in the reform caucus of the county Democratic Party and hearing my liberal 'friends' talk about how as soon as they got power they wanted to shut things down. Kick out the labor movement. . . . It was very clear their motivation was power and not principle."

"It was not exactly disillusioning but very insightful to realize they were in it just for their own self-interest and personal power," he added. "But they would never say so. On the other hand, the labor movement made it clear they were in it for their members. I thought those guys were more intellectually honest than the side that I had been on. I converted, and as a result, my selection as party chair in 1970 was greeted as a compromise choice because I had been in one camp and moved over to another."

Winograd had been given a preview of the scenario that would unfold during the 1972 McGovern campaign. As part of their plan for America, many antiwar liberals, proud adherents of the New Left, intended to change the culture and composition of the established Democratic Party. This meant above all a diminished role for labor, which was more inclined than New Left Democrats to support the war. At a famous confrontation in Manhattan in 1970, for example, union members beat up demonstrators. Labor was also aligned with unacceptable old Democrats such as Humphrey and Chicago mayor Richard Daley. When it came to changing the culture of the Democratic Party, liberals were no softies.

Disgusted by the arrogance, sense of entitlement, and what he regarded as the self-defeating politics of the antiwar left, Winograd quietly moved to the center. "A lot of people [liberals] in '72 still considered me a friend," he recalled. "The McGovern folks asked me to be a delegate to the DNC [Democratic National Committee]. I declined on the grounds that my child was due. It was an excuse. I really didn't want to be there for McGovern."

A onetime New Frontiersman, Winograd by the 1970s had also started to change his thinking about the classic liberal approach to domestic issues. He had already started down a path that some fifteen years later would culminate in his becoming a high-ranking official in the Democratic Leadership Council. "McGovern represented the political philosophy that said we needed to social engineer America to make it come out right. We needed quotas, income equality, and school diversity. All of this flowed from a fundamental belief that liberalism required good people who desired what the outcomes should be for everyone else." In Michigan, Winograd had watched how busing schoolchildren to achieve integration—offered as the prototypical example of social engineering—had torn apart the Democratic Party. "I was on the side of finding solutions that didn't involve children spending hours on buses every day," he said. "I was considered very conservative for embracing that kind of approach."

The busing issue made George Wallace exceedingly popular with a disproportionate number of white Democrats in Michigan in 1972. One of the most violent antibusing acts occurred in Pontiac, a city with a population that consisted almost exclusively of blue-collar production workers in the auto industry. In the summer of 1971, two terrorists sneaked into a bus depot and planted dynamite on the fuel tanks of thirteen buses, destroying ten of the vehicles and damaging another three. Members of the American Nazi Party often attended antibusing rallies in Pontiac, which was located in Winograd's designated territory of Oakland County.

"At the time of the assassination attempt on Wallace in [May] 1972," said Winograd, "I remember being in the Democratic Party Headquarters in Oakland County. We had to shut the blinds and turn out the lights to make sure no one shot out a window, because initially the Wallace people thought the Democrats had deliberately taken out their 'savior.'" Still, Wallace was a Democrat, although not one who appealed to Morley Winograd. In another eight years, many working-class Democrats in Michigan and across the nation, appalled at the changes sought for and achieved by contemporary liberalism, would vote for Ronald Reagan for president. But even with all the examples of liberal excess, Winograd to this day cannot accept that these Democrats supported Reagan, of all people. "Everybody could see through his economic program: cutting taxes and balancing the budget is a farce." Yet the curse of voodoo economics mattered little to working-class Democrats motivated by anger, fear, and a sense of betrayal. Indeed, Wallace had been more sensitive and sympathetic than Reagan to the economic plight of struggling families.

After the disastrous 1972 presidential election, when Michigan joined forty-eight other states in supporting Richard Nixon, the United Auto Workers (UAW) encouraged Winograd to run for state party chair. The UAW had 40 percent of the delegates, the AFL-CIO had 10 percent, and "liberals" the other share. "Rather than take on the ideology, our slogan was 'Work together to win,'" said Winograd. "It deliberately downplayed the ideological divisions in the party for two reasons: (*a*) It wasn't clear that our view was the majority view within the Democratic Party, and (*b*) it would be difficult to energize a party that spent most of its energy fighting over ideology."

Winograd was elected on the second ballot, after the AFL-CIO candidate dropped out of the race. "I inherited a party deeply in debt, and without an ideological foundation," he said. "We hired a field staff and started teaching local Democratic parties how to run elections and win. And then Watergate just fell into our lap."

As a result of the widespread corruption in the Nixon administration, Democrats in the 1974 election cycle won seats in Orange County, California, and other conservative bastions around the country that in normal times they had no prayer of winning. Due to the vicissitudes of history, Nixon's landslide reelection turned out to be the best thing that could have happened to the Democratic Party's electoral prospects. No one, it seemed, wanted to be affiliated with the Republicans in 1974. The Democrats did so well in congressional races the year Nixon resigned that their majority in the House of Representatives could even withstand Reagan's popularity. Not until 1994, more than five years after the nation's fortieth president had retired to Southern California, were the Republicans able to gain control of that chamber.

A year after Winograd became party chair in Michigan he was being hailed as a genius for overseeing the election of Democratic candidates in GOP districts across the state, including a special election in February

1974 for the seat formerly held by Vice President Gerald Ford. This was a district that had not elected a Democrat in *forty years*—since the height of FDR's popularity. "I was a national hero, on the front page of the *Washington Post*," he recalled with a smile in a subsequent interview, in November 2006. "It was an unbelievable turnaround that I had little to do with." Given Winograd's personal ambition to bring the Democrats together, and end the antipathy between labor and liberals, his modesty is understandable. During that once-in-a-lifetime election season, the idealist in Winograd yielded to the pragmatist—why go through a wrenching process to unify the party when putting up Nixon's picture was sufficient to guarantee victory at the polls? Through the years Watergate has come to mean many things to many people; for Winograd, concerned above all with getting Democrats elected in 1974, it was "a gift from heaven."

But he also knew that Watergate was not the gift that would keep on giving. At some point, the Democrats would have to resume the attempts at intraparty reconciliation interrupted by Nixon's travails. Or maybe not, an even worse prospect for the long term future of the party. After all, Watergate worked to the advantage of the Democrats again in 1976: Jimmy Carter won the presidency on the promise that he would "never lie" to the American people and Ford was politically damaged by his pardon of the previous president. "Nixon was such a threat in every Democrat's mind, as well as to non-Democrats, that we never had to return to the ideological debate, and never really did so," said Winograd. "I was chairman until '79 and there was never even a vote on my chairmanship, it was always inevitable. We never had the battles, which in retrospect might have been to our detriment, because we also never paid attention to the conservative energy that was burning."

In the 1980 Democratic presidential primary, Winograd supported Ted Kennedy over Jimmy Carter, a decision he characterized as his "last liberal hurrah." Ironically, in light of his subsequent views, he felt Carter was too conservative on economic issues, seeming to support a degree of income inequality and supply-side theory. Then in the general election,

Americans voted overwhelmingly for Ronald Reagan, which confounded Winograd but did not especially bother him. "I was glad that Carter had lost, and I didn't think Reagan would be more than a flash in the pan. This was sort of the remnants of my Kennedy frustration coming out."

Two years later, the Democrats did exceedingly well in the midterm elections, which seemed to validate Winograd's first impression of Reagan's legacy. In their account of the factors that drive American politics, Thomas and Mary Edsall claim that "the economic recession of 1981–82 . . . produced a hiatus in the conservative ascension, and the strong pro-Democratic tilt in the midterm elections of 1982 ended the immediate prospect of a full-fledged Republican realignment. Democrats picked up twenty-six House seats, and the southern Democratic-Republican alliance that had controlled House deliberations in 1981 could not be revived."[2] Not only did Reagan lack coattails, he was a liability. The Democrats effectively campaigned by frightening seniors that the president would privatize Social Security, a position that his conservative mentor Barry Goldwater proposed eighteen years before. If the '82 midterm election was an indication of the future, it was of one term and out for the Gipper.

By this point Winograd had embarked on a highly successful career in the telecommunications industry, beginning with the Michigan Bell Company and eventually becoming sales vice president for AT&T's western-region commercial markets. Though no longer involved in the day-to-day operations of the Democratic Party, Winograd remained inextricably bound up with its fate. In 1984, on the eve of the Mondale-Reagan election, he wrote a memo predicting catastrophe for the Democratic candidate. "I watched the Mondale campaign disintegrate over his convention pledge to raise taxes to balance the budget." He had seen Michigan Democratic governor James Blanchard attempt the same thing—with disastrous political consequences—a year or so earlier.

Given that Winograd remained baffled by Reagan's appeal, one can understand his feeling that the Democrats had really screwed up this time, particularly on economic issues. In fact, this was the last presidential election where the Democratic nominee was attacked primarily on stewardship of the economy and the threat of higher taxes. From 1988 forward, Republican candidates primarily ran campaigns based on the follies and fiascoes of liberalism, the culture wars, social issues, and, following 9/11, lack of resolve against terrorism.

As a result of the ensuing landslide, which enshrined Reagan as one of the most popular and influential presidents of the twentieth century, and Winograd's growing fascination with what would soon be known as the information revolution, his views on the economy and politics evolved for the third time. He had already switched from an antiwar, proreform Democrat to a prounion, antiliberal Democrat. In this latest incarnation, Winograd staked out a position on the economy and politics in opposition to the more traditional view propagated by the unions. He did so not out of anger or spite, but in the firm conviction that the economic model of the agricultural and industrial age represented an old way of thinking that could not sustain a political majority, now, or in the future. "My argument was that a political movement that was not built on information-age values, and not even on industrial-age values, but based on agricultural-age values, could not sustain itself in the long run in terms of numbers and momentum. It would be overtaken by the new ways of work and the people who work in those ways."

In 1990, Winograd cowrote a memo for the DLC arguing that the Democratic Party's values should be summed up in the phrase "opportunity and responsibility." "If we put these two things together in a way that reflected the information age in which we live, we could run on new and not old ideas." He and his coauthor shared this memo with Bill Clinton, then vice-chair of the DLC and an unofficial but undeniable candidate for the presidency. "He tested that message in DLC organizing events around the country," recalled Winograd. "He came back to us and said, 'Look, opportunity and responsibility work. But it still sounds too Republican. We need something else in there. To make it a Democratic message, we need to add the word *community*.'

"He went off and tried 'opportunity, responsibility, community,' and that became his campaign message in '92."

Winograd considered both "soccer moms" and "office-park dads"—as they've come to be known—the natural constituents for this message. "They are looking for good education for their kids, safe streets in their neighborhoods, and an opportunity to have a social affiliation with meaning that comes from church, a nonprofit activity, whatever," he explained later. "They desire a work environment and an economic outcome that allows them to do those things, [that is,] if the work doesn't so overwhelm their families because it takes forever to get there and back, or it's a twenty-four-hour-a-day job." Characterized in this way, the men and women flourishing in an information-age economy seem no different in their goals and desires from anyone else. Who doesn't want a good education for their kids or safe streets? The obvious answer is that we all do but, according to Winograd, achieving these things in an information-age economy would require taking positions and endorsing policies at times counter to those typically associated with the Democrats. In his view, a Democrat who understood twenty-first-century America would favor free trade over protectionism, oppose raising the minimum wage, embrace fiscal discipline, support low interest rates, and "invest in human resources and infrastructure."

With the exception of raising the minimum wage, which to this day remains a cornerstone of Democratic Party policy, the Clinton-Gore administration supported the core principles expressed by Winograd and other proponents of the information-age economy. Indeed, the DLC was among the most fervent backers of the North American Free Trade Agreement (NAFTA), which Clinton, aided by support from key Republicans in the House and Senate, managed to get through Congress in 1993. At the time, I was working in the local office of a historically prolabor Democratic congressman who supported the legislation and I vividly recall the intense pressure that unions applied to their traditional allies on the Hill—angry phone calls, meetings, threats to support other candidates—in an effort to defeat NAFTA.

In his 1995 State of the Union speech, Clinton included a sentence that could have been written by Winograd: "We are moving from an industrial age built on gears and sweat to an information age demanding skills and learning and flexibility." A year later, Clinton's State of the Union Speech included the famous line: "The era of big government is over." To many observers, those seven words seemed to signal the death knell for 1960s economic liberalism.

Buoyed by the sense that the White House "got it," Winograd actively promoted his views throughout the 1990s. In 1996, along with a writer and lawyer named Dudley Buffa, he cofounded the Institute for the New California (Winograd had relocated from Michigan), a think tank that sought to align state government with the needs and requirements of citizens in the information age. That same year, Winograd and Buffa published *Taking Control: Politics in the Information Age*, which looks at how technology effects politics, government, the workplace, and quality of life in the United States. The book explicitly rejected the liberal economics that had predominated since the New Deal. "In an information age, it is neither labor nor capital, nor their combination that is crucial to economic success; knowledge is the key ingredient." The authors called for a "new social contract for America," which would enhance communities by "eliminating bureaucratic regulation and establishing boundary conditions for participation that preserve the common good."[3]

In 1997, Winograd was named a senior policy advisor to Vice President Al Gore and Director of the National Partnership for Reinventing Government. He was recommended for the post by an old friend, Elaine Kamarck, who had served in the same position for Gore during the first Clinton administration. Reinventing government was a euphemism for reducing the size of government, but it also provided Clinton with the political capital to cover the costs of expanding federal programs. Winograd was not an early proponent of reinventing government, but he soon saw its value, particularly as a response to the liberalism of the 1960s and 1970s. His Wikipedia entry includes this quote: "Our titanic ship of state, the USS Bureaucracy, is on a dangerous collision course. If the ship doesn't change direction, it will hit an iceberg. Strangely, that iceberg isn't made of ice. It's a gigantic paper iceberg, frozen hard with regulation and indifference." He said there was initially "public employee angst" over the idea of reinventing government, although it diminished once the architects of this movement included union leaders in the discussion.

Clinton grasped—and Winograd learned—the political reality that a Reagan-led Republican Party was so hostile to unions that the adoption of information-age ideas by the Democratic Party would not result in a massive defection from the party over economic issues. Labor had nowhere else to go. On family leave, health care, and the minimum wage—to take just three examples—a Democratic Party in thrall to DLC ideas was still far better than the GOP alternative. As for Democrats who earned their living from the information economy, the deficit-busting economic team of Bill Clinton, Robert Rubin, Lawrence Summers, and Alan Greenspan could not be bettered. Who else but this august group could have created and managed the unprecedented U.S. economic boom of the late 1990s? Not George H. W. Bush and Nicholas Brady, Ronald Reagan and Donald Regan, or Reagan and James Baker.

Today, Republicans—Reagan and George W. Bush in particular— run up massive budget deficits and embrace questionable economic theories. In the aftermath of the 2006 Democratic takeover of Congress, many observers noted that common sense would in all probability return to the budget process and federal spending. That these predictions sounded more obvious than ironic attested to the historic shift in how voters regarded the two major parties on the matter of fiscal responsibility.

After Clinton took office, labor leaders continued to express their dissatisfaction with the right turn on economic policy, especially on free trade issues such as NAFTA. But, as expected, they remained intensely loyal to the president and his party. Today, labor is arguably the most powerful single interest aligned with the Democrats. Even during the era of GOP dominance, Republicans feared the political skills of labor, and with good reason. In November 2005, the unions defeated California governor Arnold Schwarzenegger's attempts to dilute their clout through a number of ballot propositions.

Thanks in part to the ideas of people such as Winograd and the policies of people such as Clinton, it sounds both anachronistic and politically desperate to claim in the early twenty-first century that the Democrats are intrinsically hostile to business. (However, this argument is not always doomed to fail. A skilled campaign team can get voters to believe anything.) Given the incredible economic expansion that occurred in the United States during the period from 1996 to 2000—Clinton's second term—it could even be argued that having the Democrats in power is actually better for business. We have not heard that said with any consistency or conviction about Democrats since the Kennedy administration.

. . .

If this were 1958, before the pill and counterculture, then maybe the Democrats could build a majority party for the twenty-first century, just as Karl Rove and George W. Bush tried but failed to do for the GOP. But neither the religious right nor feminists nor gay activists are inclined to leave social issues alone. One thing that Morley Winograd and George McGovern have in common is the desire to remove abortion and gay rights from the political arena and restrict them to the courts. Yet they both recognize that liberals are the prime reason that this is not the case.

For all their commitment and effort to change the way Democrats think about the economy, Winograd, Clinton, and the DLC never went through the same exercise regarding abortion and gay rights. Yet one could argue that in the last two decades the mainstream Democratic positions on both harmed the party's prospects—especially with evangelical voters—as much as "liberal" views on taxes and national security. New Democrats never developed a strong alternative position on social issues, where admittedly there is less room to maneuver than on economic matters. What would be the Third Way on abortion, for example? In the end, the DLC opted for a laissez faire approach and hoped that would suffice. "On social issues, it was suggested we ought to let people make their own choices, as long as they are accountable for the choices they make," said Winograd. "Even though the DLC was considered very conservative, there was enough of an opening there to allow the social issues side of the party to feel relatively unthreatened by what we had to say." The new Democratic position on abortion could be considered that of Pennsylvania senator Bob Casey Jr., a pro-life challenger elected in 2006 over a pro-life incumbent, Rick Santorum. Still, I do not expect that most Democratic women and Democratic men will allow Casey's view to prevail in the 2008 party platform.

Winograd acknowledges that his 1990 manifesto on how the Democrats could win the White House in 1992 "ducked the social issues." As he told me later: "Social issues are not the route to victory for the Democratic Party." Yet he had received a stark lesson in the potentially negative impact of social issues on otherwise loyal Democrats back in the early 1970s. "After I became chairman of the Michigan Democratic Party in 1973, I was taken to lunch by the Michigan Catholic Conference," remembered Winograd. "They said they planned on making a campaign out of right-to-life and the importance of right-to-life. And they asked as a Jew, didn't I feel that abortionists' lack of sensitivity to the sanctity of life was akin to Hitler's experimentation with human beings? I remember saying, 'Gee, I don't think so.'"

"I did not have any sense that issue was powerful enough to drive them out of the party," added Winograd, "but within five years, the right-to-life movement was one of the best organized groups in the state, and very capable of affecting voter turnout and election outcome. I had been wrong."

"Ducking the social issues" contributes to the damaging notion that the Democrats are not fervently committed to an essential component of their own agenda. In an era of on-the-record gay-baiting and the not uncommon opinion that "abortion is murder," it is hard to understand how the majority of liberal and progressive candidates are not more forthcoming on these issues, even given the potential political fallout.

In contrast, conservatives—especially of an ultrareligious orientation—have no such qualms. They bring up the subjects of gay rights and abortion constantly. As liberals became more quiet and uncertain over the past thirty-five years, conservatives embraced the politics of confrontation. This stark contrast contributed mightily to the perception that liberalism had no future and no soul.

CHAPTER ELEVEN

Pulling to the Right

On April 29, 1992, as my wife and I were getting ready to leave for an NBA playoff game between the Los Angeles Lakers and the Portland Trailblazers, a television set in our apartment reported a disturbance taking place at a liquor store in South Central Los Angeles. The live pictures showed black males running in and out of the establishment, grabbing whatever they could carry. The presence of the media in real time was no coincidence: an hour or so earlier, not-guilty verdicts had been handed down in the case of four white Los Angeles Police Department (LAPD) officers accused of beating a black man, Rodney King. In their inimitable style, the media had hyped the possibility of violence and anarchy in the event the officers went free. And now it appeared that the prayers of the editors had been answered.

Still, the disturbance was not yet a riot. Although the basketball game would be played only a few miles west of the besieged liquor store, there did not seem to be any reason for concern. A few squad cars filled with well-armed LAPD officers could put an end to this thing in a hurry.

Once inside the arena, we promptly forget about cops and race relations and concentrated on what was after all a very important game. Those sitting around us were of a similar mind; all radios were tuned to the Lakers station. As a result, when reality intruded, it was that much more frightening. In the third quarter, the public address announcer informed the crowd that due to "disturbances," following the game spectators would be allowed to exit only to the west of the Inglewood Forum. The teams continued to compete with the intensity that marks playoff basketball. But the spectators grew noticeably quiet.

When the game ended, my wife and I waited for what seemed like hours (but could not have been more than forty-five minutes) in a jammed parking lot before heading west. The neighborhoods were dark and the traffic was light. We decided to take surface streets home, as opposed to the more traveled San Diego Freeway. Even late at night, Southern Californians take great pleasure in beating traffic. We had just finished congratulating ourselves for making such a smart decision when we came upon an extraordinary scene: massive bright yellow flames to our left and right. An entire block of businesses was on fire.

Neither the police nor the fire department nor the media had arrived. One local amateur was filming the conflagration with his own camera; who knows how much he made selling the footage? Otherwise, the streets were deserted. We drove through the intersection, watching history unfold from the inside of a car moving much faster than the speed limit. For the remainder of the trip, we once again passed through quiet neighborhoods. When we got home we had several voice mails from friends concerned for our safety. At that point we turned on the television to find out what we had missed while watching the game.

The Watts Riots, which nearly twenty-seven years earlier covered much of the same geographical territory as the Los Angeles Riots, presaged a series of "long hot summers" in ghettos around the country. Along with assassinations, the war in Vietnam, and the Manson Family murders, looting, burning, and confrontations with the police in Watts, Newark, Detroit, Chicago, and Washington, DC, were defining features of violence in the 1960s. Although more people died in the LA riots than during Watts, Newark, or Detroit, the events that began at the liquor store in 1992 were not the beginning of a trend, but an aberration. There were no more riots of this magnitude—or anything close—for the remainder of the 1990s. By the middle of the decade, due to gentrification, fewer teenage girls giving birth, and steady reductions in the crime rate, the United States began to experience an urban revival that continues to the present. Neighborhoods from New York to Los Angeles that had been considered lost forever are now teeming with life. The image of the inner city from the late 1960s and early 1970s—angry, abandoned, and dangerous—has been supplanted by a relentless public relations campaign that promotes the rich diversity (black, white, brown, yellow, gay, straight, bohemian, entrepreneurial) and sex appeal of residing "downtown." In this new world, suburbia—or "Disturbia" to quote the title of a 2007 film—is the place to avoid.

For a few days in late April and early May of 1992, the pictures of burning buildings, smashed windows, and innocent motorists under attack from rock-throwing mobs certainly reminded baby boomers of watching the evening news during the summer of '67. But the similarities between the two eras end there. And no one recognized more clearly that the country and politics had changed dramatically since Watts than the man who would be elected president six months later.

. . .

Going into the 1992 campaign, it had been sixty years since Republicans occupied the presidency for three consecutive terms. Even then it was only President Herbert Hoover's inability to respond to an economic catastrophe in the United States that enabled his opponent, Franklin Delano Roosevelt, to win a decisive victory in 1932. Bill Clinton had to settle for challenging an incumbent during a recession, and not a depression. Nevertheless, he made the most of his opportunity. In the historian James Patterson's account: "Bad economic news dominated many headlines in 1991 and 1992. AT&T fired 100,000 workers, GM 74,000. Pan American and Eastern Airlines went under, throwing 48,000 people out of work. Japan, though beginning to lose its competitive edge, still seemed to threaten America's economic hegemony."[1] A recession calls for action, but not necessarily big ideas. Unlike 1932, the country did not seek a savior, but a manager, not to mention someone who cared. One of Bush's greatest liabilities in 1992 was that he seemed to be strangely detached from events. It is frequently the case in American politics that an incumbent grows bored with the job, and both administers the office and wages a campaign that reflects this mood. After winning the Gulf War in 1991, Bush gradually lost interest in being president.

As previously discussed, FDR governed as an unabashed liberal. Early in his presidency he openly and proudly linked the New Deal to liberalism. By contrast, the Clinton campaign sought to create distance between its own economic proposals and those of the New Deal and Great Society. Commenting on Clinton's overall approach to governance, Senator Barack Obama wrote: "He [Clinton] saw that government spending and regulation could, if properly designed, serve as vital ingredients and not inhibitors to economic growth, and how markets and fiscal discipline could help promote social justice. He recognized that not only societal responsibility but personal responsibility was needed to combat poverty."[2] These are New Democratic means (fiscal discipline, personal responsibility) to achieve liberal ends (social justice, reducing poverty). Clinton also campaigned on lowering the massive federal deficit, which, after twelve years of increased spending under Reagan and Bush, could be blamed on Republican presidents and more liberal (in the classical sense of the word) trade policies.

Clinton's pledge to reform the welfare system—specifically, limiting the amount of time people could receive assistance—and provide a middle-class tax cut was not favorably regarded by some on the left, who considered such proposals anathema to the spirit of economic equality. But if the objective of the campaign was to represent the interests of the "forgotten middle class," these criticisms, when they came, were not unwelcome. As with his famous reproach of Sister Souljah following the LA riots, Clinton was willing to engage in occasional skirmishes with members of the post-'60s liberal coalition—African Americans in that instance—so as to burnish his New Democrat credentials with moderates in both parties. It is sometimes the case in American politics that the enemy of your enemy is your friend.

The same person who as a teenager shook JFK's hand at the White House and in 1972 served as campaign coordinator in Texas for McGovern (he "performed brilliantly," according to the candidate) was now engaged in a project to pull back from some basic tenets of modern economic leftism. Along with McGovern, who had his own doubts, old-timers such as John Kenneth Galbraith and Arthur Schlesinger Jr. were not pleased with these policies. Both of them venerated Roosevelt and worked for Kennedy, and they could not understand the move to the right. According to the book *John Kenneth Galbraith: His Life, His Politics, His Economics*, the economist, then in his mid-eighties, and the historian, then in his late-seventies, grew increasingly disenchanted with the White House during the first Clinton administration. Galbraith and Schlesinger used the occasion of the commemoration on April 12, 1995, of the fiftieth anniversary of FDR's death, at which Clinton also spoke, to publicly rebuke the president for becoming too cozy with the Republicans on Capitol Hill.

There was another profound difference between the members of the Galbraith-Schlesinger generation (roughly defined as people born between 1910 and 1927) and the baby boomers. The former knew from their own experience that unapologetic liberals could win elections. In their view, it was Ronald Reagan, not Franklin Roosevelt, who was the great exception. Of course, they were unhappy with the Democrats' performance over the previous two decades, but they did not regard this either as a reason to panic or a permanent condition. On the other hand, Clinton and his peers were both impatient and increasingly in despair over recent historical trends. To put it bluntly: they were tired of losing. Better to elect a quasi liberal or a moderate Democrat than another Republican of any ideological persuasion. With the exception of Jimmy Carter's victory in 1976, which was largely due to Watergate and Nixon's resignation, Democrats had gone through twenty years of hell. After three landslide losses, and, in 1988, arguably the most inept presidential

campaign in U.S. history, Democrats under the age of fifty could toler-
ate or even encourage some tinkering if it enhanced their party's chances
of winning. A sizable proportion of these voters were living in comfortable circumstances, and though they may have empathized with the
plight of the working poor or the unions, they were not directly affected
by most of the economic policies proposed by the DLC and New
Democrats. Feeling someone else's pain is not the same as feeling pain.

. . .

Clinton's rightward drift on the economy and crime—like other gover-
nors, he displayed his macho side through unflinching support of the
death penalty—was balanced by his shameless identification with '60s
pop culture. Clinton wanted to share his good fortune at being young
when so much great rock, soul, and funk was played on the radio. Over
the years, I lost count of the number of baby-boomer parents who
breathed a sigh of relief when it turned out their kids also liked the
Beatles, Led Zeppelin, and the Ramones. There is something about having been raised during the 1960s and 1970s that inspires middle-aged
people to go out into the world and convert younger generations to
their pop music preferences. I don't recall my parents or their friends
insisting that I listen to Duke Ellington or Benny Goodman.

Clinton was the first presidential nominee to align himself with the
cultural liberalism of the 1960s. The most memorable example of his
transformative embrace of pop culture occurred during the summer of
1992, when he trumped all previous presidential candidates of the modern era who had tried to show their cool by coming out on stage and
playing "Heartbreak Hotel" on the saxophone during an appearance on
the *Arsenio Hall Show*. Clinton wore dark sunglasses for the occasion,
and any of us who watched the Democratic nominee for president that
night will never forget it. One could overlook the fact that he chose to
perform a song that had reached no. 1 on the charts thirty-six years earlier and was originally recorded by Elvis Presley, who was a figure of
ridicule—musically and politically—to liberal elites. Clinton's act of

derring-do evoked fond memories in the generation that had dared to be different.

A few weeks later, at the conclusion of the Democratic National Convention in New York, the Clintons and Gores danced and clapped on stage to the sounds of "Don't Stop" by Fleetwood Mac. Though nominating conventions in both parties had long since been turned into made-for-television extravaganzas—think of grinning nominees and their families, faces projected on overhead screens, mindlessly waving to delegates—the music was something new. Rock music was what organizers played at antiwar rallies in the 1960s and 1970s. Now it had become a promotional and recruiting tool in establishment politics. Since the '92 convention, politicians in both parties use rock or pop music to excite the crowd and establish their own credentials as fun lovers underneath it all. In fact, one of the early warning signs about George W. Bush should have been his admitted lack of interest in the albums blasting from dorm-room stereo systems during the years he attended Yale.

· · ·

Upon becoming president in January 1993, one of Clinton's first acts was to express his support for allowing gays to serve in the military. The subsequent uproar forced Clinton to accept the famous "Don't ask, don't tell" policy, which in the years since has become a catchall phrase that people routinely apply to various situations in public and private life. Clinton's retreat on the issue served as an indicator of things to come, especially in the first term. Within a year, for example, his administration abandoned its ambitious plans to reform the health-care system. But it is also revealing that Clinton chose to begin his presidency with an extension of cultural liberalism into the area of public policy. Behind the notion that gays should be allowed to serve in the military is the all-encompassing, modern-day liberal idea of tolerance. A post-1960s liberal's position is to ask, "Why not?" Liberals consistently state their basic belief that gays are people too, and should be accorded full rights, including marriage. Given that religious conservatives frequently describe gay people in terms that make them seem subhuman, to start with the simple premise that "gays are people too" is both a necessary and strategically sound approach. When liberals state this belief up front, it makes it more difficult for the other side to argue in favor of continued denial of civil rights to homosexuals. But it is not impossible—as we have seen in numerous elections since the early 1990s.

Cultural liberalism comes with its own set of values: tolerance at the top of the list followed by diversity and multiculturalism. Liberals have also been united in their intolerance toward those with whom they strongly disagree, including conservative Christians, moderate and right-leaning academics, and people who criticize groups that liberals consider family. Old school liberals—and conservatives—who believe in the sanctity of the First Amendment regard this version of liberalism as corrupt and dangerous. In the fall of 1993 (Clinton had not been in office for even a year) *Partisan Review* published an entire issue devoted to "The Politics of Political Correctness." Some twenty-five contributors, most of whom remain on the front lines of the debate over intellectual and cultural values in American society, decried the power of PC, primarily on college campuses, from a pre-1968 liberal and neoconservative perspective. The titles of many of the articles in the collection attest to a sense of crisis, in academia if not in society as a whole: "Dumbocracy in America," "Confronting the Monolith," "The Reign of Intolerance," "Soft Totalitarianism," and "McCarthyism of the Left."

In addition to universities, popular entertainment increasingly reflected the values of cultural liberalism, during the Clinton years and after. The extremely successful NBC television sitcom *Will and Grace* was a witty and well acted Public Service Announcement in support of liberal-style tolerance. Urban gay life was presented primarily through stories of normal people (by the standards of television) with normal problems. In general, gay sex on the show was portrayed in the context of the quest for love that can lead any of us into situations that do not represent our best selves. At the same time, Will, Grace, and their immediate circle did not seem to have many financial worries. The main characters managed to make payments on fabulous New York City living spaces, to eat at expensive restaurants, and of course, go to the gym on a regular basis. They were vivid symbols of Clinton-era prosperity, which was accompanied by little concern about how the working class or the poor lived. In the 1990s you could be a New Democrat and believe that gay people were just like everyone else.

The spate of reality shows that began with MTV's *The Real World* in the early 1990s is also a prime example of cultural liberalism. *The Real World* established the genre, both in terms of format and politics. From the beginning, the MTV program included at least one gay character in the mix of twenty-something strangers who fight, have sex, bond, take trips to exotic places, eat, drink, dance, and cry for our entertainment. Typically, one of the subplots involves a person in the group, usually from the Southwest or South, who has trouble adjusting to the gay housemate. Over the next several weeks, this person comes to acknowledge (at least tacitly) that being gay and the gay lifestyle have a degree of legitimacy. Thus enlightened, the chances diminish that he or she will ever become a foot soldier for the religious right.

What I have never heard or seen on *The Real World* is a reference either to the fact that America has any social, economic, or political problems other than those that directly impact the self-indulgent young people on the show; or that since 2003 their peers have been fighting and dying in Iraq. On *The Real World* and programs of its kind, reality does not intrude.

Cultural liberalism has its roots in the 1972 McGovern campaign, when for the first time gay rights and abortion were recognized at the highest levels of the Democratic Party. By the time Clinton was elected president, the post-'60s quest for personal liberation had become an American institution. From coast to coast, we are all in the process of finding ourselves. But this journey does not take place in a value-free zone. Cultural liberals deluded themselves into thinking that their own laissez-faire attitude toward personal choice would become the norm for society as a whole. The backlash to the "new freedoms" would have a profound effect on American politics that continues to reverberate today.

. . .

Richard Nixon thought everyone was an actual or potential enemy, and reacted accordingly. Bill Clinton thought he could seduce everyone into loving him. Each of these attitudes proved damaging to the respective presidencies. Derek Shearer recalled during our interview that in Clinton's first term he and another advisor, the author and journalist Sidney Blumenthal, tried to warn the president of the intensity of the hatred against both the president and his wife. Shearer said Clinton refused to believe it. "He had a view of himself that was so confident he could handle anything," said Shearer. "But he didn't understand what the National Republican Party had become. He was not prepared for the onslaught against him. He was really kind of shocked."

For once, Clinton's vaunted knowledge of the body politic and its idiosyncrasies failed him. He had forgotten the example of the 1988 Dukakis campaign, which fatally underestimated the capacity of conservative campaign consultants to portray well-meaning liberals and Democrats as destroyers of America. In 1988, Democrats did not have to worry too much about the religious right. By the time Clinton entered the White House, however, evangelicals were fast becoming the most powerful bloc of voters in the Republican Party. Their hatred of cultural liberalism and Clinton was one of the most important developments in U.S. politics during the 1990s.

. . .

Dr. James Dobson, the head of Focus on the Family, a worldwide ministry with fourteen hundred employees, might well be the only right-wing conservative in the United States whom liberals despise more than George W. Bush. Among prominent politically active ministers, Dobson can usually be counted on to issue the most contentious, insulting, and incendiary comments about liberals, homosexuals, and feminists. In his admiring biography of Dobson, entitled *Family Man*, author Dale Buss recounts how Dobson went into a three-months-long depression following the inauguration of Bill Clinton in 1993. According to Buss, Dobson despaired for a country that would elect a known adulterer as president. To be specific, a politically liberal adulterer, since Dobson was equally outraged by Clinton's naming of Dr. Joycelyn Elders as U.S. Surgeon General and Donna Shalala as Secretary of Health and Human Services. (In a 2007 public appearance, Dobson "forgave" Newt Gingrich when he admitted to an adulterous affair.) As Buss explains, "Both women were openly proabortion, favored condom distribution among children and teens, and held other liberal views on the social and moral issues that Dobson cared most about."[3] How could the American people have made such a horrific mistake?

Clinton had to be stopped. Fearing for the future of the country, Dobson emerged from his depression in the spring of '93 determined to do battle with political Satanism. "His distress about Clinton's election was one of the first times, but certainly not the last, that Dobson felt God placed an even greater mantle upon him; to become the uncompromising proponent of traditional family values in the broader social, cultural, and even political arena," notes Buss.[4]

Dobson was the first and most powerful leader within the religious right to emerge in the post-Soviet era. Entering the fray too late to warn of the dangers of "Godless Communism," instead he garnered huge support by going after abortion, homosexuality, and pornography, which in the view of many could be summarized in one word: liberalism. The back cover of *Family Man* claims that Dobson's radio program regularly attracts some 220 million listeners around the world. Not every member of the American portion of this audience votes for conservatives, but enough of them have to elect far-right, publicly pious Christian candidates around the country. Several after-the-fact assessments of the 2004 presidential campaign cited evangelical voters as the prime reason Bush won reelection. And even in 2006, the year of the Republican collapse in the House and Senate, more than 70 percent of evangelicals voted for the GOP. Following the 2004 result, nervous and especially flexible Democrats argued that their party needed to pay more attention to the concerns of what is now termed in political circles "people of faith." But the "people of faith" that made the difference at the polls seek to outlaw abortion under any circumstances and regard homosexuality as a crime. How far were these Democrats willing to compromise?

Not that long before—the 1976 race between Jimmy Carter and President Gerald Ford—evangelicals gave strong support to the Democratic nominee, who was publicly born-again. But Ronald Reagan's 1980 presidential campaign, Carter's positions (especially his support for choice), and the founding of the Moral Majority by the Reverend Jerry Falwell (who passed away in 2007) and Paul Weyrich changed the dynamic. In their study of American conservatism, *Economist* writers John Micklethwait and Adrian Wooldridge put it this way: "The Moral Majority rapidly emerged as a hard-line Christian voice on domestic issues like abortion, school prayer, women's rights and gay rights. Over the next ten years [1979–89] it would register some 2.5 million new voters. The Christian Right rapidly became to the Republicans what blacks had been to the Democrats; the people who could be counted on, who did the work of turning up at meetings, knocking on doors and getting voters to the polls."[5]

. . .

In August 2006, the official publication of the Heritage Foundation, a conservative think tank, ran an article celebrating the tenth anniversary of the welfare reform bill. That legislation, which was signed by President Clinton, replaced Aid to Families with Dependent Children (AFDC) with Temporary Assistance to Needy Families (TANF). The new formula attached a time limit to government assistance, required recipients to actively seek employment, and gave states more control over federal block-grant allocations.[6] The Heritage article praised Clinton's leadership in getting the measure passed and noted that the most vocal opponents were within his own party, including Senate Minority Leader Tom

Daschle of South Dakota and House Minority Leader Richard Gephardt of Missouri.

If Democrats had been the majority in the House and Senate in 1996,
Clinton most likely could not have secured passage of this or any other
substantive welfare reform bill. AFDC and increases in welfare benefits
were remnants of the Great Society, which was the last great period of
domestic liberalism. In addition, many advocates of the current (pre-
1996) system argued that significant changes in welfare would lead to an
increase in the number of children living in poverty. The outcry among
liberals would have been too much for even Clinton's political skills to
overcome in a Democratic-controlled Congress.

But conservatives since at least the mid-1970s had forcefully argued
that the welfare system was creating a culture of dependency, which
robbed recipients of their dignity, rewarded failure, and, as a consequence, cheated hardworking taxpayers. Even more damaging to liberals, anecdotes about clever recipients who ripped off the welfare system
and got rich at our expense had been a staple of Republican rhetoric
since the Nixon era. Though a number of these stories may have been
exaggerated or outright false, they had the gut emotional appeal that
defines a successful message during election season.

In November 1994, Republicans assumed control of the House and
Senate in part due to voter antipathy toward the then-nascent Clinton
presidency. They did not like his support for gays in the military nor the
(failed) health-care plan that his wife concocted largely out of public
view. But the Republican takeover, although humiliating to Clinton,
provided the president with an opportunity to accomplish one of his sig-
nature objectives. As a member of the DLC and a New Democrat,
Clinton had promoted the idea of "responsibility," which was a not-too-
veiled criticism of AFDC and other government programs that seemingly encouraged idleness. Now Clinton potentially had the votes in
Congress to legislate responsibility. He also had timing on his side.

During the previous two years, Republicans in the House had passed
many provisions of the Contract with America, only to have their more

sober colleagues in the Senate—led by Bob Dole, the 1996 GOP candidate for president—vote to modify or oppose outright these same measures. As a result, Republican members of the House of Representatives, the majority party for the first time in forty years, faced the very real possibility of campaigning for reelection on a record of little accomplishment. Given that the previous two Republican majorities in the House lasted all of one term, the reign of Gingrich and company could be in serious trouble.

The president also wanted a deal. Though he was running in 1996 against Bob Dole, a lackluster Republican compared with Reagan or Gingrich, the 1994 midterm elections indicated that the country was moving farther to the right. Clinton's perceived liberalism—especially on cultural issues—could pose serious problems for the president. What could he give the not-so-angry white males to prevent them from joining Rush Limbaugh's listeners in voting Republican?

In *Behind the Oval Office*, Dick Morris writes that it was on March 23, 1995, that a group of political consultants first proposed the idea of "triangulation," which the author defined rather grandly as, "The development of a fusion alternative embodying the best elements of the traditional Republican and Democratic positions, but rejecting the extremes of each party."[7] This definition implied a similarity between liberalism (the extreme wing of the Democratic Party) and the religious right (the extreme wing of the Republican Party). But by the mid-1990s liberalism was descendant and religious conservatism ascendant. The Clinton administration included New Democrats as advisors on economic policy, whereas the 1994 freshman class of the House of Representatives contained a number of openly Christian members. Liberals and liberal Republicans were quickly disappearing in Washington. Yet judged by the inventors of triangulation, liberalism was as powerful as ever. Fear of resurgent liberalism and liberalism's legacy has been an underlying theme of many Democratic campaigns from the mid-1990s to the present.

As the Heritage Foundation article demonstrates, there are still conservatives grateful to Clinton for his leadership in securing passage of the welfare bill in 1996. The legislation has since become one of the great success stories of the Clinton administration. In part due to a strong economy, welfare caseloads declined from 1996 to 2002 (then the latest available figures), according to the Heritage piece: "While previous attempts at reform resulted in only cosmetic changes, the Personal Responsibility and Work Opportunity Reconciliation Act (PRWORA) of 1996 has had a meaningful and lasting impact on the federal welfare regime."[8] Not even Ronald Reagan accomplished that.

. . .

Three years prior to the passage of PRWORA, Clinton built a coalition with Republicans and moderate and left-of-center Democrats to secure passage of the North American Free Trade Agreement (NAFTA). At the time I was working in the Southern California district office of a Democratic congressman who for more than twenty years as an elected official had compiled a near-perfect record of support for labor's agenda. His decision to back NAFTA, announced well in advance of the actual vote, prompted regular visits to our office from representatives of various unions to try to change his mind. The discussions were intense, but never heated, and invariably at the end both sides would civilly agree to disagree. Little more than one year later the election of a right-wing Congress effectively neutralized any efforts by unions to punish recalcitrant Democrats around the country. Labor now had a much more serious problem on its hands.

NAFTA, welfare reform, and the budget surplus stand as three of the great accomplishments of Clinton's years in the White House. Each of these reflects Republican economic priorities over the past forty years. Just as only a hard-line anticommunist could begin the process of establishing relations between the United States and China, only a centrist Democrat could push through legislation to expand free trade and reform welfare. A Republican president—especially after the 1980 Reagan campaign—could never have garnered the trust from all but a few Democrats to craft an acceptable compromise on such highly contentious issues affecting overwhelmingly Democratic constituencies. For example, my former boss would never have supported a Ronald Reagan bill to change the welfare system or promote free trade.

. . .

Whatever label one chooses to affix to Clinton's domestic policies—neoliberal, centrist, New Democrat, moderate—the country was in much better shape at the end of his term than at the beginning, a few months after the Los Angeles Riots. Some of the seemingly intractable social problems of the United States, including crime and teen pregnancy, were brought under control during Clinton's two terms in office. During the bleak years of the 1980s this improvement did not seem possible.

It is still not clear why urban America experienced such a positive turnaround during the 1990s. An expanding economy played a part, as did the decision of young professionals to locate in areas that had been abandoned over previous decades. Some have argued that the mere presence of Clinton in the White House gave hope to groups in society that had been psychologically and economically devastated during the reigns of Reagan and Bush. When Clinton stepped down in January 2001 the country was feeling rather satisfied with itself—much different from the mood when Jimmy Carter turned the White House over to Ronald Reagan two decades earlier.

The successor to Clinton should have been Al Gore, the nation's vice president over the past eight years. A sitting VP could not have asked for a better record on which to run. But the Gore team made a strategic miscalculation that severely damaged the candidate, regardless of how one feels about the Florida recount. Because of the Lewinsky matter and Clinton's widespread reputation for randy behavior, Gore maintained his distance from the president. Rarely did the two appear together in public. Gore wanted to avoid being too closely associated with a man who had cheated on his wife—even though Clinton's favorable ratings had increased during the impeachment hearings. I could never determine which voting bloc the vice president was hoping to appease by running on a pro-monogamy plank. If it was the religious right, he was wasting his time. As long as Gore supported choice or was friendly to gay people he could have practiced celibacy and still had no chance of receiving evangelical support.

Keeping Clinton off stage caused voters to concentrate less on the successes of the administration and more on Gore himself—a bad idea. Gore was a strange man in public. He possessed an almost neurotic self-awareness, clearly preoccupied with how every gesture and comment might be interpreted by the media and voters. In an era of bored reporters and housebound Web surfers always on the lookout for mis-statements and silly expressions, one can understand the motivation of candidates to stay always in character. But Gore's carefully controlled performances frequently made him look ridiculous, as did the highly theatrical kisses he shared with his wife at campaign appearances around the country. "Gore never seemed comfortable as a campaigner," the historian James Patterson has written. "Many of his aides found him to be demanding and brusque. Critics observed that he was 'stiff,' 'wooden,' pompous, and inconsistent."[9]

One hesitates to blame an event as momentous as a presidential election on a candidate's personality flaws, but how else to explain that despite Gore having everything in his favor in 2000 he still lost? Beginning with the thirty-six-day saga surrounding the Florida recount, in which Gore supporters were simply no match for the bullying tactics and single-minded determination of their adversaries, the period from November 2000 to November 2006 marked one of the lowest points in the history of liberals and Democrats in the United States. With a born-again Christian from Texas in the White House, a born-again Christian from Texas serving as majority leader in the House of Representatives, and members of the religious right holding key positions throughout Congress, ultraconservatives had never been so powerful. Having defeated their opponents in elections, they now wanted to smash them into dust.

The Bush years unleashed a torrent of antiliberalism in politics and the media, the likes of which had not been seen since the red-baiting days of the early 1950s. Especially after 9/11, elected officials and celebrity conservatives such as Ann Coulter, Rush Limbaugh, and Sean Hannity issued regular diatribes accusing liberals of hating God, hating America, embracing the "homosexual agenda," and sympathizing with terrorists. Liberals offered little resistance to these scurrilous attacks, just as they had during the "L-word" campaign of 1988. It was only the prospect of Bush's reelection in 2004 that finally goaded Democrats of all kinds into action, even those who had declared themselves finished with politics.

· · ·

During George W. Bush's heyday, liberals could take some solace from knowing that popular culture would not let them down. Since the late 1960s, liberals felt confident that they owned middlebrow and highbrow entertainment: theater, film, rock music, and everything on television except *The Beverly Hillbillies* and *Hee Haw*. They didn't discuss this much for fear of arousing the opposition—or confirming the opposition's own conspiracy theories—but they knew it to be true. Liberals expected that popular entertainment would validate their own political views. The bad guys on screen or on stage would be indistinguishable from the bad guys in the real world: narrow-minded, unsophisticated, misogynistic, jingoistic, and excessively Christian. The good guys practiced a kind of easygoing liberalism: gay-friendly, skeptical of religion, environmentally correct, tolerant toward blacks, Jews, and Latinos, and open to sexual and pharmaceutical possibilities, within reason, of course.

Yet by the turn of the century even the cultural supremacy of liberalism was in doubt. Right-wingers were demanding that pop culture respond more to their needs and desires, and pop culture was hearing the message. No more could liberals blithely assume that a trip to the multiplex would bring psychic relief from the horrors of life under Bush, Cheney, and DeLay. As for television . . . ah, well, there was always the theater.

CHAPTER TWELVE

Blue Culture, Red Politics

On a cool, clear Los Angeles evening in June 2005 several hundred people attended the U.S. premiere of *Stuff Happens*, a play about Anglo-American diplomacy and the run-up to the war in Iraq by the English playwright David Hare. The ironic title of the play—taken from an offensive remark by then–defense secretary Donald Rumsfeld describing the looting of art treasures in Baghdad—created the expectation of both an antiwar premise and a skewering of the Bush administration in a manner unique to angry left-leaning British writers. The left in America might despise Bush, but the left in Britain and the rest of Europe *really* despise Bush.

Liberals in the early twenty-first century still considered the theater a friendly medium, as opposed to television and radio, which from the late 1980s had turned increasingly hostile. For decades, radio had served the interests of liberals and the counterculture: President Franklin Delano Roosevelt's Fireside Chats, cool jazz, Little Richard, the Beatles, FM rock, National Public Radio, sensitive pop psychologists. I once heard someone say that the 1960s ended when hip rock stations began running advertisements for cars and furniture. But long before the second term of George W. Bush, talk radio had taken control of the AM side of the dial, entertaining million of listeners with diatribes against liberals and liberalism and praise and pep talks for conservatives. Some of the hosts were ex–rock and roll DJs who found spinning politics to be far more lucrative and ego gratifying than spinning records. The best-known rock radio personalities of the 1960s and 1970s had nowhere near the clout or fame of Rush Limbaugh. Even liberals listened to Limbaugh, although they felt guilty about it later.

As talk radio gained in popularity, with more stations switching to the format, thoughtful, concerned, intelligent-sounding liberal-minded hosts were either relegated to off-hour time slots or dismissed. To a general audience, this demotion was a symptom of the decline of liberalism. Liberal radio personalities came through to the listener as responsible, deliberate, well read, and accurate, but in the end rather dull when compared to their bullying, self-righteous, off-the-charts conservative counterparts. The advent of the talk radio network Air America in 2003—promoted and packaged as the liberal alternative to right-wing talk radio—marked one of the few times in pop culture history when the left conceded defeat. Seeking to capitalize on intense antipathy toward Bush, the network attempted with limited success to appropriate the slashing style of Limbaugh and his ilk and turn it against conservatives.

As for television: What happened to the good old days when Spiro Agnew and a host of successors denounced the liberal biases of television news? Where were the "nattering nabobs of negativism" now that we really needed them? Since the late 1990s, many liberals had acted as if their TV set received only one station: Fox. "Did you hear what they said on Fox News?" or "Those idiots on Fox are at it again" counted as conversation starters for liberals in the late twentieth century and the early part of the twenty-first. While clearly fascinated by Fox, liberals were also terribly depressed that TV—once the brightest star in the liberal-media universe—had succumbed to the right-wing wave. And all the time Fox News advertised its product as "fair and balanced," an intentionally preposterous claim that made outraged liberals decry there ought to be a law against it.

Throughout the quarter century of the Reagan legacy, only the theater remained pure and true. Judging by the reviews of productions on Broadway, off-Broadway, and various festivals around the country, liberals still owned the medium. In the weeks before the 2006 elections, for example, New York featured plays with the titles *Bush Is Bad, Dumbya's Rapture,* and *Bush Wars.* In most cases, theatergoers did not attend plays that were prowar, antiabortion, anti-intellectual, and (most of all) anti-homosexual. Liberals who go to the theater have their political opinions confirmed instead of challenged. This is not an aesthetic judgment, but a restatement of Marketing 101, that is, give the people what they want.

The theater was for the most part spared harassment from conservative pressure groups, although writers, cast, crew, and audiences include many of those people whom the evangelicals hope to convert. Practically every week Broadway and Off-Broadway opens a new play in which gay characters and gayness feature prominently, and many *New York Times* profiles on (male) writers, directors, producers, or actors includes the line, "such and such lives with his boyfriend." Even Hollywood can't match Broadway's gay demographic or product: *Brokeback Mountain* was an exception, not the rule. Yet unless your production portrays Jesus as an active homosexual or commingles religious symbols and genitalia, powerful televangelists and their swiftly mobilized Christian armies will leave you alone.

Sadly, it seems that in the opinion of the religious right, the decline and fall of Christian civilization is not contingent upon what takes place on a stage. Why bother with an "obscure" figure such as Edward Albee when you can register your disgust with a prime-time television program such as *Will and Grace?*

. . .

On the night of the *Stuff Happens* premiere, the area around the venerable Mark Taper Forum in Los Angeles had been transformed into a village square for leftists. I noted two men and two women, all apparently in their mid-twenties, gathered around a small table packed with material promoting a group called Progressive Democrats of America, or

PDA for short. Earlier in the evening PDA had sponsored a discussion in which no more than forty liberals and progressives, few of them under the age of forty, listened to an author in his thirties discuss what "they" are doing to "us." As the guests ate cold sandwiches and assorted salads off paper plates and drank white wine from plastic cups, the author talked most of all about the war in Iraq. He was angry, of course, but also calm and measured as he chronicled what he described as the lies that the Bush administration had told since shortly after 9/11 in order to justify going to war with Iraq. This was a familiar story, but one that listeners were not tired of hearing, because it reminded them yet again of why they despised this president.

A mere seven months after Bush's reelection, liberals on this night and in this place were free to indulge their political fantasies. As they walked past tables displaying left-wing pamphlets and newsletters, and the occasional author hawking an antiadministration screed, the people attending *Stuff Happens* could feel almost hopeful about the future, regardless of who occupied the White House and which party was in charge of Congress. Tonight belonged to Us.

Like kids at a movie matinee, the audience seemed to be of one mind, laughing aloud at the same things and even spontaneously hissing at the characters of Vice President Dick Cheney, and strangely enough, U.N. ambassador John Negroponte. Condoleezza Rice and Colin Powell fared better, both in the script and with theatergoers, who may have found the idea of treating rudely African American characters disconcerting.

At the conclusion of the play the United States is ready to go war with Saddam Hussein, and thanks to Tony Blair (played by the British actor Julian Sands), England stands with us. Not a happy ending by liberals' standards, and yet the audience left the theater in what appeared to be a very good mood. They were pleased that in these perilous and depressing times a play such as *Stuff Happens* could be produced at all. The country might be way too far to the right, but it was not yet fascist—a thought that provided them some consolation on a balmy summer evening.

. . .

Here is a description of the screenwriter John Milius (*Apocalypse Now, Conan the Barbarian, The Hunt for Red October* among other films) that prefaced a lengthy interview conducted with him in 2000 and 2001: "He detests 'hipness' and 'cool', belongs to the National Rifle Association, has a broad range of military contacts, and is a political conservative—a résumé that brands him as a maverick in an industry that prides itself on being liberal."[1]

In the November 7, 2006, edition of the *Los Angeles Times*—the day of the election in which Democrats took control of Congress—Patrick Goldstein, author of a weekly and authoritative column on Hollywood, wrote about Jason Apuzzo and Govindini Murty, a young married couple in the film business who launched the Liberty Film Festival and what was described as a "libertas" Web site. "To say that the site is definitely right wing would be an understatement. If it has a central theme, it would be that moviegoers won't spend money on movies populated with obnoxious liberal stars who deride President Bush and undercut the war on terrorism. Libertas blamed the box-office failure of 'All the King's Men' on Sean Penn, saying his vitriolic attacks on Bush have made him box-office poison."[2]

No matter how conservative the politics in America—the country may never again be as far to the right as it was on the morning of November 7, 2006—Hollywood will not change. Behind the safe and imposing walls of the major studios, Hollywood acts as if liberalism never went into decline. Liberals in "the business" make films that reflect their point of view, give their money and lend their names to causes that can be found on any left-wing "to do" list, and allegedly create an environment in which conservatives find it personally uncomfortable and professionally risky to trumpet their opinions. The timid self-denial of liberal politicians in Washington offers a stark contrast to the pompous and overbearing liberalism of actors, directors, and producers. In the land of artifice and lies, at least one can be an out and proud liberal.

We know about Hollywood's political proclivities because we trust our own eyes and ears (there is no denying that the industry releases a surfeit of films that skew left, although it is still not as one-sided as in the theater) and because conservative commentators write books and articles on the subject, and right-leaning programs such as *Hannity and Colmes* and *Scarborough Country* raise the issue just about every night. Like opposition to any form of tax increase, contempt for liberal Hollywood unites the conservative movement: libertarians, evangelicals, and the masses that fall somewhere in between.

Despite Hollywood's self-proclaimed reputation for tolerance and openness, the notion persists that there are even fewer Hollywood conservatives than there are Christian evangelical liberals. This would explain why Patrick Goldstein, writing for the major newspaper in the industry's own backyard, devoted an entire column to the efforts of two obscure filmmakers to promote conservative causes. A cynic would say that the film festival and Web site are a great career move on the part of Ms. Murty and Mr. Apuzzo, who would never have been featured in a column if they had championed liberal-friendly cinema. But Goldstein goes out of his way to describe their dedication, and the potential risk of being shunned or ridiculed by colleagues: "Libertas has an undeniable intellectual energy, not unlike Newt Gingrich during his rise to power in Congress. The site's contrarian ideas represent a breath of fresh air in a town where you can go to dinner parties for years on end without ever hearing anyone question liberal conventional wisdom on any issue."[3]

During the recent period in U.S. politics when conservatives wracked up victory after victory, liberal Hollywood was like Britain in 1940: assailed, assaulted, and attacked by a bigger and stronger foe, but in the end, unconquerable. Republicans may have taken control of the entire South and Midwest and most of the West, but they would never overrun Malibu. Despite being under siege by conservative groups, entertainment industry liberals would not back down in their expressions of individual and tribal politics. During seemingly every award show in the late 1980s and 1990s—the Golden Globes, the Oscars, the Emmys—millions of Americans watched stunning actresses and handsome actors sporting ribbons, usually red ribbons, on their outrageously expensive gowns or suits. This was the most evident version of "in-your-face" liberalism—although practiced at a safe remove. The camera conveyed Hollywood's famed compassion and general goodness to the folks in the American heartland. As far as I know, none of the ribbon-wearers went to the bastions of the religious right to ask that they show compassion and empathy for people with AIDS and to argue the case for additional funding for AIDS research.

From 1980 on, the productions and words coming out of Hollywood—and other branches of the entertainment industry—fostered an illusion that liberalism was still a major force in American politics. This notion was fanned by conservatives, who needed something to be against, and more important, something to fear. A popular actor or recording artist might not be the equivalent of Stalin, Mao, the Ayatollah, or Ted Kennedy, but for the short term, he or she would have to suffice.

Where liberals have nothing on conservatives is in the latter group's ability to turn hurt feelings into political crusades. The success of Sean Hannity, Rush Limbaugh, and other conservative media stars depends not only on their talent for tough talk, but their incessant whining and complaining as well. The Democrats will say something mildly offensive about Ronald Reagan, George W. Bush, Dick Cheney, or Tom DeLay and right-wing talk-show hosts immediately demand an apology. When it comes to assuming the role of victim, liberal groups such as the NAACP are amateurs compared to these folks.

But conservative critics damage their own credibility when they exaggerate the views of Hollywood liberals out of all proportion to reality. What Norman Lear says matters far less than what Newt Gingrich (when he was Speaker of the House) says, and it certainly matters far less than what Speaker Gingrich does.

. . .

When I was growing up in the 1960s and watching a slew of World War II movies on television in which American forces defeated the "Japs," my elementary school mind equated Hollywood with extreme displays of patriotism. In a deliberate attempt to offend the sensibilities of our left-leaning parents, my brother announced that his favorite actor was John Wayne, who for both of us defined the meaning of *movie star.* I recall trips to the local theater in Claremont, California, in the early 1960s, to see *Knute Rockne, All-American* (with Ronald Reagan as the Gipper), *Pt-109,* and other films that were unabashedly sentimental and pro-American. Claremont is a college town, and by the end of the 1960s it was the site of numerous demonstrations and rallies against the war in Vietnam, as well as intense campus-wide struggles over the introduction of black and Chicano studies programs. But judging by the movies that played regularly at the Village Theater circa 1962–67, one could not have imagined the presence of student radicals in such a quiet, friendly middle-class community.

I do not remember the exact moment when Hollywood turned liberal, but I do remember my father taking me to see *Easy Rider* around the time it came out in 1969 and thinking this was certainly different from the movies I had attended as a young kid. The lead actors wore their hair long, like the students I saw on the streets every day in Claremont, and the sound track featured Steppenwolf and Jimi Hendrix, who were both included in my growing collection of hard rock records. The depiction of sex, drug use, and graphic violence in the film had also not been part of my earlier cinema-going experience. At thirteen, I was probably not the target demographic for *Easy Rider,* which carried an R rating, but the film was certainly more intended for people around my age than the over-thirty crowd. And though the story did not qualify as New Left agitprop, there was no confusing the bad guys from the good, or to be more precise, the peaceful, hedonistic hippies from the uptight, violent rednecks.

Maybe liberal Hollywood—the myth and the reality—did start with

Easy Rider. By 1972, stars such as Warren Beatty and Barbra Streisand were playing a pivotal role in raising money for the McGovern campaign. The movies showing at the Village Theater were more likely to reflect left-wing sensibilities than what would come to be known as traditional values. In many of these films, the levels of sex and violence were much greater than anything seen ten or even five years earlier; older people now complained that Hollywood sure did not make 'em like they used to.

Also in 1972, the porn film *Deep Throat* opened in downtown theaters around the country, which for feminists and religious groups did not constitute a glorious moment in the history of American liberalism. Yet to the wider public, *Deep Throat* and porn in general were associated with the counterculture and liberal—in the political and general sense of the word—attitudes toward sex, freedom of expression, and culture. Beginning with Richard Nixon and continuing through Ronald Reagan and the post-1994 Republican Congress, conservatives have launched periodic hearings, inquiries, or investigations into porn or less explicit yet public activities of a sexual nature, such as the split-second baring of Janet Jackson's breast at the 2004 Super Bowl. Not all liberals were comfortable with openly sexual displays in popular culture, but they were supposed to object fiercely to the use of either law enforcement or the resources of government to expose or harass so-called smut peddlers. The new explicitness provided conservatives an opportunity to once again present themselves to the American people as society's moral guardians—merely by giving the appearance of wanting to do something.

Yet porn films and videos are not shot on the glamorous back lots of Hollywood, Burbank, or Century City, but in isolated rental homes across the San Fernando Valley. And despite right-wing efforts to link porn with liberalism and "permissiveness," the politics of the adult industry's heavyweights—almost all of whom remain anonymous to the general public—are unclear. At most, we know that the people who direct, produce, and act in porn films believe in freedom of expression, but their motivations stem more from economic self-interest than any profound regard for the sanctity of the Bill of Rights. Liberals have the choice between standing up for the adult industry or ignoring the efforts of publicity-seeking district attorneys to ban porn films and even arrest performers and directors. One has the strong sense that while the ACLU would side with the pornographers, it hopes that the issue would simply disappear.

Despite its edgy cachet and self-congratulatory expressions of disdain for traditional values (other than acquiring wealth) the porn industry does not have anywhere near the politically liberal credentials of that "other" motion-picture business. By the 1990s, in fact, it caused a minor sensation whenever Hollywood would release a film that provided a sympathetic treatment of organized religion, small-town values, patriotism, or conservatives. "If more proof were needed that Hollywood had gotten religion, look no further than the curious mix of people behind 'The Nativity Story,' brought to the screen by a former high-octane agent, a disillusioned producer and a director better known for her take on teenage sex and skater boys," wrote Sharon Waxman for the *New York Times*.[4]

In 2004, Mel Gibson smashed through Hollywood's stained-glass ceiling with *The Passion of the Christ*, which to the evident surprise of liberal and secular film executives became one of the biggest box-office successes of all time. Having already done its part to change the nature and character of American politics, the religious right, which attended Gibson's film in huge numbers, was now defined by Hollywood as a viable demographic group, alongside gays, African Americans, "chicks," and teenage boys. Like conservative Democrats, the studios suddenly recognized the importance of listening to people of faith. "After 'The Passion of the Christ' in 2004, . . . everybody understood that something had shifted; the market demonstrated that there was an underserved audience for religious fare, however, problematic Mel Gibson's movie proved to be for some viewers, particularly Jewish ones," observed Waxman in the same article.[5]

Still, Hollywood's acknowledgment of this audience did not alter the widespread notion—propagated by mainstream media—that the movie business overwhelmingly reflected liberal attitudes and positions. Cultural critics such as Michael Medved fashioned a second career by attacking Hollywood for its contempt for Real America and Real Americans. In fact, a number of observers—not all of them unabashed conservatives—regard the film industry as the most blatant example of liberal elitism. And from an artistic perspective, the sheer number of serious films where liberals are the good guys and liberal values emerge triumphant is not in Hollywood's favor.

. . .

The first overtly political rock and roll song—a folk rock song, to be precise—was "Eve of Destruction" by Barry McGuire, released in late summer 1965. The song, which went to no. 1, is all talk and no action, that is, the world is going to hell, and isn't this a rather scary thing? At best, it may have shaken a few high-school kids out of their suburban complacency. But the song does take a decidedly liberal point of view, equating the hate in Selma, Alabama, with that in "Red" China, suggesting that Christians are a bunch of hypocrites and expressing fear of nuclear annihilation. As such, "Eve of Destruction" aroused the ire of the John Birch Society and other right-wing groups, which tried (and in some cases succeeded) to get it banned from the radio. To record executives, however, what mattered above all was that the song topped the *Billboard* charts. In rock and roll, it seemed that liberal politics combined with a good beat and memorable melody could produce a gold record.

During the late 1960s and early 1970s, several rock and soul songs with a liberal theme or message sold well, including "People Got to Be Free" (the Rascals), "Get Together" (the Youngbloods), "What's Going On" (Marvin Gaye), "Love Train" (the O'Jays), and "You Haven't Done Nothin'" (Stevie Wonder), which was an anti-Nixon single that went to no. 1 in the late summer of 1974, just as the president was making the transition from living in the White House to San Clemente. These songs are typically more hopeful than angry; dominant messages are "love," "peace," and "living in harmony"—with the human race and with nature.

Probably the most controversial political song from that era, "Revolution" by the Beatles, released at the tail end of 1968, articulates the liberal position that (left-wing) violence is neither an answer to nor a solution for the ills of the world. To this day there are former New Lefties who wonder why John Lennon wrote these lyrics. They love the Beatles and always will, but they consider "Revolution" an act of betrayal.

Two of the Beatles, Lennon and George Harrison, were among the early proponents of the political rock concert, which has since become an industry unto itself. These gargantuan events either promote typically liberal causes—pro-choice, antiwar, relief of Third World debt— or address Big Problems that preoccupy liberals in particular, such as hunger, poverty, and disease in underdeveloped countries. Starting with Live Aid in 1985 (ironically a time when Ronald Reagan and Margaret Thatcher were in power), some of these (primarily) Anglo-American concerts have been telecast around the globe, reinforcing the notion that rock music and liberalism enjoy a special relationship.

In some cases, the intent was overtly partisan, such as Rock Against Reagan in the 1980s and Rock Against Bush (RAB) in 2004. Formed in an effort to get punk fans to vote against Bush, RAB put out two CD collections in April and August of that year. The proceeds funded a concert tour in so-called swing states and a voter registration drive. Among the twenty songs on the first volume are "Sink, Florida, Sink" (Against Me!), "Moron" (Sum 41), "Warbrain" (Alkaline Trio), and "No W" (Ministry).

. . .

Certain liberal or liberal groups have on occasion expressed their disappointment, dissatisfaction, or disgust with rock. I can recall in the mid- and late-1970s hearing feminist college students rail against the alleged sexism of the Rolling Stones, on the basis of songs such as "Under My Thumb" "Stupid Girl," and "Some Girls," as well as a mid-'70s album promotional poster that featured a woman in bondage. They also weren't especially happy at the time with the genre known as heavy metal, which combined macho preening with lyrics that often regarded females as sex objects. But heavy metal thrived on the opprobrium of elites. Ticking off feminists brought metal even greater respect from its core audience.

Two decades later black women and cultural critics would raise objections to rap music lyrics and videos, the latter of which invariably depicted young African American ladies in short skirts or short shorts writhing for the camera. Rap culture regarded females in a manner that made the chauvinistic '50s seem like the age of enlightenment. As Nelson George remarks in his history of hip-hop in America, "Rap made slang aimed at women like 'skeezer,' hootchie,' 'chickenhead,' and the ubiquitous 'bitch,' staples of the African-American lexicon. They've become so commonplace that many young women use them freely to attack other women and, even more alarming, to describe themselves."[6] The mind-numbing repetitiveness of "sexy" rap videos should have been reason enough for the industry to alter its product.

It is the nature and character of modern-day liberalism to object publicly to so-called offensive material, despite otherwise championing pop culture in all its manifestations. Certain liberals or liberal groups see no contradiction, inconsistency, or hypocrisy in calling for an outright ban on material they deem to be racist, sexist, homophobic, or anti-Semitic. Even this aspect of liberalism divides along the lines of identity politics: African American leaders protect their constituents from allegedly racist films, books, songs, and TV shows; women's organizations take the lead if the questionable material is considered chauvinistic, and so forth. Liberal special-interest groups direct the fight against offensive material—if the Reverend Al Sharpton declares something or someone racist then that usually suffices for the mainstream media, both because they want to be "good citizens" and because controversy attracts readers, viewers, and listeners.

.   .   .

In the contentious environment of early-twenty-first-century America, right-wing writers, producers, and directors—with rare exception— avoid injecting politics into their creative lives for fear of either retribution from liberals or ridicule from conservatives. As in the case of taxes, sometimes there is the sense that the right wishes popular culture would simply disappear, so great is the hostility to its mere existence. Regarding the "serious" arts, testimonials to the brilliance of Shakespeare and the need to preserve the canon overshadow what often comes out as a kind of reflexive hostility toward any experimentation or attempts to categorize artworks according to the ethnicity/race/sex/sexual preference of their creators.

For their part, libertarians oppose government funding for the arts, not because of any "obscene" works that have been created with taxpayer money, but in the belief that it is an example of big-government overreach. An avowed libertarian once put it to me like this: "Why should government be able to use my money to support the art of its choice?" And in the case of the religious right, it is the end product more than the principle that constitutes the prime source of its objection to the National Endowment for the Arts and similar organizations. Presumably if taxpayer funds routinely supported sculptures that exalted Jesus, paintings that celebrated traditional southern culture, or dance performances that praised the virtues and values of rural life in the United States, the Christian Coalition would change its opinion.

One assumes that it is their own fear, reluctance, or lack of interest that prevents avowed conservatives from writing plays, composing musicals, producing films, recording rap CDs, or creating modernist art. I would love to open the *New York Times* one day and read a review of a new musical that celebrates the marriage of Ronald and Nancy Reagan or an off-Broadway play that looks back fondly at the founding of the *National Review*. Not for any artistic reasons—both of these are probably terrible ideas—but for the sheer novelty of it.

Predictability is the enemy of creativity. I do not envy the theater critics who have to sit through one more play where everything gay is good, everything Republican is bad, and organized religion is the Great Oppressor. If talented artists with a view of politics and society opposed to the tenets of post-'60s liberalism invaded the galleries, theaters, recording studios, and back lots, they could unleash a fertile era of creativity that would rival the great years of 1955–75. The resultant anger and turmoil would blow the top off our stodgy and mind-numbingly predictable culture. Stepping inside a theater might make liberals feel safe, secure, and "right," but it does not do as much for those (of any ideological persuasion) who care passionately about the future of popular culture and the arts.

CHAPTER THIRTEEN

Coming Home?

In an article published in the fall of 2006, the notable historian of early America Edmund S. Morgan wrote: "The word 'liberalism' has undergone many changes of meaning and implication over the years. The political philosophers who invented the word identified it as a belief in the sanctity of individual human beings and the desirability of freeing them from needless governmental controls. In the course of the twentieth century liberalism has been associated less with limiting government than with directing it to the service of social justice and democracy."[1] Morgan's synopsis is accurate as far as it goes; one could also make a convincing argument that late twentieth-century social liberalism—its support for abortion rights, for repealing laws criminalizing homosexual activity, and for same-sex marriage—conforms to the classic desire of liberals to free the individual from "needless" governmental controls. Along with providing a broad overview of the last two hundred years of liberal thought in this country, Morgan implies that liberalism equals change. Liberalism meant one thing in the nineteenth century and something else in the twentieth. Given this historical pattern, the question naturally occurs: What form will American liberalism assume in the twenty-first century? Within the context of *Not Much Left*, which argues that liberalism has been in decline over the past thirty-five years, the question can be rephrased: How can liberals and liberalism reverse the downward trend?

. . .

In the first few days following the 2006 election results, Democrats of all kinds—liberal, moderate, conservative—were ecstatic. Their party had finally won a major national victory, but more than that, they had a tremendous feeling of relief that the United States had been "saved"— a term usually associated with conservatives and evangelical Christians. But the previous three years had seen the spectacular failure of the U.S. occupation of Iraq; a right-wing Congress that placed staying the course with the president above the interests of the country; administration policies regarding torture, the rights of combatants, and domestic surveillance that seemed to be un-American; and massive federal incompetence characterized by both the pathetic response to Hurricane Katrina in 2005 and overall fiscal mismanagement. This combination convinced Democrats that we were headed for a catastrophe like none other. They wondered whether it would come in the form of a right-wing coup, violence in the streets, martial law, financial ruin, or "collapse." This sense of approaching disaster was not limited to paranoids, cynics, kooks, or eternal pessimists.

The takeover of the House and Senate by the Democrats in November 2006 offered the first possibility of a reprieve from doom. Not since Watergate had Democrats been so grateful to the Founding Fathers for the concept of the separation of powers. It was the great hope of many of those who voted for change that a Democratic-led Congress would check, counter, and investigate the administration. Our arrogant and abusive rulers—the president and the vice president in particular—would finally be held accountable for their actions. And it only enhanced Democrats' joyous feelings that the election results dimmed the bright glow that had emanated from the studios of Fox

News for the past several years. The network for real Americans had been betrayed by real Americans, and that was a tough thing for Bill O'Reilly and company to accept.

But euphoria is not the Democrats' style. By the following weekend, many of them were asking variations of this question: What kind of Congress did we get? Liberal? Moderate? Right-of-center? Proabortion? Prolabor? Antiwar? This mood was reflected on the editorial pages of major American newspapers. Writing five days after the election, Michael Tomasky, editor at large of the liberal publication the *American Prospect*, explained that the Democrats "moved to the center and the left at the same time." Tomasky did not come to a definitive conclusion, but at least a center and a left party offered the possibility of a broad-based coalition that could remain in power for many years. He further predicted that any disagreements on social issues—which he correctly identified as marking the liberal/conservative divide within the Democratic Party—would be downplayed over the next two years in the interests of unity and strength. "Racial politics, of course, eventually tore the old Democratic coalition apart. But there's little evidence that abortion or gay marriage will do that today. Among other reasons, there will be no votes in the next two years on any divisive social issues. Why would Democrats, having finally regained control of the legislative calendar, schedule a vote that highlights their divisions?"[2]

An obvious answer is that there was no reason, and they would schedule no vote. But did this mean that groups lobbying on behalf of same-sex marriage or legalized abortion would adhere to this strategy? During the previous years of Republican rule they had no realistic chance of advancing their causes through the legislative process. At best, they could hope to stave off congressional efforts to erode abortion rights or erect further legal and symbolic barriers to gay marriage. But with Democrats now in the majority, there was no longer any good reason for these groups to shelve their agenda or remain satisfied with the status quo.

Proponents of same-sex marriage or abortion rights do not think of their issues as divisive, but as essential expressions of individual freedom and human dignity. What good did it do them for the Democrats to gain control of Congress only to say, "Sorry, but we cannot help you at this time?" And if social-issue liberals decided to go along with the official line for the sake of the party's potential short-term gain, what did that say about their commitment, passion, and idealism? Once again, liberals were being warned to keep out of sight for the sake of the team.

In his recommendation to the victors, Thomas B. Edsall, a former *Washington Post* political reporter and now the holder of the Pulitzer-Moore Chair at Columbia University, was not nearly as sanguine as Michael Tomasky. Writing in the *New York Times* eighteen days after the election, Edsall offered a stern warning to liberals to back off on a variety of fronts or face the consequences of the Republicans regaining political momentum and perhaps control of Congress. The new Congress had not even been sworn in, and Edsall had already identified liberals as the culprits should things go wrong: "When Democrats bend to the will of liberal special interest groups, even in the pursuit of laudable goals, the damage to the party's credibility can be devastating."[3] According to Edsall, it is not bending to the will of special interest groups in general that leads to problems for the Democrats, only liberal special interest groups. You can kowtow if you want, just not to liberals.

This view implies that the 2006 election was actually bad for liberals—the Democratic Party now had that much more to lose by supporting the liberal agenda on economic, social, and foreign issues. Just as in 1972 (not to mention 1980, 1984, 1994, and 2004), liberals would be held responsible for their party's failure in 2008. And just as in 1976, 1992, and 2006, liberals could expect to receive little or no credit for future successes.

It is significant that neither Tomasky nor Edsall suggest that the results of the 2006 election provided liberalism with a rare and long-awaited opportunity for internal reform. During the previous decade, as an embattled minority within an embattled minority, liberals were not in the strongest position for engaging in a constructive and public process of self-criticism and reevaluation. Why provide an apparently invincible enemy—right-wing conservatism—with additional ammunition? Given

the political situation, one could argue for a period of quiet contempla-
tion, despite what many saw as an obvious need for change. But with the
decisive victory of the Democrats, liberals had received the political protection to conduct an unvarnished and open discussion about who they
were, who they are, and most important, what they must do to regain
their prominent place in American politics.

Every congressional and presidential election that has occurred since
1972 has been in a sense about liberalism, whether the results seem to
indicate further decline, or less likely, hope for the future. Due to its historic achievements and proud legacy, liberalism retains a powerful hold
on the American people. Elected officials, pundits, political junkies, and
political scientists regularly check its condition. And as I have noted
throughout the book, even when weak, liberals are still watched warily
by conservatives for any signs of renewal. They know that a resurgent
liberalism poses a huge threat to their power. For the American right,
there must never be a recurrence of 1964.

·   ·   ·

Going into 2008, U.S. voters are confronted with several doomsday sce-
narios: global warming, the clash of civilizations, violence and anarchy in
Iraq, nuclear war with North Korea and Iran. As if these were not
sufficiently frightening, there was also the prospect of a mini-apocalypse
in the form of endless increases in the price of gasoline and the total collapse of the health-care system. When confronted with the real possibility of the end of the world, or at least life as we know it, human beings
tend to find solace in either organized religion, totalitarianism, or a kind
of easygoing denial. Discussing global warming, for example, I have
heard intelligent people say that they are not going to worry about it
because the true impact will be felt "after I am dead." Such remarks are
offered partly in jest, but the implications are appalling. The living
bequeath the nightmare of environmental catastrophe to the next generations. And it is all because we were not sufficiently motivated to take
action when there was still hope.

As noted throughout this book, one of the hallmarks of twentieth-century liberalism is that it finds its strength during national crises: the Great Depression, the post–World War II movements on behalf of the civil rights of black people, women, Latinos, and homosexuals, and the war in Vietnam. These are times that *require* new ideas and actions, both of which liberals are eager to provide. Conversely, conservatives shine—and win—when liberalism is in crisis.

Looking back, the problems and solutions confronting liberalism and American society in the 1960s and 1970s were clear. Abolish enforced segregation, provide minorities and women with the same opportunities as white males, expand the definition of civil rights to include sexual preference, and bring our troops home from Southeast Asia. We inhabit a world in which legal segregation has been eliminated, women and minorities are afforded more opportunities in business and public life, same-sex relationships have been normalized, and the troops are home from Southeast Asia. For liberals, progressives, centrists, or moderate Republicans, the hard work undertaken in the 1960s and 1970s was clearly worth it. In the political sense, liberals from that era fulfilled their responsibility as human beings to leave behind something better for the next generation.

It is not meant to minimize the accomplishments of those liberals to observe that compared to solving global warming, abolishing Jim Crow laws was easy. On the eve of the 2008 presidential election, there is plenty of evidence to strongly suggest that global warming is more than a scare tactic of anticapitalists. Only the Bush administration and its friends in industry—especially the oil companies—claim to doubt that global warming is real, and that the consequences of staying the course would be catastrophic. This administration's tepid response to global warming reminds me of Herbert Hoover's presidency during the early stages of the Great Depression.

But given its weakened state, liberalism is not in the best position to develop and implement the complex and painful strategies necessary to combat this threat. By some estimates, it will cost *six hundred billion dol-*

lars worldwide to effectively confront global warming. In the short term, a full-scale attack on global warming could rattle financial markets from New York to Beijing. For the sake of Planet Earth, would liberals be willing to absorb the criticism of conservatives and conservative Democrats if their obsession with this "problem" led to a rupture in the global economy?

Since the United States is by far the biggest contributor to the environmental breakdown that has led to global warming, it is for both moral and practical reasons that the nation must lead the way in countering its effects. But the federal government cannot acquire the necessary revenue to undertake this effort without—and here comes the part that frightens politically ambitious Democrats—raising taxes. Not just raising taxes on the superrich, but raising them on the merely rich and probably the middle class as well. Similar to 1964–66, this is one of those periods in U.S. history when the "tax and spend liberals" would seem to be in the right. But at a time when society is consumed by greed and self-indulgence, and unabashed liberals are scarce, who is willing to say what must be said, and do what must be done?

On global warming, liberals and progressives are defined as the people that are simply willing to acknowledge it is a real phenomenon. By contrast, conservatives think the whole thing is an environmentalist plot. Now that there is a growing consensus that the gloomy enviros might have a point, trading in your SUV for a model that gets better gas mileage is no longer considered a sufficient response. The candidates in 2008 who seriously propose and successfully implement the painful steps needed to combat global warming and confront the powerful institutions that contribute to it will be the leading liberals of the next generation—whether or not they choose to claim that title.

· · ·

Any press secretary based in Washington, DC, will tell you that Friday is typically a slow news day. If you have something embarrassing or controversial to report, best to send out a release late Friday afternoon, when every journalist and editor has gone home or left town. By this reckoning, Friday, March 23, 2007, was a rare day in the history of the United States. Confident that even socially active members of the Fourth Estate would put their plans on hold, Democrats chose this particular Friday to schedule a historic vote in the House of Representatives on funding for the war in Iraq. By a margin of 218 to 212, the House approved a measure that combined an additional one hundred billion dollars for military operations in Iraq with a requirement that nearly all U.S. combat troops leave the country by 2008. Only fourteen Democrats voted against the bill, and only two Republicans voted in favor of it. For the first time since the 1970s and Vietnam, Congress was declaring its intention to manage the war effort. Predictably, President Bush was furious. He regarded the vote as both a humiliating rejection of his Iraq policy (which it was) and an effort to limit his war-making authority (which it also was). Not as clear was the significance of this vote—and a similar measure approved a few days later in the Senate—for the future of liberalism.

Ten days before the vote, the *Los Angeles Times* ran a front-page story about three California congresswomen whose views on the war were now being taken very seriously by the leadership in the House. "Liberal lawmakers get place at the table," was the headline that ran above the jump. The piece profiled representatives Barbara Lee, Maxine Waters, and Lynn Woolsey, who had each endorsed a stronger measure that called for U.S. troops out of Iraq by the end of 2007. Despite pleas by Speaker Nancy Pelosi to support the bill, in the end the trio voted no.

Although the Democrats captured the House in 2006, in large measure due to their criticisms of the president's handling of the war in Iraq, these three liberals remained in the minority. A "place at the table" did not translate into official congressional policy. In the best tradition of George McGovern, Lee, Waters, and Woolsey wanted U.S. combat troops home now, and not later. They did not prevail and had to settle for the respect of their Democratic colleagues. Given what liberals had been through in the past two decades, however, even mere recognition was appreciated. As the article continued, "California's leading anti-war lawmakers admit to some satisfaction that their proposals—once mocked as far-out schemes from the nation's left coast—have become the mainstream."[4]

Among the top three early contenders for the 2008 Democratic presidential nomination, Illinois senator Barack Obama held the liberal view on the Iraq war: opposed from the beginning. In response, Obama's main competitors, Hillary Clinton and John Edwards, noted that Obama was not in the Senate in 2002, when the vote was taken to authorize support for the war. Obama said he would have cast a no vote, as opposed to Clinton and Edwards, both of whom supported Bush. Edwards later apologized for the vote, while Clinton expressed regrets but no apology. Her refusal to do so became a major issue in 2007, and gave new meaning to the term "liberal apologist," which heretofore had been considered an insult. Senator Clinton received considerable criticism from within her own party for not apologizing for her vote, which would have been the proper thing for a liberal to do.

As the situation in Iraq deteriorated, a growing number of critics drew comparisons between this war and Vietnam. In many of these stories, the word *quagmire* featured prominently. Just as in the days of General Westmoreland, the United States was stuck, with no plan for victory. For the Left, withdrawing (from Vietnam and Iraq) was the only viable solution. In both wars, the American public was told that victory was just around the corner. When it didn't arrive, the solution for both LBJ and Bush was to send more troops. How many more was a subject of fierce debate among hawks, which did not inspire confidence that either plan had any chance of succeeding.

In terms of the history of liberalism, there are differences between the two wars. In Vietnam, the U.S. increased its involvement incrementally for several years, until a massive buildup of troops in the spring of 1965. Before then, it would have been somewhat misleading to describe Vietnam as a war. There was an inadequate amount of shooting and bombing, and an insufficient number of wounded and dead on the U.S.

side. Pre-1965, Vietnam was akin to an incursion or, in the language of that time, a police action. It is difficult to mobilize a viable peace movement in opposition to an incursion. Left-wing intellectuals might be paying attention, as well as the publications to which they subscribe, but not so much the masses, even those of a liberal bent. And liberals in the early 1960s were focused more on the American South than on South Vietnam. Activists, like armies, are not inclined to fight two-front wars.

The U.S. involvement in Iraq unfolded under different circumstances. The Bush administration told one big lie (Saddam Hussein possessed weapons of mass destruction) and another almost as big (Saddam had ties to the 9/11 plotters) to get the political and popular backing for war, but it was no secret that war was their intention regardless. Clinton, Edwards, and the other members of the U.S. Senate and House knew full well the implications of their vote in 2002.

Had liberals not been in retreat, demoralized, or missing during the first term of the Bush presidency, they may have been able to mount the kind of peace movement that gets noticed by even Democratic senators. The massive demonstrations in the United States that occurred just prior to the beginning of the invasion in March 2003 were much too late to change history. They also lacked focus and strong leaders; there is no modern-day equivalent of Tom Hayden, David Dellinger, or Dr. Benjamin Spock.

A few months later, a beaming Bush addressed his fellow Americans in front of a huge banner that read "Mission Accomplished." The media did not raise many objections at the time to either the propriety or veracity of that stage-managed event. Even liberals, though disgusted by the triumphal pose of a president they already detested, signaled by their quiescence a grudging acknowledgment that victory was near. Within a few months, however, it was obvious that the only thing "accomplished" was the descent of Iraq into a violent, anarchic hell. In response to the news from the battlefront, the presidential candidacy of Howard Dean—the Eugene McCarthy of the 2004 campaign—began its swift and, in the view of many experts, wholly unexpected rise.

Part of the reason for the experts' failure to anticipate Dean's success was the absence in the summer and fall of 2003 of a strong movement for peace. Unlike in 1968, when McCarthy and Robert Kennedy ran for president on the strength of obvious and growing discontent with the war in Vietnam, Dean's candidacy served as the catalyst for people opposed to the invasion of Iraq to make their voices heard. Dean was creating a constituency for his antiwar politics, rather than stepping to the front of an already long line.

It did not take long for right-wing and neoconservative commentators to identify Dean as the antiwar liberal among the Democratic contenders, and they drew the predictable comparisons with McGovern in 1972. Quite possibly this incessant ridiculing of Dean had an impact on mainstream Democratic voters, who were desperate to see Bush defeated in November 2004. If history was any guide, nominating another McGovern would be tantamount to handing the election to the president. Once this view gained currency, it was difficult to counter. Antiwar liberals, who were still in the process of coalescing around Dean, lacked the strength and the organization of the '72 McGovern team, which as we have seen spent more than a year preparing for the primaries.

By early 2004, Democratic voters had begun to shift from Dean to the candidacies of John Kerry, John Edwards, and, to an extent, Wesley Clark, each of whom appeared to be more acceptable to the masses than the Vermont governor. The eventual nominee, Kerry, had voted in favor of the war, though he grappled with second thoughts throughout the campaign against Bush. The president subsequently defeated Kerry, in large part by asking voters if they wanted to turn the country over to some confused Democrat while U.S. troops were engaged in combat? Kerry harmed his campaign also by running *from* liberalism, despite the importance of national security—traditionally Republicans' strongest issue—in the 2004 race. By putting a label on his views from the start, Kerry would have at least spared himself the tortuous verbal maneuvers required to fend off or deflect the opposition's charge that he was a liberal.

The results of the 2004 election were for liberals—and Democrats generally—the lowest of the low points that had steadily accumulated since 1972. Nixon's landslide, Reagan's back-to-back victories, and the Republican takeover of the House in 1994 were not as depressing as the country's decision to bring back Bush. The bitter result engendered finger-pointing within the Democratic family: gays should not have pushed gay marriage; our side must heed the feelings of people of faith, as well as attend church more often; and Cold War liberalism deserves another chance.

Each of these options remains relevant for 2008. Despite Iraq, global warming, and record-breaking gas prices, one cannot discount the possibility that same-sex marriage, for example, will again rank disproportionately high on the list of voter concerns. After all, it is an issue that involves love, sex, tradition, organized religion, family, friends, and neighbors, and evokes strong emotions from people of all backgrounds. With this in mind, the current Republican candidates for president— with the exception of Rudy Giuliani—have sought to claim the unofficial title of America's number-one social conservative. The 2008 GOP presidential field would not be so preoccupied with gay marriage and abortion unless it remained enamored of the political advantages that would accrue from defining Democrats as indifferent to Christian morality and hostile to traditional values. Since Reagan, any Republican candidate's plan for capturing the presidency has had to include receiving the overwhelming support of millions of evangelical voters.

However, on the subject of the war, with the exception of Arizona senator John McCain, the 2008 Republican hopefuls were not as forthright. They harshly criticized the Democratic-led Congress for voting to set a specific date for the troops to withdraw but, other than backing the president's decision in early 2007 to send 21,000 additional troops to Iraq and offering variations on the theme that "we cannot afford to lose," did not offer their own detailed plans for victory. In contrast to 1968, when Democratic candidates broke with their president over Vietnam, none of the current Republican contenders for the White House, except

Ron Paul, openly opposed the Bush-Cheney invasion of Iraq. Other than an all-purpose isolationism, which tends to dissipate once troops are on the ground in a foreign country, modern American politics apparently does not allow for a politician to be both a proud conservative and against a particular war. The Republican candidates in 2008 could only pray that Bush would figure out a strategy for winning the war—and fast.

But the results of the 2006 midterm elections demonstrated the political perils Republicans now faced regarding the war. The need to immediately change course in Iraq united a disparate group of Democratic candidates, incumbents and challengers. They put aside substantial differences on abortion, trade, immigration, and gun control to hammer home to voters the message that Bush lied to get the United States into a war that we cannot win. For the first time, Democrats were the beneficiaries of the fallout from 9/11. In the 2002 midterm elections and the 2004 presidential race, Republicans had gained the advantage by arguing that the Democrats were incapable of protecting the nation from terrorists. But the war in Iraq, which was justified by the administration because of the attack on America, transformed a majority of the people who went to the polls on November 7, 2006, into advocates for peace, but not necessarily at any price.

Just as with Vietnam in 1972, the public had decided that bringing the troops home was more important than winning. The difference is that President Nixon had for a couple of years been decreasing the number of combat forces in Vietnam, while President Bush was preparing to do just the opposite in Iraq. Feeling invincible ever since the Florida recount went his way, Bush and company did not believe that their side could ever lose, in the political arena or on the battlefield. The president had repeatedly campaigned in 2004 on the message that "I mean what I say." Even some Democrats privately admired his consistency, especially in contrast with leaders in their own party. But the president's refusal to make any meaningful concessions on Iraq may well have cost Republicans control of Congress, and guaranteed that the next two years would be hell for his administration.

The 2006 election marked the return of antiwar liberalism to mainstream electoral politics in the United States. This time there were no peace signs, huge demonstrations chronicled by Norman Mailer, or sit-ins at campus ROTC buildings. But if you take away the romantic images, the message voters sent in 2006 is precisely the message (Democratic) voters sent in 1972 when they backed McGovern during the primary: it is time for our troops to come home. You do not need the presence of a thriving counterculture to convince a majority of voters that a particular war is bad. Beginning in the second half of the 1960s, the militancy of the antiwar movement—protestors shouting obscenities at the police, demonstrations that turned violent—combined with a perception that the New Left was anti-American made it much more difficult for the middle class to support openly an immediate withdrawal from Vietnam. They preferred instead Nixon's gradualist strategy of "Peace with Honor."

But in 2006–8, the antiwar position is almost exclusively subsumed within the familiar and safe confines of electoral politics. The most relentless advocate for peace is a clean-cut, clean-living congressman from Ohio named Dennis Kucinich. Compared with forty years ago, you can live on a neat and tidy street in suburbia and openly oppose this war without worrying so much about what the neighbors will think.

Since liberalism apparently remains unpopular, however, no one has come forward to claim this latest antiwar movement in liberalism's name. The beneficiaries of the prevailing mood, particularly the Democratic Party's main presidential contenders for 2008, are loath to affix the word *liberal* to their own views. But if opposition to the Iraq war serves as the catalyst for a major reassessment of American foreign policy in the Middle East and elsewhere, then it will invariably be stamped with a label, whether the architects of this policy choose one or not.

The dilemma for Clinton, Edwards, Obama, and others is how to campaign against U.S. involvement in Iraq without being demonized by resurgent Cold War liberals and the entire Republican Party for selling out America's interests around the world. This is the false charge that helped to bring down McGovern and continues to haunt any Democrat whose views on international relations recall his legacy. But eventually the Democrats running for president in 2008 will have to address the larger questions regarding America's role in the world. The reaction against Bush is not only caused by Iraq, but also by the perception of American arrogance and ignorance regarding Europe, China, Latin America, and Africa. In the long run, "U.S. out of Iraq" will not be enough to satisfy many voters. The Democratic candidates will be compelled to offer comprehensive positions on foreign policy, national defense, and international terrorism. Whether the candidates' views on foreign policy will be considered representative of Cold War liberalism, liberalism, progressivism, centrism, or some other ideological category is an essential question for the both the campaign of 2008 and the future of liberalism in the United States. Will these antiwar Democrats get the chance that was denied McGovern to implement a new direction for the country?

. . .

On February 11, 2007, the *New York Times* ran this headline over a front-page story about the latest Democrat to declare his candidacy for president in 2008: "Obama Formally Enters Presidential Race With Call for Generational Change." A month later the *New York Observer,* reporting on a speech by the Illinois senator at an event commemorating the forty-second anniversary of the famous civil rights march in Selma, Alabama, carried this subhead: "Barack Rhetoric in Selma Suggests J.F.K. as Senator Drives Church Crowd Crazy." The juxtaposition of these articles points out the dilemma facing younger Democrats such as Barack Obama (born in 1961): Do they truly embody a new politics or a continuation of 1960s liberalism? Consider this related question: Will the media, which typically view liberalism through the defining struggles of the 1960s, either recognize or acknowledge a new version if it comes along?

In his 2006 book *The Audacity of Hope,* Obama epitomizes the ambivalence that people born either at the end of or after the baby-boomer years (1946–64) feel toward the sixties. Like people in their early twenties today who think that the Beatles or Led Zeppelin are the greatest rock bands of all time, Obama expresses some misgiving that he was not old enough to "enjoy" the decade in real time. It is one thing to commemorate the Selma march and another to have participated.

As a teenager, Obama was attracted (not surprisingly) to the post-Selma atmosphere of open rebellion that defined the later part of the decade: Black Panthers, SDS, sex, drugs, and acid rock. "If I had no immediate reasons to pursue revolution, I decided nevertheless that in style and attitude, I, too, could be a rebel, unconstrained by the received wisdom of the over-thirty crowd."[5] To this day the 1960s represent the essence of nonconformity, a symbol of both the past and the future for young people wishing to break away from their elders and create a "self." Youth culture in the early twenty-first century is an uneasy blend of a longing to have attended college forty years ago with an aggressive embrace of new technology that befuddles one's parents and grandparents. It is typified by the teen who downloads seventy-five Beatles songs from iTunes.

But at some point a person must come to terms with the times in which he lives. This is especially the case with an ambitious leader such as Barack Obama, who cannot expect to reach his political goals by simply trading on nostalgia. Even those who relate to his rhetoric and sense of history will eventually insist that he catch up to the present. In his book the senator is both smart and honest enough to create some distance between his personal journey and events that he experienced only vicariously. After all, Obama was just nineteen when Ronald Reagan was first elected president. The vast majority of his adult life has been spent during a period of hard-right dominance in U.S. politics. As opposed to liberals in their late fifties and older, Obama does not consider it an aberration that leaders such as Reagan, Newt Gingrich, or George W. Bush would appeal to many Americans. He may not like it, but he understands it: "Nevertheless, by promising to side with those who worked hard, obeyed the law, cared for their families, and loved their country, Reagan offered Americans a sense of a common purpose that liberals seemed no longer able to muster."[6] The editors of the *National Review* could not have said it any better.

Obama is neither a Reagan Democrat nor, it would appear by the above passage, an anti-Reagan Democrat. Although he does not come out and say it, one gets the sense that Obama wants to be the next choice for those who work hard, obey the law, care for their families, and love their country. After all, there is no inherent reason why people who fit these criteria must vote Republican. But Obama will need to find a way to appeal to them in decidedly non-Reaganesque terms. At the end of the day, he is still a member of the Democratic Party.

If Obama was the liberal candidate on the war, John Edwards was the liberal candidate on domestic issues. At many campaign appearances, the North Carolina senator touted his detailed plan to provide health coverage for all Americans—an idea that Harry Truman first embraced sixty years earlier. Edwards acknowledged that paying for his proposal would require raising taxes, but he insisted on taxing only the rich. Yet with millions uninsured and millions more paying ever-higher premiums, Edwards might well have found an issue that matters more to more Americans than bringing the troops home from Iraq by mid-2008.

If Edwards were able to secure his party's 2008 nomination, we know that his plan for universal health coverage would be viciously attacked, just as Republicans and the health-care industry went after Hillary Clinton's plan in 1993–94. To this day many experts argue that the humiliating collapse of that plan was among the key factors in the Newt Gingrich–led takeover of the House. In the months following the '94 elections, I spoke with angry Democratic members of the House who argued that Bill Clinton should have tackled welfare reform early in his administration and health care later down the line—if ever. Never again in Clinton's two terms in office did his administration offer a plan to reform the health-care system.

While universal health care harked back to the liberal agenda of the late 1940s, another major component of Edwards's 2008 platform, ending poverty in the United States, recalled the early years of the Johnson administration. The senator even occasionally used the Great Society phrase "War on Poverty" in outlining his plans to audiences around the country. Had Edwards run for president in 2000, he would not have dared to address this issue in such a forthright manner. Along with the Republicans, DLC Democrats who drove the party's economic policies would have harshly criticized his dream of eliminating poverty as archaic, antigrowth, impossible to achieve, and politically foolish. But after nearly eight years of an administration that blatantly favored the rich, and with the results of the 2006 midterm elections offering at least a tacit endorsement of economic liberalism, Edwards may well have chosen to emphasize an issue that resonates with voters in 2008.

. . .

The 2008 Edwards campaign is a vivid reminder that American liberalism, despite its current slump, has always been a work in progress. Back when Michael Dukakis was a student at Swarthmore, liberals discussed how the federal government should provide health coverage for all Americans. Back when Rick Tuttle was an undergraduate at Wesleyan, liberals were advocating an end to hunger and poverty in the United States. Even some of the historic liberal crusades of the 1960s represented a continuation of efforts to expand progress and freedoms that had originated long before. For example, the civil rights movement sought to achieve for black people what was supposed to have been secured in the decade after the Civil War. It was not until the shift to affirmative action, quotas, and Afro-American studies programs—plus the rise of a more militant and younger group of leaders in the black community—that racial politics assumed its uniquely "sixties" character. The antipathy that neoconservatives and other disaffected or former Democrats have felt toward domestic liberalism since the death of Martin Luther King is the result of bitter disagreements over these issues.

The environmental movement also had its antecedents in the turn of the century (if not before), with the conservationist policies of President Theodore Roosevelt and the actions and words of naturalists such as John Muir. The counterculture no more discovered the need to preserve America's natural beauty than it discovered sex. Of course, in the six decades since Teddy Roosevelt was in the White House, America had emerged as the world's biggest industrial power and, not coincidentally, the world's biggest polluter. It was therefore not surprising that post-'6os environmentalists spoke in grand terms about saving Planet Earth; cleaning up the air above America would also make it easier for people to breathe in other countries. In the case of global warming, which had not yet been officially acknowledged during the 1960s and 1970s, the negative effects of U.S. energy consumption on the rest of the world is disputed by only a stubborn and vocal minority.

Nearly fifty years prior to the founding of the National Organization for Women (NOW) in 1966, the Nineteenth Amendment to the United States Constitution granted women the right to vote. Looking at the ambitious scope of political activity by women for women in the 1920s makes it evident that here, too, women's liberation and feminism came out of a rich tradition. Indeed, the modern character of the women's movement during the 1920s is striking. As the historian David Kennedy wrote in *Freedom from Fear:* "The Equal Rights Amendment, first proposed by Alice Paul of the National Women's Party in 1923, sought to guarantee full social and economic participation to women. An organization movement for birth control, founded by Margaret Sanger in 1921 as the American Birth Control League, heralded a growing feminine focus on reproductive control and erotic liberation."[7] The key difference between the two eras is the emphasis on abortion rights, which, as was noted earlier, triggered a backlash that helped to launch the religious right as a major force in U.S. politics.

Only the gay rights movement that began in the late 1960s does not have any obvious predecessors. *We Are Everywhere: A Historical Sourcebook of Gay and Lesbian Politics* devotes 150 pages to the period before the 1970s and nearly five hundred pages to 1970 through 1995. The symbol of the closet plays a role in the late arrival of homosexuals to American liberalism: gay men and women could choose to hide their true sexual selves rather than suffer insults, discrimination, harassment from the authorities, and perhaps violence. But in the political and social environment of the late 1960s and 1970s, homosexuals felt increasingly free to publicly declare their sexuality. By the time I started working at a suburban California Tower Records store in 1978, the gay employees were as open about their desires and as willing to share details of their wild weekends as the straight ones. I can't imagine it would have been like this even five years earlier.

Nonetheless, 2009 will mark the fortieth anniversary of the Stonewall Riot, which is generally recognized as the catalyst for the gay rights movement. The novelty has long since worn off. Since Stonewall, millions of Americans have grown up in a world where being gay or bisexual is no big deal. The efforts by some religious groups to "change" a person from gay to straight are widely viewed as either bizarre or cruel. While one must always offer the caveat that there is more work to be done, it seems to me that a gays in the United States have never had it so good. Like the civil rights movement and feminism, the gay rights movement must be regarded as a success.

. . .

"We have nothing to fear but fear itself." Franklin Roosevelt's famous words could also apply to liberals during the first decade of the twenty-first century. Liberals have nothing to fear but fear itself—and, apparently, losing elections. Throughout this book I have attempted to demonstrate that liberals are primarily responsible for liberalism's steady decline since the early 1970s. This process began with the defeat of George McGovern in 1972, when liberals started backpedaling, and continued through the tempered liberalism of the 1976 Carter campaign; the founding of the Democratic Leadership Council in the mid-1980s; the "L-word" fiasco of 1988; and the open retreat from liberalism by Democratic candidates during the 1990s and the first half of the 2000s. The mixed messages of post-1960s liberalism—exemplified by political correctness and the confusing and contradictory nature of identity politics—contributed to this bleak situation. Many old-line liberals were appalled by the repeated tendency of various groups to claim the role of victim despite the obvious and historic gains in their political and social status.

In the meantime, conservatives took full advantage of the opposition's self-doubt and incessant agonizing. Beginning with Reagan, attacks by the right on liberalism's failures—real or imagined—were all the more effective because very few liberals were willing to offer a forceful counterargument. It was as if they conceded that Reagan had captured the moment. By the end of Reagan's first term as president, the idea of a "third way"—between Reagan on the one hand and 1960s liberalism on the other—looked increasingly attractive to power-hungry Democrats in their thirties and forties. The founding of the DLC in 1985 was one important consequence of this new approach to the left/right divide.

But today liberalism has its best opportunity in four decades to claim a prominent place within American politics. One of the indicators is the reemergence of George McGovern. During a single week in April 2007 he was profiled in *Rolling Stone*, speaking out about the significance of his 1972 presidential campaign in ending American involvement in Vietnam, and wrote an op-ed piece in the *Los Angeles Times* responding to attacks on that same campaign from Vice President Dick Cheney: "He [Cheney] also said that the McGovern way is to surrender in Iraq and leave the U.S. exposed to new dangers. The truth is that I oppose the Iraq war, just as I opposed the Vietnam War, because these two conflicts have diminished our standing in the world and our national security."[8] McGovern has lived long enough—he was eighty-four in the spring of 2007—to witness the beginning of a turnaround in his own political standing with fellow Democrats. As a result, I expect we are going to hear more people in the party saying "McGovern got it right" over the next few years. The unwritten rule that Democratic presidential contender must never appear on the same platform as McGovern, at least in the midst of the campaign, might well be officially retired. A new generation is getting the chance to learn the truth about McGovern's political legacy as the country heads toward November 2008.

As McGovern's fortunes go, so do liberalism's. Given that the end of the McGovern campaign marked the beginning of a three-decade cycle in which liberalism went into a steady decline, is the restoration of his good name a sign that liberal politics will soon be on the rise? As we have seen throughout this book, a significant component of liberalism's decline is the calculated refusal of leading Democrats since the 1980s to acknowledge liberalism's relevance to their own political histories. Yet this did not stop the opposition from making the connection, which had the unfortunate but not unexpected consequence of exaggerating liberalism's failings for younger voters who did not know any better.

The recovery of liberalism won't happen in a single election cycle. An apparatus is in place—Fox News, talk radio, politically engaged fundamentalist ministers, right-wing elected officials who adore Reagan—that will continue to perpetuate the wild charges about what liberalism has done to America since the 1960s. Liberalism has shown a historic embrace of freedom and progress and an ability to lead the country during periods of anxiety and turmoil. I believe that a growing number of voters will recognize that liberalism offers the best hope for the future.

Epilogue

Who Are You?

In the late summer of 2006, the Democratic nominee for U.S. senate from Ohio, Congressman Sherrod Brown, met with a small group of confirmed and possible supporters at a law office in downtown Los Angeles. Over a lunch of Subway sandwiches, chips, bottled water, and four different kinds of cookies, Brown outlined his strategy for defeating the incumbent, Republican Mike DeWine. Accompanied by his wife, Connie Schultz, a Pulitzer Prize–winning columnist for the *Cleveland Plain-Dealer* (and on leave for eight months to write a book about the campaign), Brown talked about raising the minimum wage, the friendly reception oil companies receive in Washington, the conduct of the Iraq war, and the Republican right's demagoguery on social and national security issues. When I asked him to describe his ideology, Brown answered "progressive." A follow-up question as to why he didn't say "liberal" elicited the response that liberalism is fine—as far as it goes. Progressives and liberals agree on many ideas, explained the congressman, but it is only the former who will combine these ideas with an aggressive, confrontational approach that can actually make a difference.

In a subsequent e-mail, Brown, who was elected by a wide margin, elaborated on his earlier point: "Liberals support generous government programs like LIHEAP [home heating and cooling assistance for the

elderly]. Progressives support LIHEAP but also fight oil and gas industry price gouging. Similarly, liberals want an adequate prescription drug
benefit (not the privatized, Part D written by the pharmaceutical companies). Progressives, every day, on the other hand, challenge the drug
companies' pricing practices."

He ended: "Liberals and progressives alike want to help people.
Progressives are more likely to go after and fix the root cause." Brown's
definition implies that the progressives of today are not unlike the liberals of yesterday: confident, robust, and fearless.

In 2005, voters elected Antonio Villaraigosa as mayor of Los Angeles
by a wide margin. He was the first Latino to hold the position in over a
century. The musical lineup at his election-night victory party, which
drew thousands to an outdoor venue, reflected the wide-ranging (in
terms of ethnicity and class) coalition that supported his campaign: a
jazz ensemble, a solo opera singer, a Jewish musical group, a salsa band,
and mariachis. Villaraigosa went into office tremendously popular in
neighborhoods across one of the most ethnically diverse cities in the
world. You saw his picture prominently displayed in Persian restaurants,
Korean-owned grocery stores, Little Armenia, and historic African
American communities.

As a onetime Chicano activist, labor organizer, and member of the
ACLU, Villaraigosa (born in 1953) has the classic liberal pedigree of his
generation. Though elected in a city that is friendly to liberalism, his
landslide victory a mere seven months after the reelection of George W.
Bush was a miracle to many people on the left. Their side never won
anymore. But with Villaraigosa's huge victory, maybe liberals were not
finished yet.

Then again, it was only one election. Asked to describe his own political philosophy, the mayor, on the occasion of his first anniversary in
office, answered with the phrase "proud progressive," which sounded
suspiciously like a concoction created as a poll-tested replacement for
something else, that is, the "L-word." A *proud progressive*—I had never
heard the term before—is someone whose beliefs, opinions, and policies

are obscure and suspicious. Why shouldn't a progressive be proud? It would have been historic for Villaraigosa to have called himself a "proud liberal," and the message would have been heard across the country proclaiming him one Democratic officeholder who would not be intimidated by liberal-bashers—unlike John Kerry. In reality, Villaraigosa is a tremendously ambitious politician with barely concealed dreams of someday moving on to Sacramento and maybe Washington, DC. To have "proud liberal" or even just "liberal" on his resume might get in the way of reaching those goals—or so it would appear. Yet if an elected official of Villaraigosa's popularity and celebrity will not admit to being a liberal, what hope is there for a revival of liberalism? How many more landslide victories will be necessary before the situation changes?

. . .

In addition to charting the decline of liberalism as an inspiring force, a fount of good new ideas, and an advantage at the ballot box, *Not Much Left* has discussed the consequences of this phenomenon for American politics as a whole. To put it bluntly: Why does the decline of liberalism matter? What does it mean for all of us, the left, the right, and the center, that so many liberals have taken early retirement, gone into hiding, or denied their political legacies? Consider the following three points:

First, serious political commentators, many voters, and some oddballs too, routinely argue that American politics functions as a one-party system. According to this view, there is no significant difference between the Democrats and Republicans, and you can forget about viable third or fourth parties. Elected officials with an "R" or a "D" by their names are captive to special interests, concerned only with staying in power, moneygrubbing, and fiercely protective of the political and financial establishments. Disagreements over ideology or issues, and partisan bickering, are a mere sideshow to this grim reality.

I do not agree with this theory, although there are times when it has a kind of perverse logic. In a representative democracy, politicians are alternately solicitous of and terrified by "the people," who, after all, control their fate. Constant anxiety leads to public acts that make sense only to those who derive their living in and from politics. We see it when Illinois-born Hillary Clinton claims to have been a lifelong New York Yankees fan; when Al and Tipper Gore kiss at campaign rallies as if they were auditioning for a Hollywood love story; and when Republicans who fled military service channel John Wayne or Clint Eastwood. There is a "political personality"—regardless of affiliation—that contrasts with what most of us would consider normal behavior for people of a certain age. But this should not be confused with the existence of a one-party system.

Nevertheless, the decline of liberalism has all but eliminated a viable intellectual and political challenge to post-Reagan conservatism. You cannot expect wisdom and insight to emerge from a debate between aggressive conservatives and timid liberals. Nothing in the contemporary political world resembles, for example, the marvelously entertaining clashes between John Kenneth Galbraith and William F. Buckley in the 1960s and 1970s.

Blustering, anti-intellectual, right-wing media stars have dominated the debate today because liberals are confused, embarrassed, and ashamed. They exhibit little strength or resolve to resist the pummeling of political bullies. Archconservatives in Congress and the White House get away with it because liberals past and present are reluctant to defend liberalism's honor and legacy. Dismayed by this political equivalent of a "missile gap," liberals have lowered their expectations, demanding neither vengeance nor retribution, but only occasional satisfaction. When "they" say something outrageous or merely disagreeable, "we" should respond with something outrageous or agreeable. Isn't that the way American politics is supposed to work?

Second, the younger generation, whose only knowledge of the civil rights and antiwar movements, women's liberation, and ecological activism is from books, articles, and the History Channel might wonder why old-timers act so resentful and nervous when they are called liberals. How can *that* generation revel in the accomplishments of the '60s and at the same time create a distance from the ideology that helped to make those accomplishments possible? Either the '60s were not that great or liberalism is a failed belief system.

The Clintons, Kerry, and others whose politics were formed in the 1960s have never conducted an honest and thorough examination or reexamination of the past, present, and future of liberalism. Through the auspices of the Democratic Leadership Council, Bill Clinton, starting in the mid-1980s, redefined liberalism at the margins. He was mainly concerned with the perception that liberals are hostile to business and enamored of government giveaways. But the essence of liberalism, including such fundamental questions as what liberals believe today, how liberals define freedom, and consistencies or inconsistencies between social and economic liberalism, has not been adequately addressed. How could it be addressed when liberals have dropped the word *liberalism* from their vocabularies? You cannot hold a summit on liberalism without first acknowledging its existence.

Third, the absence of robust liberalism from contemporary politics diminishes the viable options for left-leaning college students. Veterans of the New Left and the liberal causes of the 1960s and early 1970s often lament that kids today just do not possess the political acumen, ambition, and spirit as they and their friends did forty years ago. You hear this gripe especially often when aging feminists talk about younger women, whom they regard as insufficiently grateful for the sacrifices made on their behalf way back when.

But how many viable choices do "kids" today really have? With communism thoroughly discredited, socialism on the run, and liberalism in crisis, what are twenty-year-olds supposed to do, where are they supposed to go? One answer would be to the "other" side. In the 1980s, Reagan garnered considerable support from students in part because he and his movement represented the true revolutionary force of the time. Never underestimate the role of sheer excitement in determining the politics of young people. Middle-aged and senior Democrats were appalled that a young person could have anything other than contempt for Reagan. But they missed the point. Reagan was the guy that your '60s-loving, comfortably liberal parents, aunts, and uncles despised. That was good enough.

Another answer would be for young activists to break with "old" liberalism and in effect create a new liberalism. Start a newer left. This would pose a grave challenge to the editorial staff of the *Nation* magazine and other remaining guardians of the liberal-progressive tradition in the United States, garnering further support for reform, and not only from people in their teens and twenties. Whether the new version requires a return to First Principles or a declaration of the Beginning of History would be one of the primary issues to consider. In 1962, Tom Hayden and fellow authors wrote the "Port Huron Statement," which is either condemned or credited with creating a framework for left-wing campus politics over the next decade. Perhaps a twenty-first-century equivalent will galvanize a new generation of liberals, people who entered the world when either Reagan or George H. W. Bush served as president.

NOTES

INTRODUCTION

1. Noam M. Levey, "Congress Sets Terms of Iraq Exit," *Los Angeles Times,* April 27, 2007.

2. Max Lerner, *America as Civilization* (New York: Simon and Schuster, 1957), 731.

3. George McGovern, *The Essential America: Our Founders and the Liberal Tradition* (New York: Simon and Schuster, 2004), 74.

CHAPTER ONE. IN LOCKE'S STEP

1. Charles Murray, *Human Accomplishment: The Pursuit of Excellence in the Arts and Sciences, 800 B.C. to 1950* (New York: HarperCollins, 2003), 49.

2. Peter Gay, ed., *The Enlightenment: A Comprehensive Anthology* (New York: Touchstone, 1973), 71.

3. Quoted in ibid., 75.

4. Henry Steele Commager and Allan Nevins, *A Pocket History of the United States* (New York: Washington Square Press, 1968), 85.

5. Quoted in Morton J. Frisch and Richard G. Stevens, eds., *The Political Thought of American Statesman: Selected Writings and Speeches* (Itasca, Ill.: F. E. Peacock Publishers, 1973), 37.

6. Ibid., 164.

7. James M. McPherson, "What Did He Really Think About Race?" review of *The Radical and the Republican: Frederick Douglass, Abraham Lincoln, and the Triumph of Antislavery Politics* by James Oakes, *The New York Review of Books*, March 29, 2007, 18.

8. Hugh Brogan, *The Penguin History of the USA* (London: Penguin Books, 1999), 415.

9. Richard Hofstadter, *Anti-Intellectualism in American Life* (New York: Vintage, 1963), 208.

10. Victor Davis Hanson, "Solid Virtues," *Times Literary Supplement*, February 16, 2007, 10.

11. Brogan, *Penguin History of the USA*, 478.

12. Wendell Willkie, *This Is Wendell Willkie: A Collection of Speeches and Writings on Present-Day Issues by Wendell Willkie* (New York: Dodd, Mead and Company, 1940), 185.

13. Frisch and Stevens, *Political Thought of American Statesmen*, 305.

14. Ibid., 329.

15. John Kenneth White, *Still Seeing Red: How the Cold War Shapes the New American Politics* (Boulder, Colo.: Westview Press, 1997) 35.

16. Isaiah Berlin, *The Proper Study of Mankind* (New York: Farrar, Straus and Giroux), 629.

17. Paul Johnson, *A History of the American People* (New York: Harper-Collins, 1997), 764.

18. Tony Judt, *Postwar: A History of Europe Since 1945* (New York: Penguin Press, 2005),102.

19. Richard Parker, *John Kenneth Galbraith: His Life, His Politics, His Economics* (New York: Farrar, Straus, and Giroux, 2005), 260.

20. Johnson, *History of the American People*, 792.

21. Gore Vidal, *At Home: Essays 1982–88* (New York: Vintage, 1990), 125.

22. Brogan, *Penguin History of the USA*.

23. Quoted in William L. O'Neill, ed., *American Society Since 1945*, A New York Times Book (Chicago: Quadrangle, 1969), 9.

CHAPTER TWO. WHICH WAY DID THE '60S GO?

1. Godfrey Hodgson, *America in Our Time: From World War II to Nixon— What Happened and Why* (New York: Vintage, 1978), 220.

2. Quoted in ibid., 286.

3. Laura Pulido, *Black, Brown, Yellow, and Left* (Berkeley: University of California Press, 2006), 69.

4. Ibid., 113.

5. Hodgson, *America In Our Time*, 410.

6. Quoted in Mark Blasius and Shane Phelan, eds., *We Are Everywhere: A Historical Sourcebook of Gay and Lesbian Politics* (New York: Routledge, 1997), 380.

7. Neil Middleton, ed., "How Earth Day Was Polluted," *I. F. Stone's Weekly Reader* (New York: Vintage, 1974), 3.

CHAPTER THREE. UNHAPPY TOGETHER

1. John Sinclair, interview by Dean Kuipers, 3rd Degree, *Los Angeles City Beat*, July 27–August 2, 2006, 16.

2. Ethan Rarick, *California Rising: The Life and Times of Pat Brown* (Berkeley: University of California Press, 2005), 362.

3. Todd Gitlin, *The Sixties: Years of Hope, Days of Rage* (New York: Bantam, 1993), 247, 230.

4. Robert Reich, *Why Liberals Will Win the Battle for America* (New York: Knopf, 2004), 13.

5. Stokely Carmichael, "What We Want," in *The American Experience: A Radical Reader*, ed. Harold Jaffe and John Tytell (New York: Harper and Row, 1970), 90.

6. Quoted in ibid.

7. Author interview with Derek Shearer, July 2005.

CHAPTER FOUR. 1968 IN AMERICA

1. Stanley Karnow, *Vietnam: A History* (New York: Penguin Books, 1983), 581.

2. Lewis Chester, Godfrey Hodgson, and Bruce Page, *An American Melodrama: The Presidential Campaign of 1968* (New York: Viking, 1969), 633.

3. Jeff Shesol, *Mutual Contempt: Lyndon Johnson, Robert Kennedy, and the Feud that Defined a Decade* (New York: W. W. Norton, 1997), 472.

4. Alan Brinkley, "The Making of a War President," *New York Times Book Review*, August 20, 2006, 11.

5. Quoted in Robin Abcarian, "Back to '68 and the Way We Were," *Los Angeles Times*, November 24, 2006, E2.

6. George McGovern, interview by Alex Simon, *Venice Magazine*, November 2005, 61.

7. Katrina Vanden Heuvel, ed., *The Nation: Selections from the Independent Magazine of Politics and Culture, 1865–1990* (New York: Thunder's Mouth Press, 1990), 274.

8. Chester, Hodgson, and Page, *American Melodrama*, 633.

9. Sidney Blumenthal, *The Rise of the Counter-Establishment* (New York: Times Books, 1986),127.

10. Robert Caro, *Master of the Senate: The Years of Lyndon Johnson* (New York: Knopf, 2002), 445.

11. Ibid., 446.

12. Commager and Nevins, *Pocket History of the United States*, 569.

CHAPTER FIVE. CURIOUS ABOUT GEORGE

1. Edmund Wilson, *The Sixties* (New York: Farrar, Straus and Giroux, 1993), 498.

2. Karnow, *Vietnam*, 627.

3. Ibid., 636.

4. Norman Podhoretz, *Why We Were in Vietnam* (New York: Touchstone, 1983), 197.

5. John Micklethwait and Adrian Wooldridge, *The Right Nation: Conservative Power in America* (New York: Penguin, 2004), 214.

6. Peter Knobler and Greg Mitchell, eds., *Very Seventies: A Cultural History of the 1970s from the Pages of Crawdaddy* (New York: Fireside, 1995),145.

7. Hunter S. Thompson, *Fear and Loathing: On the Campaign Trail '72* (New York: Warner Books, 1973), 174.

8. Gitlin, *The Sixties*, 256.

9. Karnow, *Vietnam*, 626.

10. Garry Warren Hart, *Right from the Start: A Chronicle of the McGovern Campaign* (New York: Quadrangle/New York Times Book Company, 1973), 77.

11. Ibid., 169, 186.

12. *Newsweek*, "Can McGovern Put It All Together?" June 19, 1972, 23.

13. Ibid., 24.

14. Thompson, *Fear and Loathing*, 248.

15. *Time*, July 24, 1972, 25.

CHAPTER SIX. MODERN TIMES

1. "... for the people," the 1972 Democratic Party Platform, page MR 8.
2. *Time*, July 24, 1972, 17.
3. *Time*, May 8, 1972, 19.
4. Hart, *Right from the Start*, 297.
5. Frank Rich, "Five Years after 9/11, Fear Finally Strikes Out," op-ed, *New York Times*, August 20, 2006, 10.
6. Tony Judt, *Postwar*, 408.

CHAPTER SEVEN. I AM WOMAN, SAY IT LOUD

1. The Mojo Interview, *Mojo*, October 2006, 47.
2. Gillian G. Gaar, *She's a Rebel: The History of Women in Rock and Roll* (Seattle: Seal Press, 1992), 116.
3. David Ehrenstein, "A Liberating Booty-Shaking," *Los Angeles Times Book Review*, July 17, 2006, R9.
4. Ronald Brownstein, *The Power and the Glitter: The Hollywood-Washington Connection* (New York: Vintage, 1992), 243.

CHAPTER EIGHT. SEXUAL POSITIONS

1. Author interview with Lillian T., January 2006.
2. James T. Patterson, *Restless Giant: The United States from Watergate to Bush v. Gore* (New York: Oxford University Press, 2005), 52.
3. Kay S. Hymowitz, "The L Word: Love a Taboo," in *Backward and Upward: The New Conservative Writing*, ed. David Brooks (New York: Vintage, 1993), 83.
4. Biancamaria Fontana, "On the Defensive," *Times Literary Supplement*, August 11, 2006, 27.
5. Jane DeLynn, "I Flunked Masturbation Class," in *Very Seventies: A Cultural History of the 1970s from the Pages of Crawdaddy*, ed. Peter Knoebler and Greg Mitchell (New York: Fireside, 1995), 281.
6. Anemona Hartocollis, "For Some Gays, a Right They Can Forsake," *New York Times*, sec. 9, July 30, 2006, 2.

CHAPTER NINE. OUT OF TIME

1. Jules Witcover, *Marathon: The Pursuit of the Presidency 1972–1976* (New York: Viking, 1977),155.

2. Steven Hayward, *The Real Jimmy Carter: How Our Worst Ex-President Undermines American Foreign Policy, Coddles Dictators, and Created the Party of Clinton and Kerry* (Washington, DC: Regnery Publishing, 2004).

3. David Hempton, "For the Poor," *Times Literary Supplement*, September 8, 2006, 24.

4. Jimmy Carter, *Our Endangered Values: America's Moral Crisis* (New York: Simon and Schuster, 2005), 32.

5. Quoted in Elaine Woo, Jean O'Leary obituary, *Los Angeles Times*, June 6, 2005, B7.

6. Stanley Crouch, *Notes of a Hanging Judge: Essays and Reviews, 1979–1989* (New York: Oxford University Press. 1990), 231.

7. Hayward, *Real Jimmy Carter,* 229.

8. Philip Jenkins, *Decade of Nightmares: The End of the Sixties and the Making of Eighties America* (New York: Oxford University Press, 2006), 152.

9. Jenkins, *Decade of Nightmares,* 220.

10. Lou Cannon, *President Reagan: The Role of a Lifetime* (New York: Simon and Schuster/Touchstone, 1991), 511.

11. Patterson, *Restless Giant,* 189.

12. Ibid., 376.

13. Louis Uchitelle, "Here Come the Economic Populists," *New York Times*, Week in Review, November 26, 2006, 1.

14. Joan Didion, *Political Fictions* (New York: Knopf, 2001), 43.

15. Patterson, *Restless Giant,* 223.

CHAPTER TEN. YESTERDAY'S GONE

1. Kim Phillips-Fein, "Be Dull, Mr. President," *London Review of Books*, October 19, 2006, 17.

2. Thomas Edsall and Mary D. Edsall, *Chain Reaction* (New York: W. W. Norton, 1991),169.

3. Dudley Buffa and Morley Winograd, *Taking Control: Politics in the Information Age* (New York: Henry Holt, 1996), 2, 257.

CHAPTER ELEVEN. PULLING TO THE RIGHT

1. Patterson, *Restless Giant*, 247.
2. Barack Obama, *The Audacity of Hope: Thoughts on Reclaiming the American Dream* (New York: Crown, 2006), 34.
3. Dale Buss, *Family Man: The Biography of Dr. James Dobson* (Wheaton, Ill.: Tyndale House Publishers, 2005), 150–51.
4. Buss, *Family Man*, 152.
5. John Micklethwait and Adrian Wooldridge, *The Right Nation: Conservative Power in America* (New York: Penguin Books, 2005), 85.
6. Dick Morris, *Behind the Oval Office: Getting Reelected against All Odds* (Los Angeles: Renaissance Books, 1999), 298.
7. Ibid., 389.
8. Michael New, "Welfare Reform at 10: Analyzing Welfare Caseload Fluctuations, 1996–2002," Heritage Foundation, August 17, 2006.
9. Patterson, *Restless Giant*, 407.

CHAPTER TWELVE. BLUE CULTURE, RED POLITICS

1. Patrick McGilligan, ed., *Backstory 4: Interviews with Screenwriters of the 1970s and 1980s* (Berkeley: University of California Press, 2006), 275.
2. Patrick Goldstein, "Doing the Right Thing," *Los Angeles Times*, November 7, 2006, E5.
3. Ibid.
4. Sharon Waxman, "They Have Seen the Light, and It Is Green," *New York Times*, November 5, 2006, 4.
5. Ibid.
6. Nelson George, *Hip Hop America* (New York: Penguin, 1999), 188.

CHAPTER THIRTEEN. COMING HOME?

1. Edmund S. Morgan, "Inventing the Liberal Republican Mind," *New York Review of Books*, November 16, 2006, 32.
2. Michael Tomasky, "How the Dems Did It," *Los Angeles Times*, November 12, 2006.

3. Thomas B. Edsall, "The Struggle Within," *New York Times*, November 25, 2006.

4. "Their Antiwar Cries Are No Longer in the Wilderness," *Los Angeles Times*, March 15, 2007.

5. Obama, *Audacity of Hope*, 30.

6. Ibid., 32.

7. David M. Kennedy, *Freedom from Fear: The American People in Depression and War, 1929–1945* (New York: Oxford University Press, 1999), 28.

8. George S. McGovern, "Get It Straight, Mr. Cheney," *Los Angeles Times*, April 24, 2007.

SUGGESTED READING

Liberals who came of age in the 1960s are in the habit of romanticizing their political biographies. Ask them about their formative experiences and they will invariably mention having attended the "I Have a Dream" speech, the March on the Pentagon, Woodstock, or various other demonstrations, concerts, and love-ins, including ones never reported in the media.

For the purposes of this text, I sought interviews primarily with liberals or in some cases ex-liberals who first became politically active in the 1960s. I did so because I believed that their personal histories would help provide valuable perspective on what happened to liberalism between the Kennedy administration and the second term of George W. Bush, but also because I was almost certain that they would have real stories to tell, involving joy, heartbreak, disappointment, retreat, and, perhaps, a reawakening.

Having worked in politics for more than a decade in Southern California, I had a good sense from the start of some of the people I wanted to interview for this book. As an example, I knew Bill Rosendahl, who is now a member of the Los Angeles City Council and had played a key role in the McGovern campaign. I had casually known Rick Tuttle for several years, and was aware of both his passion for liberalism and his reputation for being able to speak lucidly and at length about modern American history and politics. Tuttle led me to Judge Terry Friedman, who not only shared invaluable insights about his stint working for McGovern in 1972 but also provided me with a treasure trove of documents from the campaign. Morley Winograd, whose political evolution encompasses an entire chapter of the book, and I met in the mid-1990s at various Democratic Leadership Council events. Until I sat down to interview Winograd, however, I had no idea of the extent of his transformation from liberal to New Democrat.

I also interviewed several conservatives in doing research for this book, some of whom I knew and others I found through the Claremont Institute and other means. Although their personal stories are largely absent from the text, these discussions provided further insight into how and where liberalism went wrong beginning in the 1960s and continuing, in their view, to the present day.

Given its centrality to the American experience, there is no shortage of books and essays that feature liberalism in either a supporting or lead role. I consulted key writers of the past (Max Lerner, Dwight MacDonald) and the present (Robert Reich, Thomas Frank) to acquire a better understanding of liberalism's influence and meaning at various points in the history of the United States. Richard Parker's lengthy and, one would expect, definitive biography, *John Kenneth Galbraith: His Life, His Politics, His Economics* (New York: Farrar, Straus and Giroux, 2005), provided invaluable insight into what it meant to be a lifelong, unapologetic liberal through much of the twentieth century. I doubt we will see Galbraith's kind in this century. Still, liberals or potential liberals remain on the contemporary political scene, even though they may be reluctant to apply that description to their own views. One of the best-written and most intelligent assessments of liberalism's modern-day difficulties and possibilities that I encountered in my research was Senator Barack Obama's *The Audacity of Hope: Thoughts on Reclaiming the American Dream* (New York: Crown, 2006). It will be intriguing to see if Obama is willing or able to lead an effort to reassess and redefine liberalism on behalf of a generation of activists for whom the triumphs and tragedies of the '60s are tales told by parents and grandparents.

My quest for secondary sources also yielded pleasant surprises. For example, the classic text from the early twentieth century, titled simply *Liberalism* (New York: Oxford University Press, 1979), by the English journalist and writer L. T. Hobhouse, is a lucid, succinct, and highly relevant synopsis of liberalism's unique strengths. It should be required reading for every Democratic presidential candidate in 2008 and beyond.

A friend provided a long out-of-print collection of speeches by Wendell Willkie—the losing candidate to FDR in 1940—that vividly demonstrated there was a time in American history when some leading Republicans were proud to be counted as liberals (Wendell Willkie, *This Is Wendell Willkie: A Collection of Speeches and Writings on Present-Day Issues* [New York: Dodd, Mead and Co., 1940]). In fact, the Willkie-FDR race, a battle between two New Yorkers, may have been the most liberal-friendly presidential campaign in American history. *Memoirs of a Revolutionist: Essays in Political Criticism* (1957; Reprint, New York: Viking, 1970), a collection of essays and columns by the aforementioned Dwight MacDonald that I snagged in a used-book store in Riverside, California, offers a trenchant and running critique of Franklin Roosevelt's presidency from a left-wing perspective. Twenty-five years later, liberals would be repeatedly assailed by the far left, which deemed them insufficiently prepared for or committed to the "inevitable" revolution.

There is no shortage of articles in the daily media and political magazines that either condemn liberals and liberalism to eternal hell or offer a blueprint for liberalism's renewal. Votes in Congress and state legislatures and key elections are analyzed for signs of whether liberalism is on the rebound or falling further behind. I consulted the obvious sources— the *New York Times*, the *Los Angeles Times*, the *Washington Post*, the *Wall Street Journal*—and the not so obvious—the *New York Review of Books*, the *London Review of Books*—to assess liberalism during this highly volatile period in American politics. My readings included articles discussing the state of feminism, gay politics, the civil rights movement, and the environmental movement as these causes struggled to stay vibrant and current.

Finally, popular culture provides its own map for charting the direction of liberalism in the past fifty years. Everything from the way African Americans, women, and gays are portrayed in various eras to the lyrics of popular songs provides a sense of how art and entertainment influence politics and how politics influences art and entertainment. Publications such as *Rolling Stone* and *Mojo* helped me to frame this discussion, as well as numerous articles and essays in mainstream publications that seek to connect punk, disco, rap, and porn to contemporary politics. The love/hate relationship of liberalism with mass entertainment in this country is a fascinating subject in itself.

INDEX

Text:	10/15 Janson
Display:	Janson
Compositor:	BookMatters, Berkeley
Indexer:	Barbara Roos
Printer and binder:	Maple-Vail Manufacturing Group